Frances Ryder was employed as a company director and worked in the engineering sector for over thirty years, mostly responsible for the statutory reporting and compliance requirement of a limited company. She is also a person-centred counsellor (Rogerian Theory) and has a Master of Arts in human relations.

To the whole of my loving family, close and extended, to my partner of over forty years, my son, and every friend and colleague who has ever been by my side when I needed them.

Frances Marian Ryder

An Ethnographic Study into the Social Organisation of a Small Medium Enterprise a Snapshot from 1983 to 2009

Austin Macauley Publishers™
London * Cambridge * New York * Sharjah

The story, experiences, and words are the author's alone.

A CIP catalogue record for this title is available from the British Library.

ISBN 9781035847129 (Paperback)
ISBN 9781035847136 (ePub e-book)

www.austinmacauley.com

First Published 2024
Austin Macauley Publishers Ltd®
1 Canada Square
Canary Wharf
London
E14 5AA

Table of Contents

Introduction

Utilising a qualitative inductive approach, this work is an autoethnographic study of the social organisation of a highly technical, 3-D engineering small medium enterprise in which I was employed as the Operations Director and organisational manager for twenty-six years, from 1983 to 2009.

In this organisational ethnography, Trice & Beyer's (1984) typology of rites and ceremonials became a heuristic and sensitising device to explain the diverse organisational events and activities of this small medium enterprise which are reported on in the research.

As participant observer, the data gathered was derived from the everyday organisational cultural events. Observational data was collected as narrative which was then simultaneously iteratively coded, categorised, memoed and sorted into main categories, the ethos of the constructivist grounded theory interpretive approach. Each cultural event was analysed separately, but was not empirically distinguishable.

An element of complexity is brought to the project because I had more than one role in the organisation, including that of the ethnographic researcher. A comprehensive literature review was undertaken at the beginning combined with more focused and concentrated reading throughout the lifetime of the project.

Chapter 1
Background

This chapter introduces the research background and content in which I outline the history of a small medium enterprise called Newland Limited, including an account of my organisational roles. Details of Newland's commercial activities between 1983 to 2009 are provided. First, I define and put into context the socio-economic perspective of SMEs in UK and Europe. Subsequently, the research focus and justification is given.

The Small Medium Enterprises (SMEs)

An SME is a legally defined entity that is sometimes called a company, a firm or a business that is incorporated by law and registered in England at Companies House, an agency of the Department for Business, Innovation & Skills (BIS). SMEs are defined by company law as a privately owned entity, an ongoing concern, which is limited by shares.

The European Commission (Enterprise And Industry Policies) defines the enterprise categories for determining whether a company is an SME as being (1) the number of employees and (2) either turnover or balance sheet total. The table that follows gives an overview of those European Commission (Enterprise And Industry Policies) enterprise categories:

European Commission Small and Medium-Sized Enterprise Definition			
Enterprise Category Size	**Headcount**	**Turnover or...**	**Balance Sheet Total**
Medium	< 250	< €50 million	< €43 million
Small	< 50	< €10 million	< €10 million

Micro	< 10	< €2 million	< €2 million
SOURCE: European Commission Enterprise and Industry Policies...Facts and Figures...SME Definition http://ec.europa.eu			

The European Commission (Enterprise and Industry Policies) also recognises that SMEs are of social and economic importance, making great contributions to entrepreneurship and innovation, as each gives provision of employment to millions in the private sector working communities of the European Union.

SMEs have political significance as their efforts provide the lifeblood to the European economy through improved market access to overseas markets and the promotion of European standards. SMEs are regarded by the European Union to be of crucial importance for the future development of the EU. They have potential for long term sustainable economic growth, creating employment through an entrepreneurial mindset that is now to be promoted and encouraged, especially amongst young people, by both the EU and the current UK government coalition.

All legal entity companies worldwide, whether large, small, medium or micro, have to operate compliantly, efficiently and effectively in order to conduct their business activities successfully and protect their market positions.

In the UK, SMEs are governed corporately through The Companies Act and The Employment Rights Act. These Acts are all subsequently consolidated, modified or reenacted from time to time, in order to underpin the statutory obligations and legislations of all UK based SMEs. Recorded in the Department for Business, Innovation & Skills (BIS) Statistics for the UK and Regions 2009, released on 13 October 2010 through The National Archive, is the following statistical data for UK based SMEs:

Department for Business, Innovation & Skills (BIS) Statistics for the UK and Regions 2009	
Estimated Private Sector Enterprises (At the Start of 2009)	4.8 million
Numbers of SMEs Start-Ups (Since the Start of 2008)	51,000
% Numbers of SMEs Start-Ups (Since the Start of 2008)	1.1%

Estimated Number of Employed Persons	22.8 million
Estimated Combined Annual Turnover	£3,200 billion
% SMEs Compared to All Enterprises	99.9%
% Private Sector Employment	59.8%
% Private Sector Turnover	49%
% Gross Domestic Product (GDP)	50%
Estimated Turnover in SMEs	£1,589 billion
Turnover Increased by Since the Start Of 2008	£88 billion
% Turnover Increased Since the Start Of 2008	5.8%
SOURCE: The National Archive, For Department of Business, Innovation & Skills (BIS) Released on 13 October 2010, www.nationalarchives.gov.uk	

From the statistical information held online by The Insolvency Service and Companies House for the period 1984 to 2011, there were 414,000 company liquidations in England and Wales, comprising of compulsory liquidations, creditors voluntary liquidations, corporate insolvencies, receiverships, administrative receiverships and company voluntary arrangements:

Company Liquidations in England and Wales for the Period 1984 to 2011	
Period in Years	Number of Insolvencies
2001 to 2011	162,000
1991 to 2000	164,000
1984 to 1990	88,000
Totals Insolvencies	414,000
SOURCE: www.insolvencydirect.bis.gov.uk	

These statistics are reported by The Insolvency Service as a generalised report of Company Liquidations for England and Wales. From these statistics, it has not been possible to separate out the insolvencies of SMEs from other corporate insolvencies. From the numbers shown, it is possible to determine that such corporate failures are a significant fiscal loss to the UK and European economy which the UK government is trying to avoid.

In the UK, help is on hand from coalition government initiatives to encourage SME activity. These initiatives set out to motivate banks to lend money, spark entrepreneurship, ignite new start-ups and rescind inhibiting legislation. In the May 2010 budget, to help to reduce the burden on cash flow, The Chancellor George Osborne took on board the need to support the entrepreneurial flair of the UK's start-ups and SMEs by increasing the Entrepreneur's tax relief from £2 million to £5 million.

In November 2010, the government brought out new initiatives to encourage SME start-ups that should be a quick, simple and viable option for anyone who wanted to set up in business and maximise their opportunities. By November 2011, the government pledged to improve its engagement with small businesses and offered business growth packages to help Britain's SMEs to create jobs, export to new markets, secure finance capital and cut red tape.

In his speech, Start Up Britain, in Leeds on Monday, 23 January 2012, David Cameron made reference to Winston Churchill's comment on private enterprise. Churchill said it is either a predatory tiger that needs to be shot, a cow that needs to be milked but not enough see private enterprise as a healthy horse pulling a sturdy wagon. David Cameron emphasises that small high growth firms are the engine of new job creation and they punch well above their weight.

Making direct reference to the current unaffordable lease terms of three years for SMEs with limited start-up capital, Cameron announces that the coalition government is now promoting the use of the spare empty spaces in the public sector to help such SMEs to start up and to grow.

Even though SMEs are governed and systemised by bureaucratic officialdom, each one of them remains capable of maintaining modern day diversification into business activities that provide for their shareholders and workforces. SMEs stay viable through years of successful trading by the effective management of people, relationships and cash flow. It can be seen from the statistical information that is currently available that SMEs provide legal, economical, commercially viable and social contributions, European and UK wide, that benefits the government and the wider societies that each provides for.

Newland's Organisational History

To help to get a stagnant British economy moving, Margaret Thatcher's 1980's government encouraged the start-up of SMEs. Start-up capital was easier to obtain as the government monetarism policy promoted the concept that new private business enterprise would help to stabilise economic downward trend.

In January 1983, a former work colleague invited me to join an organisation that he intended to start up and for which he had already developed a three to five year business plan. This SME was called Newland Limited. As part of their initiatives for new start-ups and to help to reduce unpopular unemployment levels, the government of the day offered a financial incentive called the Enterprise Allowance. Newland's was able to take advantage of this wage assistance scheme.

Newland's was located in one of the new Science Park concepts that had sprung up in the North West of England. Even though the shape of the new Science Park was defined by the mid-80s, expansion was an ongoing activity as it became part of a New Town encompassing town facilities, retail complexes, housing, schooling, and recreational forest parks. Newland's owner was able to negotiate an affordable long lease term with the New Town. Having a viable business plan, finance capital available, an office from which to operate, and staff already employed to manage its organisational needs, Newland's was ready to trade.

At the start of the business enterprise in January 1983, there were three dimensions to Newland's business plan. The first aspect was to sell a new range of modular office furniture as it was being utilised in an organisational setting known as Newland's business centre activity. This showroom type actual working environment was a live demonstration space with real people at work doing their everyday business activities.

The second aspect of the business plan was to service these smaller scale office spaces. Entrepreneurial individuals could run their own business enterprises, renting desk space in the business centre, on a weekly basis, without the commitment of a long term lease. Reception and administration services would also be provided on an as required basis, week by week, which were billable upon demand.

Newland's third aspect to generate revenue was to supply temporary (contract) mechanical, electrical, electro-mechanical and instrumentation engineering labour to the oil and gas high value engineering maintenance service sector in UK, Europe and worldwide.

Later on, an opportunistic prospect was taken up that became, from 1986 onwards, Newland's single provision of revenue generation. This was referred to as the supply of 3-D engineering data service which has now evolved into data life management services.

When Newland's started up, my organisational role was not defined by a title. I was not a director of the company but I had the broader responsibility to manage the business activities on a daily basis. I was responsible for the everyday financial matters of this newly incorporated company which employed only one other person, its owner and main shareholder, who also acted as a marketing individual. Newland's first formal trading day, 5 February 1983, was of great significance and remained so.

In this section, I have given an overview of Newland's organisational history and its three to five year business plan. I will now briefly chronologically detail the three dimensions of the business plan starting with the supply of serviced office space followed by the provision of temporary (contract) engineering labour.

1983-1986: Supply of Serviced Office Space

In line with the business plan, modular units were set up as open plan individual desking stations with file storage. These pod-like arrangements were rented out on a week by week basis to individuals who wanted to set up their own businesses. Larger companies, moving into the new Science Park area, also rented space from Newland's. For them, it was a way in which key staff could be working immediately in a local office environment whilst the relocation from other parts of the UK and/or overseas was taking place.

Newland's provided, as part of business centre support, reception type meeting and greeting, conference room hire, typing service which then eventually became word processing service, photocopying facility, facsimile service, and telephone answering services.

The demand for the telephone answering service was popular and telephone lines were installed and uninstalled on almost a weekly basis. There were times however, when the complex mechanical wiring of 1980s telecommunications in the building failed. Two telephone engineers, Mick and Nick, who always introduced themselves as “Taking The Mick” Mick and “You’re Nicked” Nick, were frequent visitors to Newland’s. Their regular attendance to the building made them part of the social aspects of Newland’s and they were a source of entertainment, joking and amusement.

Such social aspects of the workplace were evident in the way the open plan and reception area was used. The positive side of the open plan arrangement was that, although it was a working environment, it was also a socially communal one. If someone had a bad day, then it was felt by all and the relevant support was given. When someone had a commercially successful day and wanted to share their good fortune with others, the mood of the business centre reflected the sense of achievement, coupled with hope and optimism.

Although, the occupants of the pod-like desk centres were not commercially connected, like a group of employees are in a company, each were connected in some relational way. As business partners, myself and Newland’s owner, were often addressed by clients saying that the open arrangement of the business centre helped them to allay any feelings of isolation or fear.

These individuals realised that each were not always alone in their own particular commercial states of affairs; that other individuals experienced the same business and/or personal situations at times and that other people, who ran their own small businesses, sometimes felt the same way.

Newland’s set up a coffee area in the reception space which offered a complimentary drink to visitors and other building occupants. The coffee counter unit had a bar top type shelf which became a good spot for leaning and discussing the wider implications and struggles associated with being a business man or woman in 1980s Thatcherite Britain, including gossip, because the business centre was a place where people did their own kind of commercial transactional business, but also interacted in friendly and supportive ways with each other

Generally, sales potentials, the difficulties in procuring resources, cash flow, compliance issues and staff matters were all subjects of discussion however, the confidential business always took place in the conference room.

This sense of workplace community extended to Christmas time when we would have a party and Newland’s would supply buffet food and soft drinks for the whole business centre. If Newland’s had a particularly good year, it would also supply a glass of champagne for each person. Some people brought in their own alcoholic beverage and one client who was a professional singer always entertained the party.

Newland's annual party was of great interest to its client group and as December approached each year, we would be asked time and again if the party was to go ahead. It most often did and was a very enjoyable occasion. Employees of other companies in the building often sneaked in to have some food and to listen to the music.

When Newland's was running the business centre, most of the building was full and although it is difficult to quantify exactly how many individuals we had daily contact with, over the years hundreds of people came and went through Newland's reception area.

The business centre, however, was not the only business activity that Newland's conducted, there was also an engineering aspect at the heart of its core.

1983-1994: Supply of Temporary (Contract) Engineering Labour

As a chartered mechanical engineer already with long experience of working on gas turbines and compressors for the high capital value maintenance service sector, Newland's managing director's principal interest was in engineering. When the time was right, business activity moved to the next phase of the business plan, the provision of service contract labour to the oil and gas industry.

Newland's won a contract to provide service labour, anywhere in the world or offshore, for both the installation and maintenance of large rotating machinery such as gas turbines, gas compressors, pumps and all of the associated mechanical equipment, the instrumentation and the electrical. Newland's billed companies at an hourly rate, taking a small pence profit margin for each engineer. There were large teams of engineers working on one or more than one machine, so a financial gain would be made on the consolidated project.

The payroll was a significant weekly event running for the whole of the installation of the on/off maintenance timetable, which often extended to years.

Newland's conducted this type of business for over fifteen years, but it phased out as the large engineering machine installation projects started to decline. Meanwhile, the potential for a new engineering business activity emerged. Newland's called this the supply of 3-D data acquisition services.

1986-Present Day: Supply of 3-D Engineering Data Acquisition Services

In 1986, Newland's was given the opportunity to purchase a piece of innovative software from a chemical company that had been using it to conduct in-plant equipment replacement.

A trained engineer could survey a particular piece of equipment, a structural element, a vessel, a tank or a pipeline in-situ and take readings using a universal measuring device, a theodolite. Then, by using the software and a mechanical stereo-comparator, the engineer, or a team of engineers, could analyse the readings and define where a particular piece of equipment was in 3-D space, its orientation and its dimensions.

The ability to produce accurate dimensions of any piece of equipment in-situ, meant that a particular piece of equipment or pipeline could be fabricated in a workshop elsewhere and installed as a replacement item first time thus, eliminating the need for further modifications and prolonged site shut down delays. Consequently, oil, gas, nuclear, petrochemical, paper pulp and pharmaceutical plants could ensure that any planned shut down time did not exceed economically acceptable limits.

Newland's purchased the software and started a service that provided 3-D models to companies that had a requirement to replace expensive vessels, equipment and/or pipeline in their processing plants. Although for Newland's, it was a lucrative chance to develop a new commercial engineering service, it was also a financial risk because the work was labour intensive and time consuming.

Newland's recruited an experienced engineer who eventually became one of the directors of the company. Afterwards, the service was technically and financially streamlined. As part of the third phase of development, Newland's recruited a software development engineer, who re-coded a new 3-D modelling package. This software provided greater data accuracy and remained the intellectual property of Newland's.

Newland's expanded this 3-D modelling engineering activity and it became the main stay of its trading capacity for the next twenty-three years. The engineering concept remained the same but the advancements in computer and laser technology highly improved its innovative and technical capabilities.

Newland's ultimately came to employ thirteen individuals on a full-time basis. Up to 2009, Newland's employed nine modelling skilled engineers who made up the site and analysis teams; eight were employed locally in the UK and one engineer lived and worked overseas. Three employees were administration and marketing.

Employees were deployed in various roles, boardroom activities, strategic planning, marketing, software development and bespoke creation, engineering technical service providers, 3-D data acquisition consultancy, business finance, accounting and administration.

Newland's eventually became the market leader in the supply of 3-D data acquisition services, to a global market, from which it generated income in a flexible arrangement that had been progressively refined to three streams of engineering services.

The first stream of revenue was a service supply related to a type of work such as model conversations, data translation and the meta-labelling of data for asset management solutions. The second stream was to conduct a site survey, the building of a 3-D model, the transfer of the data into a 3-D design package from which the client could do their modification work. The third stream of revenue was the development of bespoke software solutions in accordance with client requirements.

These three streams of engineering service formed the bases of Newland's sales income from which employment opportunities were derived.

The Research Focus

According to Trice & Beyer (1984) studies of organisational culture often focus on discrete cultural forms and fail to place phenomena studied within an overarching conception of culture, like rites and ceremonials that have distinguishable characteristics.

Rites and ceremonials are elaborate planned sets of activities, conducted through social interactions for the benefit of an audience with defined roles for people to perform. Significantly, the social consequences link rites and ceremonials to other characteristics of the organisations that have interest for organisational researchers. Rites and ceremonials hold meaningful and relevant organisational information and their visibility makes them easily recognised and accessible for researchers.

Trice & Beyer (1984) also suggest that it is extremely difficult for organisational researchers to pursue true ethnographic research which entails long term, full-time participation observation unless they belong to the organisation being studied. Here lay my ethnographic research advantage. My organisational roles were a director of the company, a manager of the enterprise, a member of the work groups and an individual at work. I, therefore, had full-time access to research Newland's organisational culture to investigate what rites and ceremonials, if any, existed.

A research opportunity arose for me after Newland's directors, of which I was one, had resolved internal organisational difficulties due to poor management supervision between 2005 and 2009. My idea for a research project was not solely triggered by the significant events that took place but more by recognising the diversity of the daily activities of Newland's organisational culture.

As part of my managerial role when dealing with Newland's workforce, I often contemplated questions such as "what are the threads that bind us together?", "how do changes impact upon the group", and "what does it all mean to the group as a whole or, how does the group make sense of what is happening?"

Additionally, I learned that individuals brought their personal matters to the workplace and in some instances, involved work colleagues in such events. Visibly, moods, happy and difficult events, etc. affected the workforce. As a manager and part of the workforce, I had several other questions: "is management isolated or part of this group?", "does the group pretend to bring into the fold the management team or does the group deliberately and selectively isolate the individual managers?"

I recognised the opportunity to design a qualitative ethnographic research study to write a book. Exactly like my Post-Graduate Diploma in Person-Centred Counselling and MA in Human Relations some years earlier, the purpose of my research was personal gain.

The research setting was Newland's office where we all worked in groups and teams, conducted our daily work activities, interacted in relation to aspects of work and personal issues which sometimes resulted in conflict but ultimately, all gained personal benefit from the reciprocal efforts of the communal whole. So it was from this familiar vantage point, that I aimed to capture what was contained within the organisational setting. All of these events became my research focus.

These types of interactions within an organisation have been identified by Fineman, Gabriel & Sims (2010) who suggest that the focus should not be on the organisation, but on the organising activities and the processes of doing things in organisations. According to Schein (2010) organisational culture is a pattern of shared basic assumptions that have been learned by a group as it problem solved its needs for external adaptation and internal integration. If the adaptations work well for the group, then these new ideas are passed onto new members as a way of sharing and contributing in group life.

Trice & Beyer (1984) suggest that organisational culture has two basic components. The first is substance; a network of meanings contained in its ideologies, norms and values. The second is the forms and practices in which this substance, a network of meanings, is manifested through the expressed affirmed and communication to its members including rites, rituals and ceremonials.

In relation to leadership and the role of this within the complexities of relationships within an organisation, Berson & Sosik (2007) examined the types of influences that self-aware leaders can demonstrate to encourage quality and innovation in their organisations. Focus has been placed upon the interpersonal aspects of taking charge and the challenges awaiting new managers as they try to establish productive working relationships (Manzoni & Barsoux 2009).

The emphasis of existential communication and leadership is turned from it being an essential and prime leadership skill to the justification for it being considered as an important aspect of communication (Ashman & Lawler 2008).

Research on gender (Koch 2005, Kyriakidou 2012, Scott & Brown 2006, Servon & Visser 2011) suggests that a considerable amount of bias exists against females who aspire towards leadership positions, especially in highly technical organisational environments. In particular, Scott & Brown (2006) suggest one possibility for change is to encourage organisational cultures that promote equality and values of fairness in the workplace, in order to circumvent encoding biases.

Future research should investigate whether there are any circumstances or situations that advantage females or place them on an equal footing. They hope their paper serves as an impetus for other organisational scholars to consider encoding biases in leadership, which remains scant in the current body of literature.

Teams are regarded as an important social unit within organisations (Ambrosini, Bowman & Burton-Taylor 2007, Hanson 2006, Hrebiniak 2006, Koch 2005, Williams, Parker & Turner 2007). To retain the competitive advantage, organisations need to effectively mobilise knowledge resources

(Joshi, Sarker & Sarker 2006). When delivering increased customer satisfaction, Ambrosini, Bowman & Burton-Taylor (2007) have specifically demonstrated that inter-team coordination was a critical factor in the delivery of service but did not connect any of these outcomes to organisational performance and hence, survival.

It can be seen from these examples of explicit organisational topics that the focus is on the internal activities of the organisations and have not included the broader picture of the work based social activities and events that contribute to organisational performance and survival. This broader view is supported by writers such as Das T. Hari (1983) who has suggested research into the socially organised SME, their organisational cultures, the combined factors of the organisational activities and its members. These aspects will be the focus of the literature review which in turn, will inform the developing focus of the research to be undertaken.

Historically, Newland's as an SME has always been an arena of organisational activity.

Schein (2010) says that suddenly, we have become aware that the occupations that govern activities in these arenas of activity are themselves cultures, about which we know little.

In the varied social and cultural aspects of Newland's organisational life, I could see similarities to the work of Malinowski (1922) who focused on the norms and values within the organisation of island natives, their methods of work and practices, accomplished by the reciprocal working arrangements of its members, and the upholding of ritual and ceremonial traditions.

Similarly, Trice & Beyer (1984, 1993) focus on rites and ceremonials and offer a practical approach to the study of cultural forms, operating in concert and thus, uncover networks of interacting meanings that characterised its organisational culture. Once uncovered, their concepts then need to be extended and explored.

Newland's organisational environment was a centre of engineering innovation coupled with social aspects of people being in their workplace. Between 1983 and 2009, Newland's generated income by turning strategic planning into pragmatic action, adequately resourced by sufficient financial underpinning making it a long term viable organisation. Norms, values, methods of work, practices and networks of interacting meanings that characterised the organisational culture therefore, must have existed and functioned successfully.

Undoubtedly, Newland's longevity attests its engineering socio-economic importance to the UK and world economy however, without a willing workforce trade, profit, tax and employment would not exist. Earlier, Schein (2010) confirmed we know little about types of organisational cultures in SMEs like Newland's.

Fineman, Gabriel & Sims (2010) place focus on the "doing" in organisations. They liken the organisation to a river, viewed from a helicopter above, looking calm, smooth and tranquil, yet the closer lower view shows turbulence and choppy waters. My thoughts aligned with theirs. To me, however, Newland's was an organisational swan swimming on a lake, serenely sat on crystal water, paddling like mad underneath!

Hence, Newland's events would be examined in the rest of the thesis based upon the research aim of discovering Newland's organisational culture to explain how its members worked together.

Inside Newland's, corporate governance, management and employee roles, reciprocal working arrangements, group interactions and teaming activities certainly manifested in visible and relevant types of rituals and ceremonies, as planned activities, conducted through social interactions. These diverse exchanges will also be investigated and consequently, aspects of Newland's organisational cultural activities will be the focus of the literature review in the next chapter.

Chapter 2
The Literature Review

In this chapter, I examine and review the literature on small medium enterprises (SMEs) and their organisational cultures. I identify a gap in the research to enable a contribution to the knowledge of organisational culture in SMEs.

Current Research View on SMEs

To conduct this literature review on SMEs, I used my University Athens off campus access to view the databases JSTOR (www.jstor.org) PsycInfo (Ovid) and later, ISI Web of Knowledge (now Thomson Reuters).

Prior to using the full online services, I manually ordered journal articles, which were then delivered by mail, supplied from the British Library, Library Privilege Service (www.bl.uk). Online JSTOR provided access to an archive of electronic journals primarily in the humanities and the social sciences. Using PsycInfo (Ovid) I was able to view professional and academic literature in counselling, psychology, related disciplines and also, sociology. The ISI Web of Knowledge (now Thomson Reuters) gave me access to multiple products of the world's leading citation databases held in external collections.

To begin the search, I defined the first set of terms based upon those activities deemed normative for organisations and private limited companies. What emerged were groups, emotions at work, knowledge, leadership, learning, organisational wisdom, private limited companies, qualitative research in organisations, teams, team working, technology, tools and the concept of family.

I also used search terms salient to qualitative research studies. They were ethnography, constructivist grounded theory, organisational culture, organisational ethnography and SME activity. The work of theorists Y. Agazarian, W. R. Bion, Kathy Charmaz, Sigmund Freud, Barney Glaser, Martin

Heidegger, Soren Kierkegaard, Bronislaw Malinowski and Carl Rogers were also reviewed.

Reading was continuous. All material included in the research was obtained from two hundred and six journal articles, hundred and fourteen books and twenty-six internet/media based articles. My search rationale lacked an inclusion/exclusion criteria. All of the material was considered because their discrete aspects were relevant.

The outcome of the first level of response did not give a clear overall picture of the social organisation of SMEs. The search results revealed an absence in the emergent literature that specifically matched and exclusively responded to this first set of terms. What emerged was a large amount of literature based upon one single feature or discrete aspect of an organisation for example, strategy, management, leadership and teams.

As the literature branched off into these single features and discrete aspects, I could follow that content and synchronise the search results as normative for the internal activities of an SME, that were relevant to my experience.

I categorised the search results into organisational wisdom, knowledge management, management and leadership, groups, teams and team working, technology and tools, gender/women and the family concept. In harmony with the rationale I adopted, I was able to use this literature to review these discrete organisational cultural activities together with all of their social multi-faceted aspects.

I observed from the volume of literature available to review, there is a universal endearing quality about a small medium enterprise. An SME attracts and encourages both quantitative and qualitative researchers to study the discrete, but diverse commercial activities and features of organisational life contained within them. Yet still and more important for the context of this research is that the literature volume focuses on the discrete, yet ignores and pays little attention to the social organisation of SMEs.

The following section is a review of the literature on the organisational cultures of SMEs.

Organisational Culture of SMEs

The everyday activities of an SME are complex, intricate and multi-parted and research has indicated that each separate discrete area can be interesting to study. Researchers are taking up the challenges to discover how and if human resources systems, organisational forms, management practices and operational capabilities relate to organisational intelligence in SMEs, including the ethical and social dimensions of it (Kessler 2006).

Co-workers who gain personal experience of another's work activities and its steps of process, can through personal reflection, bring about a change in their understanding which can lead to development in an organisation. Learning, therefore, is seen as social practice that takes place in specific contexts, like an organisational culture (Schulz 2005).

Inside SMEs, there are the complex issues that corporate boards have to deal with in terms of strategy and legal compliance (Conger & Lawler 2009, Kirchler, Hoelzl & Wahl 2008). There are board decisions to be made to promote their market positions.

Does trade remains domestic or strives to become internationally diverse (Brouthers & Brouthers 2003, Zimmerman, Barksy & Brouthers 2009)? Networks help the newly incorporated SMEs to overcome the liabilities that their lack of commercial and market experience can engender (Jorgensen & Ulhoi 2010).

An SME's collective inside civilisation has company specific abstract relationship patterns for working and communicating together and this is often referred to as organisational culture (Fineman, Gabriel & Sims 2010, Gallos 2006, Mitroff & Kilman 1976, Schein 2010, Trice & Beyer 1984). Research studies on organisational culture dates back to the 1970s (Trice & Beyer 1984). Culture was rediscovered when various aspects of organisational behaviour was analysed in the work of Mitroff & Kilman (1976) who studied the stories of working managers to discover their concept of the ideal organisation.

The Gallos (2006) organisational cultural definition is about organisational development (OD) its foundation, scope, focus, purpose and methods, in terms of how changes affect the development of the organisation, through an effort that is planned, organisation-wide and managed from the top. Schein (2010) defines organisational culture as a pattern of shared basic assumptions, taking into consideration the influences of leadership, that have been learned by a group, as it problem solved its needs for external adaptation and internal integration.

If the adaptations work well for the group, then these new ideas are passed onto new members as a way of sharing and contributing in group life.

Organisational cultures also give homes to rites, rituals and ceremonial activities that become part of their internal society, firstly through substance, a network of meaning contained in its ideologies, norms and values (Trice & Beyer 1984). Secondly, there is the forms and practices in which this substance, network of meaning, is manifested through the expressed affirmed and communicated to its members (Trice & Beyer 1984, 1993).

According to Fineman, Gabriel & Sims (2010) there are many possible vocabularies of motives that provide explanation to behaviours in organisations and a strong organisational culture can be a blueprint for commercial success.

Ethnography has been used to study the different dimensions of the same organisational behaviour phenomenon yet, what is still lacking in the research are studies on the social organisation of an SME with all of these interrelated organisational features (Das T. Hari 1983).

The organisational cultures contained within any SME are functioning working community environments. Employed individuals bring their willingness to work, their experiences, their training and place all of that into a combined action with others. The maintenance of that sense of community and its good atmosphere are important components of all processes of work (Collin 2006).

In an organisational environment, individuals can be given the opportunity to learn new skills that will ideally and practically contribute to the collective whole, through their sense of self and through belonging and contributing (Kivetz & Tyler 2007). This pooled workforce is then reinforced by the individuals who make up the internal society (Neri 2006) the interpersonal skills of the managers who provide guidance (Hatch, Kostera & Kozminski 2006) and the persons who are in places of management with leadership persuasion (Wilhelmson 2006).

According to Dubreuil (2008) human cooperation takes such a vast array of forms that extends to so many individuals, that its existence still remains a social puzzle. In his work, Malinowski (1922) has given researchers one anthropological definition of how social cohesion, strong reciprocity and the ceremonial traditional can function in a society that works jointly for the common good.

In spite of the good of altruism and human cooperation there is however, experimental economics research that determines, through the selfishness axiom, that individuals seek to maximise their own material gains and anticipate that others will do exactly the same (Peacock 2007). To contrast this self-interest, there is research that has determined that food rituals help to reduce anxiety and stress, sustain continuity and develop a strong sense of social harmony (Thomson & Hassenkamp 2008).

Decision making processes are conducted by the officers of the company, its representatives, on its behalf, legitimately and in accordance with current law. Any company is, therefore, considered to be more than simply an entity or a unit (Tyler 2006, Kirchler, Hoelzl & Wahl 2008). Although, it is not a living thing or considered as a scientific object, there is such a thing as company life and the expectation of its organisational civility to society and the law.

An SMEs social community existence is to be conserved to enable the preservation of the entity, as a commercially viable legal ongoing concern. This is the foundation from which the SMEs representatives can take full advantage of the generation of organisational wisdom to remain corporately successful (Kessler 2006). In doing so, the existence of the SME is perpetuated and it remains as an employment provider to the internal society. The occurrences of organisational daily life can predictably go according to the business plan.

At our research fingertips, however, is the capacity to capture the intrigue and phenomenon of the unpredictable events that can change and divert organisational circumstances (Summers-Effler 2007).

Being a willing part of any organisational life places us all, as workers, inside the organisational culture that exists and functions within our choice of workplace. In an organisational environment each assembly of persons can be different, but all are linked by the need to gather with each other and use the work place for doing duty, sharing information and negotiating conditions for advantages or limiting disadvantages.

When we all act together, we act jointly, by having a participatory intention towards collective action, in order to meet the needs of the common good (Kutz 2000, Trice & Beyer 1984). Belongingness increases employee cooperative helping and compliance (Den Hartog, De Hoogh & Keegan 2007). As long as we have a sense of belonging, through strong reciprocity, we can take ownership and pride in our work effort. We can feel connected with others so that we can aspire for our own success, the success of others and the organisation in which we work (Dubreuil 2008).

The activity of working together helps to develop a sense of community that can represent a cooperative social system for doing things together and learning from that experience (King 2004, Lightsey 2006, Schulz 2005).

The underpinning culture is the concept of organisational wisdom which will now be explored.

Organisational Wisdom

Organisational wisdom is an emerging domain of research because it reflects the realities of the business climate, one that is perpetually complex, diverse, fluid and interdependent. Included in this, is also the individual wisdom that makes use of the institutional and social processes, such as organisational structure, culture and leadership (Kessler 2006). What is scant in the literature is the synthesis of all of this knowledge, its asset potential and subsequent practical implementation (Kessler & Bailey 2007).

In terms of organisational knowledge, the research question still remains for an organisational researcher to determine how does any employed workforce, in their unique SME setting, know what each needs to know and how does their own unique knowledge become shared (Arthur, Defillippi & Lindsay 2008, Dias 2007).

This question is philosophically addressed from a phenomenological point of view by Gibbons (2001) in terms of how the truth of one's beliefs, or perhaps, facts about a setting, will be involved in the explanation of an action and what he refers to as knowledge in action. Yet, still it does not fully address the recognition of, the identification of and the perception of the human capital asset of knowledge that is generated through the organisational activities of even the smallest of SMEs.

The effective performance and output of team working in SMEs is vital to commercial success. Using a theoretical framework to determine the utilisation of knowledge and intelligence in the performance of teams in organisations, Ringer (2007) found that effective leadership and management required a pooling of all the organisational knowledge called collective thinking.

The four core elements of collective thinking were proposed as a shared clarity of purpose, emotional and psychological mature functioning on the part of the key players, the necessity for psychologically safe thinking spaces and shared responsibility for building, maintaining and utilising the thinking space. The findings concluded that the research on collective thinking still remains organisationally challenging, complex and elusive.

A positivist research approach, one that assumes the priori that there are discoverable relationships between organisational values and knowledge management behaviours and outcomes, has been undertaken and indicates that **organis**ational culture has a more complex relation to knowledge management than first thought (Alavi, Kayworth & Leidner 2005). However, there is still participant observation research work needing to be done to capture all of the dimensions of organisational cultural knowledge that is embedded in practice based working environments (Suzuki et al 2007).

In doing so, any additional research studies could further inform small and large organisations on the fundamental multi-faceted aspects of the working knowledge that is contained and shared within their teams (Joshi, Sarker & Sarker 2007).

In the literature on knowledge management, there are absences of criteria that could be helpful to the organisational needs of an SME, with limited resources, that is unable to invest in the adoption of an integrated knowledge management system yet still regards knowledge as both intellectual and relational capital (Cegarra-Navarro & Dewhurst 2006, Schrire 2006, Stake 1995). We are able to see from the literature that the concept of knowledge management remains of interest to researchers.

Knowledge Management

In their research on knowledge management issues in knowledge-intensive SMEs, Nunes et al (2006) state that although knowledge management has been successfully applied in large companies, it is disregarded by SMEs. This disregard has been attributed to the lack of sharing, recording, transferring, auditing and exploiting of organisational knowledge, together with the lack of the utilisation of available information technologies.

All businesses require the adequate management of their financial resources and SMEs usually have limited cash flow. It could, therefore, be a tough job to try to predict which SMEs might be ripe for the implementation and adoption of a knowledge management and/or an enterprise system (Ramdani & Kawalek 2009). For some SMEs, it could simply be the longevity of their commercial success that proves that their knowledge assets are being successfully managed and utilised effectively without the implementation of a dedicated knowledge management information system (Delahaye 2005).

These kinds of SMEs may be focusing outwards on their current and future trade potential, implementation and competitiveness as opposed to continuously strategizing around a board table on the administration of internal knowledge

(Singh, Garg & Deshmukh 2008). Their proven success of organisational learning will continue to come from an ongoing ability to record, document and manage all of their unstructured knowledge, which is difficult to capture and augment, yet invaluable to any practice based SME (Dias 2007, Espedal 2007, Schultz 2005).

Difficulties are still encountered when organisations make attempts to initiate change because new approaches cannot succeed in cultures that are bound up in their old ways of working (Filson & Lewis 2000). There is an opportunity for researchers to highlight the strategies and techniques that management in organisations develop and use in order to face, overcome and avoid any resistances to any organisational changes (Griffiths & Light 2009). Literature on management and leadership therefore, remains current for organisational researchers to review.

Management and Leadership

Leadership in organisations has been previously examined in terms of the influence of leaders covering subjects such as leadership effects, communication and the need for transparent leadership. This literature determines that leaders, because each are also part of the whole community at work, have to remain effective in terms of their direct actions, their communication styles, their perceptions of others, others perceptions of them and their connected diverse team involvement (Ashman & Lawler 2008, Hambley, O'Neill & Kline 2007, Vogelgesang & Lester 2009, Williams, Parker & Turner 2007).

The attention and involvement of the organisational leadership can be the one consistent component that can contribute to that organisation's ethical and moral behaviour (Velthouse & Kandogan 2007). The literature on leaders and managers has demonstrated that by its very nature, leadership is a human endeavour and **self-awareness** can be a powerful tool for social influence (Sosik 2001, Vogelgesand & Lester 2009).

A modern day manager must guide discussions through to resolution and have the good grace and sense not to overburden the process with personal ambition and ego (Sheard, Kakabadse & Kakabadse 2011).

There are absences in the research literature that demonstrate how organisational leaders can or have in fact met these aspirations of ethical behaviour, style, perception and leadership connection. There is a research need to determine if leaders can actually use their **self-awareness** and emotional intelligence when dealing with employees who have to comply to unyielding organisational aims and objectives (Berson & Sosik 2007, Melita Prati, McMillan-Capehart & Karriker 2009).

In doing so, this will help to determine some traits of the constructive leader, which ones advertently or inadvertently act out destructive leadership traits and if and how, these traits could be more commonly defined (Einarsen, Aasland & Skogstad 2007, Tepper 2000).

Research has determined that managers that have to mindset switch may not be most effective in their subsequent decision making. Ambivalently, if the tasking arrangements require both cooperation and creativity, then optimal performance does require the synthesis of regular switching between collectivistic and individualistic perspectives (Goncalo & Staw 2006, Hamilton et al 2011). There is a difference between being a good manager and being an effective leader and just simply equating leadership with management is a common, yet unhealthy business practice (Hatch, Kostera & Kozminski 2006).

If researchers are given the opportunity to measure the interaction styles and differences of real life managers and leaders at work, then it could be determined what leadership styles and behaviours are most effective in actual teams (Kets De Vries 2007, Hambley, O'Neill & Kline 2007, Wageman, Fisher & Hackman 2009).

The management and employee relationship may well be friendly but it is rarely based upon friendship (Jeske 2001). There is very little literature available on whether there is a connection between the impact of this omnipresent leadership involvement on employee proactive behaviours and the social influences that a charismatic leader can innovatively have (Den Hartog, De Hoogh & Keegan 2007).

Some literature on joint leadership states that there is a need for these kinds of leaders to have a perception of their own learning and development needs for example, their social and intrapersonal competencies (Wilhelmson 2006). Wider research conducted on a broader selection of organisational managers could give some additional results on the ubiquity of joint leadership, the relationships of these joint leaders and their impact on the organisational culture and work processes (Conger & Lawler III 2009, Manzoni & Barsoux 2009).

The research approach when dealing with managers and their organisational politics seems to have importance. According to Manzoni & Barsoux (2009) who provided managers with insight into the links between political behaviour and leadership action, the word "politics" was considered by managers as a taboo subject that each themselves regarded as the "shadow side" of leadership action.

If SMEs strive to become innovation pioneers in their fields of industry, their board members and management teams need to pay attention to their organisational cultures and its shadow sides, as contained within these cultures are individuals with the capacity to hinder both the implementation of new strategy and the practical implementation of the existing ones (Einarsen, Aasland & Skogstad 2007, Naranjo-Valencia, Jimenez- Jimenez & Sanz-Valle 2011, Tepper 2000).

SMEs do also have contained within them leaders who have the constructive capacity to turn the organisational noxious into organisational learning and improve rather than damage performance and progress (Clair & Dufresne 2007).

My own qualification as a person-centred counsellor brought me to consider how the work of Carl Rogers could be relevant in the workplace. Hannabuss (1997) encourages managers, trainers and supervisors to remove themselves from their managerial comfort zones and place themselves, sometimes, into the more unfamiliar world of counselling by using Carl Rogers' core conditions to enhance their effective workplace management skills.

In a study undertaken by Gatongi (2007) there is a migration of the use of person-centred counselling skills from the organisational domain to the educational one. Despite the obvious differences of these two environments, it can be seen how effective Carl Rogers' core conditions can be. In schools, the skills are shown to diminish and alleviate disruptive behaviour in classrooms, as teachers let pupils know their feelings and explain why standards of behaviour are important.

Hannabuss (1997) says that all organisational managers and leaders can develop their interpersonal skills through an increased understanding, a portrayal of acceptance and be authentic in all of their managerial dealings. Researchers should then assess the results.

Taking a critical perspective and hoping to broaden the sights of management perspectives, each of us are led to believe by Bolle (2006) that Heidegger (1962, 1966, 2010, 2010) still shows us why management is necessary, what it needs to react to and on what it is founded. Leadership and people management has something really existentially ambivalent about it and in this way, Heidegger (1962) phenomenologically, could be appreciated in terms of offering a care and concern dimension for the assessment of management skills.

Groups, Teams and Team Working

It would be an impossible task for any researcher to ignore groups, teams and team working when conducting a literature review on SME activity. Researchers have had a historical interest in interpersonal and intergroup cooperative behaviours that are based on trust, monitoring, cooperation and reciprocity (Ferrin, Bligh & Kohles 2007, Malinowski 1922).

One viewpoint has been taken that play in adulthood still matters because creativity is borne by being removed from the more constraining reality that individuals function in at work, thus providing the freedom to explore and experiment with new ideas and innovative thought patterns (Goldmintz & Schaefer 2007).

According to Goncalo & Staw (2006) current research in organisational behaviour suggests that organisations should adopt collectivistic values because they promote harmony, cooperation and productivity. Their results, however, indicate that individualistic values, although they can incite the destructive, conflict and opportunism, are more beneficial if the spark of creativity is not to be extinguished.

The findings in one research study on unitary workplace fun, concluded that fun is fundamental and fun in the workplace, as a multi-dimensional construct, is one **organisational** characteristic that is still missing in the current research literature (Tews, Michel & Bartlett 2012).

A 1960s viewpoint taken of working with the concept of the team-as-a-whole potential determines, then, that there must be existing some excellent models, theories and techniques for working with teams that are not yet well enough known to the wider business world (Whitaker & Lieberman 1964).

There is one argument that defends using the work of Bion in the study of the human relations that exist inside organisational cultures and in society as a whole (French & Simpson 2010, Bion 1961, 1962, 1965). Interest in Bion's work continues to increase. Appreciation and application of his extraordinary insights into group life justifies further study, which could be adjusted to take into account the more modern day organisational SME team setups (Fraley 2007, Friedman 2006, Lipgar 2006).

Some literature on teams was focused more on the role and emphasis that the team leader played in team building (Ambrosini, Bowman & Burton-Taylor 2007) whilst other authors said that frequent communication was the emphasis required to help to build the team's social capital that was nested in the member's relationships (Joshi, Sarker & Sarker 2007).

Emotions are part and parcel of group organisational life and there is a space in the research for identifying the different types of group emotions, their influences and their consequences in small groups and work teams (Kelly & Barsade 2001). According to Troth (2009) organisational researchers could do more work on further determining the findings of their research by considering how team levels of emotional intelligence and task complexity might impact upon team conflict behaviours and team decision making performance.

Other philosophical research has determined that collective action is the product of individuals who orient themselves around a joint project, regarding their own actions as contributing to the collective outcome (Kutz 2000). If researchers could bridge these existing gaps, findings could define the widespread social phenomenon of the collective actions of these jointly acting individuals, who reciprocally help each other in all kinds of practical tasking arrangements, whilst working in teams.

Technology and Tools

The virtual world has also made an impact upon team working and the use of modern day technology and the internet makes it possible for SMEs to use virtual teams in their production work (Hardin, Fuller & Davison 2007, Potter, Balthazard & Cooke 2000, Potter & Balthazard 2002). What is also important when working with an overseas based virtual team is that cultural backgrounds are a factor for consideration by all members of the organisational culture (Hardin, Fuller & Davison 2007).

In particular, the perception of leadership is a critical factor for these geographically distributed teams and their successful outcomes (Hambley, O'Neill & Kline 2007). Virtual leadership, however, might lack the integral leadership presence that can inspire team working and performance, so more research would assist to further understand the impact of virtual leadership and the related virtual team interactions styles (Potter & Balthazard 2002).

The literature on the continued use of web-based technology and the everyday exposure of workforces to it confirms that directors and owner-managers need to start to pay attention to the potential addictiveness of the internet at work and if its continual daily use is being conducted in healthy ways

(Guadagno & Cialdini 2007, Taylor, Fieldman & Altman 2008, Whitty & Carr 2006, Yellowlees & Marks 2007).

The computer can be regarded as an extension of the self. Internet based activities are now a unique and vital tool for organisations to utilise in order to optimise their performance however, misuse of the internet will continue to occur until the levels of exploitation are identified, more fully understood and effectively addressed (Whitty & Carr 2006). Technology is now part of the organisational social collective related with the commercial activities of an SME, so its use and impact is really worth addressing in any social organisational research.

Gender/Women

Gender research has discovered that 21st century thinking has brought some change in Western ideologies for woman managers, but women are still underrepresented in leadership positions (Koch 2005). One laboratory and field study determined, clearly, that teams led by a woman were much more affectively expressive than the teams led by a man and all women teams were the most expressive (Koch 2005).

The gender bias against females in leadership positions has been widely expressed in both the academic literature and the popular press. The work of some early authors still remains available in the modern day literature. However, their viewpoint on the personality of women, the professional domain and the domestic domain could be too controversial for today's organisational leadership thinking (Lewin 1935).

By researching organisational cultures that promote equality and values of fairness, these gender biases could be avoided and researchers could also investigate what advantages, circumstances and situations place females on an equal footing with their male counterparts (Scott & Brown 2006).

Women now participate more in the fields of science, engineering and technology (SET) but little research exists on how women, especially those in management positions, are performing within these chosen fields. Unfortunately, some findings have determined that some barriers do still exist (Servon & Visser 2011). Theoretical research suggests that women engineers have found a way of redefining themselves in order to achieve balance between their female and engineering identities.

Questions still remain for organisational researchers to make some redefinitions of this in social and psychology research to answer further career questions and make engineering an attractive profession for women (Kyriakidou 2012).

The role of gender is significant to the ways in which one can be online persuaded as some research has identified that men rely more on the rationality of the argument and women prefer face-to-face contact in order to be rationally persuaded (Elsbach, Cable & Sherman 2010, Guadagno & Cialdini 2007).

To sum the literature argument up for whether women or men make better leaders, the making of the final point comes not from specific gender related leadership, but speaks for the neutrality that effective leadership demands. Leadership is genderless and down to the capabilities of the individual leaders concerned and leading the teams when the time is right. The best team leaders are the ones who have learned to shift their orientation, depending on the situations that their teams face.

Sometimes these leaders can act swiftly and at other times, these leaders defer action until considerable observation and analysis has been determined (Wageman, Fisher & Hackman 2009). These gender differences are worth considering by further social research.

The Family Concept

Systematic studies have previously examined the concept of the family construct in organisations and one study in particular, highlights the need for SMEs to pay attention to the boundary conditions of the use of the family metaphor in organisations. There is a need to address if it is being misused or when it is simply inappropriate for their organisational setting (Brotheridge & Lee 2006).

One research study identifies the person who fosters the group members sense of belonging and identity (Neri 2006). This person embodies and inspires organisational functions through reciprocal arrangements. Because this individual is more than just the spokesperson, the qualities, characteristics and impact of these key players could make a contribution to research on organisational culture. Through their personal capabilities, they also have the ability to encourage and foster organisational transformational change and development (Beaver & Hutchings 2005, Neri 2006).

SMEs may also find it helpful to unravel some of the complexities related to employee performance in family firms and construct a framework that helps them to determine if the firm is heading for success and/or failure (Gibb Dyer Jr 2010). From both the teams perspective and the perspective of others in the team, the age differences for young members has already been evaluated.

Age differences are important when considering perspective taking to understand the dissimilarities in teams based in highly technical environments (Williams, Parker & Turner 2007). Whereas, the personal capabilities of key players in organisational development has placed the emphasis on prior experiences (Beaver & Hutchings 2007).

This literature on team working did not highlight if there is any impact on younger people working in teams of older and more experienced individuals, especially in highly technical environments. Organisational researchers could determine what kind of working relationships exist in age diverse work teams, that include both young and older team members in particular, in single disciplines like engineering and/or software development SMEs (Beaver & Hutchings 2007, Williams, Parker & Turner 2007).

There are still some research gaps for determining the right fit of the person when recruitment decisions are being made. According to Sekiguchi & Huber (2011) future research should examine all of the pertinent contextual right fit factors, in the organisational structure and the organisational culture, that influence these right kind of fits (Sekiguchi & Huber 2011).

On employee well-being, very little is known about the decision making processes that determines whether work interferes with family or family interferes with work, especially the psychological conflict that individuals can experience, if and when family and work compete (Greenhaus & Powell 2003).

I have reviewed the literature currently available on organisational wisdom, knowledge management, management and leadership, groups, teams and team working, technology and tools, gender/women and the family concept.

Included in organisational wisdom is the individual wisdom that makes use of both institutional and social processes like organisational structure, culture and leadership (Kessler 2006). The synthesis of all of this knowledge remains scant in the literature (Kessler & Bailey 2006).

The impact of the culture on knowledge management is raised in the literature by Filson & Lewis (2000) Griffiths & Light (2009). Organisations encounter difficulty as they initiate change. Resistance and conflict is encountered in cultures that are bound up in old ways of working.

Ashman & Lawler 2008, Hambley, O'Neill & Kline 2007, Vogelgesand & Lester 2009, Williams, Parker & Turner 2007 say that managers and leaders are members of the organisational community at work and need to remain effective in terms of direct actions, communication styles, perceptions and involvement. Wilhelmson (2006) places the emphasis on social and intrapersonal competencies. The literature also conveyed that leadership is a human endeavour and **self-awareness** aids social influence (Sosik 2001, Vogelgesand & Lester 2009).

A research account of how managers and leaders have met aspirations of ethical behaviour, style, perception, and leadership connections is welcomed.

A current study by Ferrin, Bligh & Kohles (2007) and a much earlier one by Malinowski (1922) demonstrate that researchers have an historical interest in interpersonal and intergroup cooperative behaviours that are based on trust, monitoring, cooperation and reciprocity. Other studies by Ambrosini, Bowman & Burton-Taylor (2007) and Joshi, Sarker & Sarker 2007 focus more on the role and emphasis of team leaders and social capital nested in member relationships.

Technology is now part of the organisational social collective making the work of virtual teams possible and undertake the commercial activities of an SME. Hardin, Fuller & Davison (2007) Potter, Balthazard & Cooke (2000) and Potter & Balthazard (2002) have demonstrated that virtual teams exist in organisational formats. Hambley, O'Neill & Kline (2007) emphasise that leadership is critical for the successful outcome of virtual teams. Potter & Balthazard (2002) says more research would highlight the impact of virtual leadership and virtual team interaction styles.

Servon & Visser (2011) have demonstrated that women now participate in the fields of science, engineering and technology but little research exists on how women managers perform within these fields in terms of social and psychological research.

In terms of the family concept, Neri (2006) has identified an organisational member, not necessarily a manager, who cultivates the **well-being** of the group. This person also has the ability to encourage and foster organisational transformational change and development. Brotheridge & Lee (2006) however, highlight the concept of the family metaphor in organisations and also, its appropriateness and misuse.

The majority of the literature used qualitative methods such as observation, interviews, focus groups, semi-structured survey questionnaires, narrative analysis, comparative study and secondary information by researchers who were not full-time participant observers or key organisational workers, and therefore, more comfortably distanced from their subjects.

Because I was a director of Newland's and a manager of the workforce, conducting interviews and focus groups unrelated to Newland's commercial activities and my role responsibilities could have placed undue pressure on an organisational member who did not wish to participate. The same consideration would apply to the completion of a survey questionnaire.

As a key worker and potential immersed researcher, ethnography would be suitable for the study of Newland's cultural events and its workforce. Ethnography is inductive and primarily based upon the direct observation of people in particular settings. Newland's naturally occurring data would underpin this study therefore, non-intrusive observation was my only option. Autoethnography permits the inclusion of self in research and therefore, my chosen research option.

According to Muncey (2010) autoethnographies are characterised by text that evoke the imagination and increase the reader's understanding of the research topic.

What I particularly noted in the literature was that very few studies used grounded theory as a philosophical approach and a way to interpret and explain their findings. A creative and intellectual interpretation on the use of grounded theory was demonstrated in qualitative research by Turner (1983) which had been personalised by the researcher's justification for the sometimes ordinary and mundane.

In the Turner (1983) work, examples are given that show it is possible to lessen the purist grounded theory methodological approach in order to gain a better understanding of the everyday human interactions that take place in an organisational setting, life and the wider world in general.

Even if the outcome was deemed descriptive, grounded theory, would still contribute greatly to my study. The belief was that constructivist grounded theory, as a philosophical approach, would always reveal the nature of Newland's organisational culture, produce the greatest of insights and provide a better understanding of the research participants organisational life as it unfolded in their own unique world of work (Charmaz 2006, Glaser 1978, 1998, 2001, Glaser & Strauss 1967).

Obviously, not all research on organisational culture and work based activities used qualitative methods. One quantitative study on knowledge management by Alavi, Kayworth & Leidner (2005) used correlation analysis to analyse their data. O'Regan & Ghobadian (2006) conducted a study to produce findings on the applicability of generic strategies in SMEs. They addressed the limitations in their research and the benefit of augmenting quantitative data with qualitative in-depth case studies or an ethnographic approach.

All of the literature, however, gave results on the organisational activities of SMEs and were worth considering in the planned research.

The following section of the literature review will focus on the authors who specifically call for ethnographic research to be conducted in SMEs and give their reasons why each say it is effective for the study of an organisational setting like Newland's.

Using Ethnography and Autoethnography

Quantitative studies may be well suited for the measurement of success, but there are limitations with this method when examining the social organisation of an SME and the social complexities of organisational culture. There are challenges in relation to how the researcher quantifies, mathematically analyses, measures and correlates how one individual at work is thinking and feeling about their employer, job, manager and work colleagues.

One quantitative study on organisational culture made use of single informants, the company CEOs, using a previously tested questionnaire. The researchers admitted that the use of multi-informants would have enhanced further the validity of their findings (Naranjo-Valencia, Jimenez-Jimenez & Sanz-Valle 2011). Not all quantitative analysis techniques, therefore, have provided strategic and organisational performance researchers with the breadth of results that were sought and desired.

Any future research on strategy and organisational performance should consider a more in-depth approach (O'Regan & Ghobadian 2006).

Collective organisational groups have the ability to become qualitative research multiple informants because their complexities, ideas and skills are very applicable to their organisations. The researcher, however, needs to remain focused on the fact that the whole point of the observation work is to understand people in their work roles and how each might feel and act at work (Barnes, Ernst & Hyde 1999, Ferrin, Bligh & Kohles 2007).

It is the goal of Anderson (2006) to champion the potential and promise of an alternative to evocative autoethnography, one that is qualitative consistent, referred to as analytic autoethnography, derived from traditional symbolic interactionism. This approach was encouraged by the work of Arthur Bochner and Carolyn Ellis, who according to Anderson (2006) have tested and well-documented variations of autoethnography (Bochner & Ellis 2001).

In addition, Vryan (2006) believes researchers can more usefully establish what analytic autoethnography is and also what it can be, so to be able to enhance the abilities to learn and teach about human life in new ways.

Atkinson (2006) steps up to rescue autoethnography from the analytics by implicating that the self of the ethnographer is always, to some degree, connected to the ethnographic process. Ethnographers do, however, have to be a safeguard against any implied supposition of reflexivity, that self-transformation through personal reflection, will be the outcome of their research processes.

Muncey's (2010) view on the creation of autoethnographies is that there has been an increase in the number of papers published and reports of autoethnographic studies have found a place for their dissemination in the academic world. In spite of this increase, very few studies of organisational culture within small to medium-sized enterprises exist and even fewer use ethnographic methods to explore the complex phenomenon of these working environments (Brooks 2008, Fineman, Gabriel & Sims 2010, Gingrich-Philbrook 2005).

Storey (1994) provides organisational researchers with the opportunity to conduct future research as there still remains the need to focus on studies of universal definitions of organisational cultures within SMEs. Organisational cultures are an integral part of organisational life and due to their complexities, the establishment of a universal definition for such cultures could be too complex to standardise.

Organisational researchers do have the opportunity to conduct studies on organisational cultures in SMEs and give illustration to the unique complexities that exist within them, which could add to the definitions for organisational culture, but not necessarily universally define them (Peel 2006).

Trice & Beyer (1984) have also appealed to organisational researchers to conduct studies that place the micro-detail of their organisational phenomena into a framework concept of culture. Later, Trice & Beyer (1993) extend these concepts by offering the opportunity for organisational researchers to study the cultural processes that underlie much of the daily activities of modern day organisations using their typology of rites.

Trice & Beyer (1984) make reference to substance, a network of meanings, manifested, from which practices emerge that express and communicate those meanings. These authors, however, state clearly that they do not expect that their typology of six major characteristics of organisational culture, as rites and ceremonials, is exhaustive, but it is a very good starting point from which organisational researchers could add refinements and enhancements.

In particular, there has been an increase in the focus of the use of qualitative methods to gain understandings of the work practices used in software engineering based SMEs (Bodan, Muller & Nett 2011).

Whilst all of this literature is pertinent to the operational activities of an SME and its organisational culture, I have been unable to uncover any literature that is based specifically upon the experience of an employed solo director cum manager, acting also as the researcher, like myself.

Although Mitroff & Kilman (1976) studied the experiences and stories of working managers to discover their concept of the ideal organisation, neither were the researcher, who was also a key worker, inside an SME based organisational culture in which one or the other were employed.

According to Kessler (2006) the modern day strategic corporate social and ethical complexities of organisations have cast doubt upon traditional models of management, highlighting a need for new perspectives and approaches to the behaviour within, as well as the stewardship of organisations.

To summarise, it is clear that some researchers have focused their sights on one organisational cultural element, discrete feature or a single aspect of an SME, like strategy, knowledge management, leadership, management and teaming.

Even though the research literature demonstrated the variety of working elements of an organisation, it lacked any insight or focus on the social organisation of SMEs.

Additionally, the literature failed to demonstrate how the organisational culture could be grounded in the work activities. My developing thoughts aligned with those of Dubreuil (2008) who identified that despite all of the research that is available, human cooperation and reciprocity in SMEs still remains a social puzzle.

Having summarised the salient points from the literature that I consider applicable to this research study and an exploration on ethnography and autoethnography, the following section focuses on the opportunity to make a contribution to the gap in the research to date.

Research Opportunity

Using ethnography, Newland Limited will be the site for the study. The research participants are Newland's workforce. The people and their interactions are the focus of the research.

Because similarities existed, I will use Trice & Beyer's (1984) typology of rites as a way to explain Newland's organisational activities, socialisation, ritualising, celebrations and the joint undertaking of work in groups and teams using modern day tools and technology (Atkinson & Delamont 2006, Peel 2006).

Grounded theory analytically fragments narrative textual data into codes, categories and their properties and dimensions, from which an interpretive hypothesis of the subject being researched will emerge. My aim was that this principle of constructivist grounded theory would reveal the abstract nature and reality of Newland's organisational culture and members.

I will need to seriously consider my own organisational roles of director and manager and their impact upon this study.

In my professional roles, I used management ethical behaviours, leadership styles and self-awareness to promote rather than hinder Newland's organisational performance, including Carl Rogers' counselling skills to help me do this. It was also my aim to remain aware of any preconceptions that might exist in these roles and question my interpretation of them in the observation work, data collection and analysis (Charmaz 2006, Silverman 2005, 2011).

Gender researchers may also be interested in this research because I was a woman manager that worked in the highly technical environment of an engineering SME that remained market leader in its field greater than the twenty-five years that I was employed there.

The employed workforce of Newland's was made up of different age categories and individuals, with diverse characteristics and professional qualifications and training, that encompassed engineering, technical and administration. The teaming arrangements included both young and older group members who were expected to take full responsibility for their own actions and decision making. In this research, these age differences have not been taken into consideration to determine whether age in team working has any significance and whether people with higher qualifications have different expectations.

The internal organisational culture of an SME are group based societies that thrive through a combined, collective effort that benefits all, something like the tribal life that Malinowski (1922) defined as a framework of social cohesion and stability through the concept of solidarity. Similarly, through a unique sense of community, an organisational life, people, interactions, corporate governance, organisational systemisation, the manifestation of a combined effort and the undertaking of duty, Newland's continued as **an** economic success.

Hayano (1979) says of Malinowski that no matter how exhaustive his knowledge of the Trobriand Island society was, he (Malinowski) could never be considered a native by his or their standards. Speaking on behalf of Newland's own organisational cultural social diversity and organisational life, I do not strive to be one of the natives to gain a natives view, I already belong as one of the natives and have to continuously question my native view (Eberle & Maeder 2011, Silverman 2005, 2011).

I am able to describe an organisational functionality, coupled with social complexities, from being central in the mix, influenced by my roles as an employed person at work, a director of the company, a manager and leader of the workforce, a work colleague and a group member with a desire to belong. It has been proposed by King (2004) that we, as people, establish meaning by belonging, doing and understanding what we all do.

Because I was central to Newland's organisational core and part of the workforce, I would not singly adopt a researcher's metaphorical understanding of my work colleagues and Newland's events (Alvesson 2010).

Longevity of time enabled my development of successful working relationship with all of Newland's members upon whom I could place some value judgements and trust. As Ashleigh & Nandhakumar (2007) indicate, trust is engendered from closely located, tight-knit teams that have worked together over long periods of time, all aiming for the common good (Trice & Beyer 1984).

After providing a general, statistical and political picture of the small medium enterprise (SME) I was able to review the current literature that is available on SMEs and the segmented aspects of their organisational activities. From this review, I could determine what absences existed in that literature.

There is an opportunity for organisational researchers to conduct the ethnographic study on the social organisations of SMEs. These types of studies would make a significant contribution to the existing body of literature, as currently, it only demonstrates the single discrete aspects of organisations and their cultures.

Research Aims, Objectives and Research Approach

The research aims and objectives were to reveal Newland's naturally occurring organisational cultural events undertaken by personnel in their work setting. The objective would therefore address three main areas of interest:

(1) To reveal, describe and explain how the individuals and groups work together; negatively and positively.
(2) To generate an understanding of what processes are at work in the group(s).
(3) To reveal and make known the functions, methods and processes of the groups and the "threads that binds us together".

In order to achieve the approved objectives it would be necessary to use a research approach to fit.

Working inside Newland's held prospective for me to become a full-time participant observer. My place gave me the opportunity to become a non-intrusive researcher. Ethnography, therefore, would naturally provide the research design in order to gather material. The coding, writing of memoranda, sorting and re-sorting associated with the grounded theory approach would be used for analysis of narratives.

Using an autoethnographic approach for the study would give an account of my experience in the place in which I worked. It would also give an account of the ways in which the whole of Newland's workforce functioned jointly, influenced by the expectations of an employer and the external commercial conditions that prevailed. Grounded theory would reveal the reality and nature of Newland's organisational culture, including the work that I conducted on behalf of the company.

The investigation would focus on Newland's organisational cultural life. The autoethnography would emanate from an in-house managers perspective of which there are very few current studies. I would provide details of Newland's organisational work functions, its social interactions and how its employees went about their everyday activities in the workplace, including having social interactions.

Further, I was aware of the need to maintain research focus and the risk of disregarding the influences that the complexities of my own organisational roles would bring.

Having provided an aim and several objectives for the research and a brief overview of the research design, I will now describe the methodology employed.

Chapter 3
The Research Methodology

This chapter covers the methodology of the study and it is divided into four sections.

In Section I—Subject, Scope and Method, I give an account of my role history that addresses, as a pre-research event, an important role change for me. I put my duties and communication skills into a context and place emphasis on the aspects of these roles that would have influence on data collection. Section II—Data Gathering outlines the method of data collection. Section III—Analysis of Data outlines my use of grounded theory in an organisational ethnographic approach.

In Section IV—Reflexivity, I provide a perspective of the influences placed upon my researcher position by my employed responsibilities.

Section I – Subject, Scope and Method

The absence of literature on the social organisation of SMEs provided me with the opportunity to conduct an ethnographic study of the organisation in which I worked. Established in 1983 and still operating in March 2009 when I retired as one of its directors, Newland's had stood the test of time as a UK based highly technical engineering SME. Innovative 3-D engineering capabilities made Newland's a market leader conducting business activities worldwide. The ethnographic study of Newland's organisational cultural activities, through rites and ceremonials, would be a worthwhile endeavour (Trice & Beyer 1984).

Using Trice & Beyer's (1984) typology of rites as a framework, the diverse activities of Newland's organisational culture was to be studied. Newland's employees would be observed as the business activities were conducted each working day. I was also a Newland's employee. From my director and managerial position, I had access to information and records that shaped the business-related activities, thus giving me exposure to the commercial engineering events that occurred inside Newland's.

The principles of grounded theory were used to analyse the data. The findings revealed a framework of the socially organised characteristics of Newland's unique and diverse cultural activities through rites and ceremonials (Charmaz 2006, Malinowski 1922, Trice & Beyer 1984). The methodology was generalised so that another ethnographer can use it in any other organisational setting.

Ethical Considerations and the Demography of Newland's Employees

I was a director of Newland's and a key manager of the enterprise. Researching Newland's workforce activities, inside an organisation in which I also worked, meant that ethical considerations had to be reviewed.

As part of the research proposal, I prepared a punch list for ethical considerations that addressed certain areas of concern. These I identified as priorities of work vs. research, directorship obligations, management responsibilities, being a researcher, confidentiality, anonymity, workforce participation autonomy, consent from Newland's owner, consent from the workforce, assessment of risks, impact upon Newland's image, shareholder and workforce and any impact upon other institutions.

I conducted a risk assessment which determined that all risks were low. Each employee was given an information sheet about the research scope, aims and objectives. The owner of Newland's gave consent in writing. Letters of consent were signed by each director and employee who agreed to be a research participant.

The research data was collected from April 2008 to the end of December 2008. The demography for Newland's employees during that time is shown in the following table:

Demography Of Newland Limited Employees									
Dates	**Total in Group**	**Number of Males**	**Number of Females**	**% Males**	**% Female**	**Male Age Range**	**Female Age Range**	**Average Male Age**	**Average Female Age**
Start 1 April 2008	12	9	3	75%	25%	24 to 64	53 to 60	36	54
End December 2008	12	9	3	75%	25%	22 to 64	53 to 60	35	54

Autoethnography

Ethnographic focus is on culture, observing the related events as a participant or non-participant observer and exploring the relationship between the culture and behaviour. The ethnography is a product of the interaction between the researcher and the social world, the researcher is setting out to capture and describe (Atkinson 2006, Gray 2004).

This research is organisational ethnography because it is based inside an organisation and is about that same organisation, but more importantly for the research, one in which I worked (Eberle & Maeder 2011). This ethnographic endeavour is always, in some degree, autoethnographic because my ethnographic self is always linked with the process of construction (Muncey 2010).

Comparing the work of the anthropologist ethnographer Bronislaw Malinowski (1922) to that of the existentialist Martin Heidegger (1962) Malinowski keeps his world succinct, straightforward, understandable to the reader in the narrative of the events of village life. I see Heidegger addressing his concepts in a more complex way grasping the meaning of Being in the world through his concept of *Dasein*.

Generally, Heidegger's (1962) concept of *Dasein* is that *Dasein* is essentially an invitation for all human beings to take a different perspective of being in the world, not in the context of things and objectives, but in meaning and understanding the world as it is seen, known, understood and interpreted, as an exploration of self. Curiosity is a tendency of *Dasein's* being as it has a potentiality-for-seeing. Awareness lets what is ready-to-hand, available, and what is present-at-hand, perceived, be encountered 'bodily' in themselves with regard to the way they look.

According to Carman (2001) Heidegger understands the work of the phenomenologist to be a drawing out and revealing that which is covered up and buried over in what ordinarily shows itself.

My research aims and objectives were to reveal, describe and explain how Newland's individuals and groups worked together, to generate an understanding of what processes were at work and to reveal and make known the functions, methods and processes of the groups and the "threads that binds us together".

As a qualitative researcher who is expected to inquisitively question all interpretations made in the research process, I see connections of Heidegger's (1962) curious and aware *Dasein* with Silverman's (2011) interpretation of reflexivity or, the self-aware analysis of the dynamics between researcher and participants, the critical capacity to make explicit the position assumed by the observer in the field and the way in which the researcher's positioning impacts upon the research process.

Although, I am always persuaded by what is external through my own consciousness of duty and even though scientific enquiry insists it is possible, I cannot transcend the world in an attempt to treat it dispassionately or objectively (Ashman & Lawler 2008).

Observational work is multi-sensorial as it has the potential to include all that we see, hear and smell from which the researcher sets out to establish meaning that is later conveyed to a reader (Suzuki et al 2007). This research on Newland's and its organisational culture is ethnographically focused. My success as a researcher, however, would also depend upon my ability to understand and interpret the organisational community where the data was being gathered.

Even at this early critical juncture, I accepted that there would have to be considerations for my own roles in the study. I could not be distanced from all of the employed functions that I conducted in the organisation. When I was thinking in the role of participant observer, I would be considered in the same directorship, managerial and leadership role by myself and colleagues with whom I worked and was observing. My employment duties would always have to take priority over the study.

I would always be reflecting upon old collective experiences and somehow juggling and managing the new strategies and concepts, striving to keep the rickety harmonious present day activities in a state of balance and commercial liquidity. My experience of events would always influence my interpretation of them.

The daily social interactions, joint group activities, reciprocal working arrangements and the odd ceremonial events that were celebrated in Newland's, helped me to appreciate Malinowski's (1922) observations and compelling understanding of the micro-detailed aspects of village life events of tribes in the Trobriand Islands. I however, lacked the tranquillity of the tropical island that Malinowski so obviously enjoyed. Inside Newland's, an SME based upon engineering innovation, we too had our own kind of organisational village life.

Within, there was the impact and ramifications of the everyday social implications of being at work that tested the boundaries of management and personal tolerance. As appealing as it was, functionalism would not suit my research.

As well as being an ethnographer in Newland's, I had different employment obligations to fulfil in two roles. I was Newland's Operations Director and I was a manager of all of its daily organisational activities. On a personal level, I was a qualified person-centred counsellor and I sometimes used counselling skills to assist me in the workplace. Inevitably, these circumstances were unchangeable therefore, it is important to mention that my role duties could have implications for the materials gathered.

To give clarity to Section I of the methodology chapter, I will start with my role as manager.

My Role as Manager

As a manager, I sometimes felt frustration at the external and social interruptions that occurred inside Newland's community especially when such disturbances had to be placed above the work priorities. I wrote this comment in my field notes because I often had a empathic sense that:

Work/life balance is tilted too much to social needs.

I was a woman manager that worked in the highly technical engineering environment of an SME. I had a caring management attitude that was not always well balanced by the other two Newland's directors who were male. I could sense that my approach was regarded with some suspicion and there was a lack of trust in my ability to manage the engineering capabilities of the group. Although, I was perceived as a popular manager, I was not an engineer with highly technical abilities. My background was company law and accountancy.

Realistically, I knew there were moments when my kinder and caring attitude was taken advantage of.

During pressurised production times when Newland's engineers wanted to take time off and it was in the company's best commercial interests that staff absences should be minimised, I was always approached from the family angle. At this perspective, I admit that I found it difficult to object to the grant of absence, but I always found a way to compromise the position and negotiate terms that kept all parties content, including the family.

I did, however, have the capacity within me to tackle any liberty taking and put my management foot down (Brotheridge & Lee 2006). I was aware of not going too far and micro-managing, by pulling back the reins and taking up too much control of the detail to the detriment of us all (Einarsen, Aasland & Skogstad 2007, Wilhelmson 2006).

I strived to keep my self-awareness as a way to influence my leadership tactics and to keep my role as manager close to the workforce, amenable but not too overtly friendly (Berson & Sosik 2007, Sosik 2001, Sosik & Jung 2003, Yukl 2002).

Even though we all strived mostly for the work day ideal, sometimes uncomfortable events happened that strained Newland's organisational seams. Incidents occurred that required a person to uncomfortably reassert themselves, confrontations arose, uncomfortable silences were evident, negative interpretations were voiced and frosty glances were followed by squaring up (Smith 2007).

Although I could not prove it, I heard over the grapevine that two of Newland's engineers actually got into a physical fight when they were away at site, offshore on the west coast of Australia. I was never formally told this information, but somehow the news was given to me. I made a constructive management decision to ignore it.

As a director, manager and member of the workforce, I felt that I was accepted and liked. I knew also that some level of incongruence existed in Newland's organisational culture that disregarded the popularity of all of the management staff. I was never given a reason to believe that Newland's employees would or did deliberately mislead me or any of the other directors yet, I was certain that not all information was passed onto me, even when it was in my best interests to receive it. The success of the grapevine intervened.

As a manager, I organisationally connected myself to Newland's commercial activities and as a person, I made every effort to be part of the community. As a manager and person, I regarded this incongruence, withholding, as the shadowy part, the dark side, of Newland's organisational culture. Management staff were kept in the gloom and secret conversations took place that related to matters that were unpopular, sensitive or in direct disagreement with management requirements, needs or wishes.

This pushing away of management is likely the pattern for how Newland's group members protected themselves from any sense of a manager's invasive presence or an inhibiting leadership pressure that can create relationship tension (Kivetz & Tyler 2007, Manzoni & Barsoux 2009). The perception of leadership intrusion might have stemmed also from the concept of the pressures of seniority and authority, even when the manager might have been a popular group member and an associated work colleague (Einarsen, Aasland & Skogstad 2007).

However, the attitude of Newland's organisational culture towards making the manager's feel organisationally homeless and estranged changed when it was deemed that there was an advantage to be gained (Bolle 2006, Espedal 2007).

Even though I could not change the situation, it is important to mention that such exclusions of my manager role, could have implications for the materials gathered, because the information that was withheld could have been useful to the research.

The counsellor in me helped to find the required levels of frustrated acceptance (Gatongi 2007, Hannabuss 1997). I often wondered, however, if the counsellor in me helped or hindered. It helped me to understand Newland's workforce in an empathic way, but it also helped the workforce to sometimes manipulate the softer side of me. Because I could and did empathise with the workforce, as their manager rather than as a researcher or counsellor, one state of Newland's group culture leapt out and grabbed my attention.

The counsellor in me sensed that a conditions of worth relationship (Rogers 1951, 1980) existed within Newland's organisational community. I made particular reference to it in my field notes:

There is a limit to openness because a conditional relationship exists.

The researcher in me flagged up a warning about not jumping to conclusions about why a situation exists and reiterated the need to simply record the presence of a phenomenon, that is later analysed from a researcher's viewpoint.

From my managerial standpoint, its presence caused me some concern, because it was in direct contradiction to the idealised values of my own managerial objectives aiming for openness and respect towards each other. I intended to do something about it. Managerially, I was assisted by the sense of empathy brought to me through counsellor training. I was aware also of the possibility of a research slip.

From the organisations point of view, I sensed that the limitations of the group were governed by a historical feeling of not being able to be open and to act authentically because of the fear related to the historical experience of having a bad managerial experience (Espedal 2007, Einarsen, Aasland & Skogstad 2007, Tepper 2000).

Sometimes indirect sarcasm or light prejudices were vocalised in the group which I thought belonged elsewhere and outside Newland's organisational walls. From a managerial point of view, I judged that these were not too serious to formally address as such comments did not cause embarrassment to the company (Robbins & Parlavecchio 2006). I took notice of them because from a research point of view, such comments could have some social significance in terms of the influences of Newland's organisational life.

My Role as Operations Director

The work production teams had a level of autonomy to conduct the practical methods of work that were synonymous to the technical requirements of the tasking arrangements. Leading as the Operations Director, I was not responsible for the technical content of the work, but I was responsible for ensuring that the technical content met the contract specifications, delivery dates were met and an invoice was raised. I, therefore, adopted a policy to sometimes remain at a distance, as an observer, in watchful waiting.

The exception to this was in matters relating to compliance with corporate governance, which was the direct responsibility of the Operations Director and where there was no place for negotiation. When these circumstances arose, it could be difficult to keep everyone satisfied and smoothly integrate the incompatible, when the legal and morale demands just simply had to be compliantly met (Hermans 2006).

The other exception was to become involved if asked, or invited to do so. Even though as the Operations Director I could still distance myself when necessary, my message to the group was to stay in direct contact with each other, for all of the times that it was practical to do so.

Facets of leadership are linked to the personal development of the manager whose influences are informed through an increased self-awareness (Andersen 2009, Berson & Sosik 2007, Clair & Dufresne 2007, Greenleaf 1970). In attempting to achieve effective communications, I personally maintained an approachable stance by being accessible. I offered an approbative review for any exemplary effort made by an individual or a team.

I would openly offer praise when an intricate and complex 3-D model was presented to me and I could recognise pride in the team. I genuinely admired the integrity of the 3-D engineering models and the team effort that was required to produce the precise levels of required accuracy.

I kept an autonomous hands-off approach that did not interfere, even when the going got tough and only asked for unquestionable compliance when corporate governance demanded its full acquiescence. I was comfortable to become the observer only, in watchful waiting, as and when it was necessary. I could demonstrate patience and detachment in the expectancy that deadlines would be met. I could trust the teams to produce their work on time and I demonstrated my trust by remaining non-interfering and tolerant.

These were complex management interaction tumblers that I constantly had to organisationally juggle. An important part of my work duties was to maintain the appropriate levels of communication to maintain boundaries that kept a level of contact with the workforce and keep the process of commerce in action.

For all managers in business, there has to be a positive and constructive method for communicating needs and wants in order to pass on directions, instructions, wishes or at times, demands (Ambrosini, Bowman & Burton-Taylor 2007). The communication has to be effective enough to provide the right kind of direction and guidance that enhances organisational performance without the need for dominance (Claire & Dufresne 2007, Einarsen, Aasland & Skogstad 2007, Hannabuss 1997).

My experience as a company director, an engineering manager and training as a person-centred counsellor helped me to do this. I give some indications of the impact of my management style when one work colleague said to me on quite a few occasions:

I can sometimes see the counsellor in you.

Another colleague addressed the changed teaming issues:

It felt like we are now working as a team.

and, I was told by a co-worker that in the twenty years that we had worked together:

You've never lost your temper nor diminished a person in any way whatsoever.

I was told though that I could be impatient with computer equipment. This observation of me by a work colleague was correct. Although it was regularly upgraded and updated accordingly, Newland's network could get very slow, especially when production times were high. I sometimes felt the frustration with my work computer and my face must have demonstrated this as at times, I addressed Newland's network as:

the not-work

The network, eventually, was re-cabled with new junction boxes fitted throughout the whole of the office space after which it worked extremely satisfyingly well.

In the summer of 2006, my role in the organisation expanded when I inherited the day-to-day management of the engineering production team. I will now provide a picture of the events that occurred in Newland's during that phase.

Pre-Research Events

Intermittently between 2005 and 2006, Newland's had been experiencing management problems. For what, eventually, manifested as a significant amount of time, Newland's had been continuously encountering difficulties with the engineering production group. Morale in the work groups had reached an all-time low and there were performance and output negative ramifications. Work errors meant that some 3-D modelling analysis work had to be repeated. Due to the threat of financial penalties, Newland's was placed at commercial risk.

Due to tensions in the workplace, several employees had threatened to leave and one experienced engineer actually gave written notice. After a positive intervention, this engineer had a change of mind and decided to stay. Shortly afterwards, the technical director responsible for the organisational diminishment and reduced production output resigned and I inherited the extra managerial responsibilities.

Although, I did still remain as a director and the manager of the operational activities of Newland's and conducted those same duties, my role change brought me in closer contact with all of the production team members. I was now perceived as being their first point of contact in relation to all production work matters.

My first task was to introduce the concept of team working and a formal announcement about my more involved role was made. The purpose of my brief was to bring the group back into a more efficient and effective working process and assist in the improvement of the overall morale of the workplace in the best way that I could.

The Person-Centred Counsellor at Work

During the period of 1998 to 2002, in my free time, I had re-trained as a Rogerian person-centred counsellor. I often used these counselling skills as a point of reference to assist me in all of the organisational duties that I had been assigned (Rogers 1951, 1980).

From past experience I knew that, as a combined organisational workforce, we were lacking insight on how teams worked, good communication skills and an awareness of the impact of group behaviours. There was also a lack of regard for the intra-organisational community and there had been some criticisms of the company image (Barnes, Ernst & Hyde 1999, Ferrin, Bligh & Kohles 2007, Fraley 2007, Friedman 2007, Schon 1987). I had to rely heavily upon my own personal judgement in what I used and how I delivered the information setting out to make the right but relevant points.

Newland's employees were familiar with the services of ACAS, that benefits both employees and employers, so I used an ACAS free online training e-course available to small businesses. My intention was to jointly agree how improvements could be made organisation-wide. One objective was to insist on the recognition, owning up and acceptance of certain behaviours of those persons who had, in the past, contributed to the lack of group spirit, intentionally or unintentionally.

All of Newland's employees were responding to the atmosphere that existed at the time and there was a valid reason for that as well. I made an informed judgement on what I understood could have been wrong.

For many years, Newland's engineering work group had been used to a more heavy hands on management supervisory approach that left little space for any autonomous, creative and original thinking. I had clashed on several occasions with the technical director about such an approach, as I felt that it was limiting the undiscovered abilities of the workgroup and diminishing productivity. Often, I was just shot down in flames as I was told that my subjective, softer approach was regarded as too weak for the engineering objective environment.

I was told that I would just get walked all over, but I didn't believe a word of it. At that time, my connection with production was only initiated when the task was completed and the billing procedure was invoked. So I was more removed from the day-to-day processes of the technicalities of the engineering workgroup and I was merely an observer of what sadly became more and more negative and prohibitive effects. I had a strong sense of empathy that I found difficult to ignore and I pushed for what I felt was fair.

Dealing with individuals in a constructive and humanistic way would begin to build confidence and group stature (Clair & Dufresne 2007, French & Simpson 2010, Whitaker & Lieberman 1964). Though I lacked engineering capability and talent, I trusted that Newland's technically competent individuals would recognise their own slippage and their professional pride and integrity would carry any possible threats to the attention of the management (Baker & Sinkula 1999, Siu Loon Hoe 2007). That was my pitch for the endorsement of confidence in Newland's engineering staff and I won the point (Pfeffer 2010).

I thought of it as a new era however, Newland's employees were genuinely anxious about all of the changes and how these would impact upon them and their job reliance. A long term serving employee and director had resigned and it would take some time for the organisation to settle. We encountered some attitude and communication difficulties because uncertainty existed in how to respond and to whom.

As a concerned manager, I encouraged each employee, that if any person wished to do so, to talk it through with me. The intention was for employees to come to terms with all of the changes and how the changes would affect them and their future employment (Gatongi 2007, Hannabuss 1997, Rogers 1951, 1980, Rogers & Freiberg 1994).

Employees told me of their feelings of a grief type sense of loss (Dunn 2000, Worden 1991). A cloud lingered over the group for many months and it took some time before everyone settled down and began to get used to the idea that the individual concerned would not be returning. The person was still talked about by the work group on many occasions, sometimes directly with me and at other times, just amongst themselves. Their response to me was positive and always in agreement with the management decisions that had been made.

Concerns were most often related with Newland's ongoing ability to win new work, the longevity of the existing work and the pressures of balancing work and family life.

Although I was a director and manager, I was also part of the group, so I too was impacted by all of Newland's organisational events as I conducted my duties and this research project.

Having laid out my organisational roles and the significant events in Newland's that created a deeper level of contact, experiencing and understanding with the workforce, I will now address the data gathering.

Section II – Data Gathering

As the ethical considerations for this study had been addressed in the research proposal, the plan would be that I would observe Newland's group of employees in their place of work, which was also my own. I would make field notes of the various interactions and activities that occurred, throughout the course of each working day, as the employees routinely conducted their employment duties and I conducted mine.

Following the principles of grounded theory devised by Barney Glaser (1978, 1998, 2001) and Glaser & Strauss (1967) I started to gather the observation material from 1 April 2008. I collected the data for a period of six to nine months during my second year of study. At the same time that I gathered the data, it was simultaneously coded, memoed and re-memoed in the grounded theory process. Although I knew that everything I collected would be research data, I devised three ways, triangulation, in which I could identify the sources from which the data sprung to validate the research.

From this source, I made field notes and file managed all of those field notes accordingly (Glaser & Strauss 1967, Schwartzman 1993). I called the narrative Core Data, Background Notes and Intelligent Narrative, and I shall start with Core Data.

Core Data

This was the first planned way of collecting research data. It was my intention to record the group meetings and any one-to-one dialogue between myself and other employees of Newland's and make transcripts. This collection idea did raise some ethical issues and I had to change the process immediately. I realised that there was a great deal of discomfort and nervousness around any thought of my taping conversations with individuals as I was a manager and a director of the workforce. I replaced it with what I called a technological helping hand.

Technological Helping Hand

This was the replacement data collection method for Core Data. As a way of gaining data, I used emails that went electronically back and forth between myself and others. I regarded the emails as forms of written conversations between a minimum of two individuals or more and at times, a group of people. In them, questions were asked of others and there would usually be a response to a question.

At other times, statements of information were provided to an addressee, who in turn, would re-inform and build up a set of data that was constructive to the process it was developing. Often these contained descriptive, implicit and explicit recollections of events demonstrating a flow of the process of Newland's business activities in written text.

The originators of the emails did not object to my having access to such information. My use of Newland's emails remained uncontentious throughout the study even though I printed them off and removed them from Newland's premises to use as research data. This process did not seem to create any tension or upset any individual who was using technology as a means of communication throughout the many parts of their working day.

I could gather this data unobtrusively, having access to a set of privileged company information that was uniquely pertinent to the commercial activities and business practices of Newland's. What I could not see were the written communications and/or texts that any Newland's employees sent to each other of which I was not copied. I could have, at any time, used my position of authority to access these records, via the assistance of Newland's computer network manager.

Because I was already linked with Newland's corporate governance requirements, its financial status, its contractual obligations and the engineering project processes, I felt that the written communications that came my way, across my desk, were sufficient enough to use for this research project.

The next way that I collected my research material was through a type of personal journal and/or diarised expressions of events.

Background Notes

These were field notes which were based upon my personal experience of being at work and I called them Background Notes. These reflective journal type notes, an existential diary, came from a personal perspective taken of the events and circumstances that occurred in Newland's.

This method of collection was privately unobtrusive and did not interfere with any employee routines as I worked quietly alone in the process, simply making field notes and diagrams. Background Notes, however, were limited by my managerial role. As I either sat at my desk or moved around the office, I sensed that there were limitations to the openness of others and I was at times, deliberately being kept in the dark. Next is the method on how I collected a second set of field notes, Intelligent Narrative.

Intelligent Narrative

This is a set of field note narrative based upon the observation of others at work and the associated activities that manifested as each person conducted their Newland's organisational duties. The ethical considerations for this part of the collection process had been covered. The workforce was aware that I was collecting research field notes however, this process did not disturb or alarm any employee or their routine as I worked alone in the collection process.

Intelligent Narrative included the recalling of historical events and everyday happenings within Newland's that were based upon the observations of others. Parts were the observations that developed from my direct involvement in the day-to-day organisational activities. This data was from a lone viewpoint gained from discussions and day-to-day contact with others. Parts were written formats that developed from the observations of conversations that took place between other employees, in which I had no involvement.

The viewpoint was that of the lone researcher's experiencing of what had been discussed and the interpretive outcome of the events.

This section now completes the methods that I used to collect the research material. I would now like to address the analysis of that data using grounded theory as a method. In the next section, I show how I put that process of grounded theory into action.

Section III—Analysis of Data

The analysis for the research data used the coding and memorandum techniques of grounded theory as devised by Glaser (1978, 1998, 2001) and Glaser & Strauss (1967). I did not have access to a computerised analysis programme so all of the work was done manually. Each cultural event was analysed separately, but was not empirically distinguishable.

As earlier described, the data had been gathered, collected, coded, memoed, re-memoed and filed in three different sets of records called 'Technological Helping Hand', 'Background Notes' and 'Intelligent Narrative'. Microsoft Excel diagrams and charts were used to aid the grounded theory analysis and coding.

From these three sets of records, early categories were formulated. This phase I referred to as the 'Pink Coding' stage. From this stage of pink coding sheet categorisation, came a set of more detailed memoranda called 'The Skeletons Of'. I then reviewed, sorted and re-sorted this early memorandum work continuously developing subsequent sets of detailed memorandum note making called 'Memorandum Skeletons' and later, 'The Combined Skeletons'. From these extended memorandum notes, I identified categories relating to Newland's events.

In the analysis phase, I spent an extensive amount of time interpreting, manually coding, writing memoranda, sorting, re-sorting, filing and managing large volumes of narrative data created from shared experiences and relationships with research participants in line with the constructivist approach (Charmaz 2006). I considered all of the data and compared incident to incident to determine if data was either new material that was dissimilar, inconsistent enough to create a new category or similar, consistent enough to be integrated into the existing categories as a property or a dimension.

To demonstrate reliability, I maintained an audit trail of all of the analysis processes and concept of theory work as a 'Proof of Concept'.

Section IV—Reflexivity and my Role as a Researcher

As I start to consider my role as a researcher and reflexivity in this research study, I have included an extract from the first field background notes that I made in my reflective journal so that the reader can hear my voice:

Here lies the real secret to what I am trying to achieve, I think. I am looking at what is regarded as intangible, what is known, not known and can be known. I am not removed from the research, I play a real part in the everyday matters that relate to the research and the primary purpose for which each person is employed and that is to make the company successful for its owner. I am closely related to all of the matters involved in the day-to-day happenings in the company and I am much more than frustrated by them, most of the time and I don't really know why.

I know that I feel that I am in too deep, too closely involved with its employees and they expect too much from me and of me. Some larger companies have whole departments dealing with what I spread myself around in one day. Small to medium-sized companies don't have such a luxury. I know I don't solely provide in the success of the company, it would be arrogant and short sighted of me to think so.

I know wholeheartedly, that all of its employees are involved in all of the company's economic success, but my feeling is associated with the responsibility that goes alongside the position of a director of the company. The single responsibility of it all is a lonely and scary place to be.

My words emerge from an employed person, a director with responsibilities, who realises that there is no separation in any of the roles and that all my role boundaries are seamless or seemingly non-existent.

My statement identifies the different roles that I fulfil and the difficulties I experience daily in wondering where the responsibility boundaries of the director, manager, group member, work colleague and now researcher are set. I also question if they exist at all. As a person, doubt manifests in the opening statement. As a researcher, I seek out the intangible and I cannot be impassively removed from the impact of the organisation around me, whilst also, my actions impact upon the participants daily (Ashman & Lawler 2008).

Ethnographers are encouraged to use their own personal experiencing, yet be open and transparent about their intentions. Following Silverman (2005, 2011) reflexivity is defined as the self-aware analysis of the relationship between researcher and participants, a critical capacity to make explicit the position of the researcher in the field and the way in which the researcher's positioning impacts upon the research process. Reflexive self-reflection is to be used correctly and not mistakenly defined as the self-questioning of the researcher (Silverman 2005, 2011).

Researchers are to adopt a principle of reflexivity, derived from ethnomethodology, that defines that nearly everything that is being observed cannot be separated, isolated and treated independently of the other matters that exist.

According to Malinowski (1922) the first condition of the ethnographic work is to deal with the totality of it all, the communities social, cultural and psychological aspects, because these aspects are so interwoven that not one cannot be understood without taking into consideration all of the others.

Suzuki et al (2007) say that the success of the researcher is also dependent upon an ability to gain an understanding of the community under research and make sense of every piece of data that is collected. Additionally, researchers are to capture the assortment of the social characteristics of the research settings and let be heard, the voices of those being researched (Suzuki et al 2007, Silverman 2005, 2011).

The next consideration of being a researcher in my own work environment was the level of complexities that accompanied that task. As with all of my other roles, this would be another phased one that was inextricably connected, seamlessly linked with all of the others and from which I could not be removed. My role as the silent observer was never going to be easy because my organisational role as a manager and member of the group structures could not be a silent one (Barnes, Ernst & Hyde 1999).

Even though I was a researcher in my own organisation, the aim of the ethnographic task was straightforward. I was to conduct observational work based in an organisational setting in line with the approach described by Koch (2005). I would be seeking out and describing the organisational routine, the ordinary everydayness of it all, the mundane and the stirring of Newland's daily commercial events (Fetterman 1998, Muncey 2010, Silverman 2005, 2011).

However, as an employee of Newland's with directorship and managerial responsibilities, it would be impossible for me to have no influence, when my influence was needed on a daily basis to meet the organisational needs.

Although, I knew that my own management interactions would be beneficial to the research, I had to constantly review any preconceptions because I knew they would exist. This dual role resulted in a lack of clarity in my decision making.

For me, there was no opportunity to stand on the sidelines as a participant observer and just watch what unfolded before my eyes. I lacked the comfort of being the outside observer looking in. I was an encompassed proactive insider employee within the organisational setting that I was studying (Trice & Beyer 1984). I was observing the work activities and the social interactions, but I was part of doing those activities and connected in a social way.

As Newland's manager, I had to assess timely and effectively, what needed to be done, in terms of job responsibilities and provide a solution, based on knowledge of the circumstances and previous experience of handling situations. As a researcher, I had to just observe the whole event as it unfolded and continually question my interpretation of it. I did also take into consideration the fact that my work colleagues knew that I was conducting research and this role was accepted by them but they did not divulge how this role affected them.

To summarise, as individuals we are never outside the turbulent togetherness of being touched by the involvement of being with other people (Summers-Effler 2007).

Realistically, as a researcher, an idealised level of unobtrusiveness will be compromised by my employers need for me, as a manager, to have a deep level of influence, involvement, authority and at times, interference. This concept is supported by the writings of Blaxter, Hughes & Tight (2001) Charmaz (2006) Denzin & Lincoln (2005) Roldan (2002) and Strauss & Corbin (1998).

Whether the effort in using grounded theory was worthy for this project still remains in question though, I did enjoy the detailed work of the coding and categorising processes.

I worked full-time for Newland's, so planning and programming was a consideration for the research study. Business plans and research strategies however, rarely proceed completely in accordance with the planned and both have the potential to stray (Strauss & Corbin 1998).

In this chapter on subject, scope and method, I have given an account of the influences of my professional role within Newland's, given an outline of the collection of the data and analysis, together with a perspective of my role as the researcher and reflexivity. All of these details complete the content for the research methodology.

The next chapter is the first of the results chapters called New Staff.

Chapter 4
Results: New Staff

This chapter covers the recruitment of Newland's new staff using Trice & Beyer's (1984) citing of rites of passage as a way to explain how new employees were recruited and socialised. First, I will summarise Van Gennep's (1909-1960) concept of rites of passage. Then, it is important to set the Newland's organisational scene as the background for the pre-recruitment phase and also, the recruitment event, using data extracts where applicable. In conjunction, I will use the contexts of rites of separation, rites of transition and rites of incorporation as examples to illustrate Newland's experience of recruiting new staff.

Rites of Passage

In life, there are common events such as pregnancy and childbirth, the onset of sexual maturity, betrothal, marriage and death. Van Gennep (1909-1960) observed the commonalities across customary behaviours that typically accompany these "common and unavoidable events" (Trice & Beyer 1984, p. 657). Because these events create significant change for the individuals involved, Van Gennep (1909-1960) named the accompanying sets of behaviours "rites of passage".

Of rites of passage, there were three distinctive, consecutive subsets of behaviours which Van Gennep called rites of separation, rites of transition and rites of incorporation (Trice & Beyer 1984). The intent of these rites were to assist individual members of a social system to re-establish an equilibrium in their social relations that had been disturbed by their moving from one social role to another.

Using the induction and basic training process of the United States Army, Bourne (1967) cited in Trice & Beyer (1984) provides an example of rites of passage and its consecutive behaviours of separation, transition and incorporation. Separation begins on the first day as new army recruits report to their assigned training centre.

Transition occurs as learning takes effect and familiarity with the basic training builds. Incorporation is the transformation from untrained new recruit to skilled soldier (Trice & Beyer 1984).

Although, Bourne (1967) clearly illustrated the recruitment processes of the US Army and stated they provided a good example of rites of passage in "modern organisational life" (p. 658) this account is visibly limited by the fact that the viewpoint taken is restricted by the events and behaviours of military life only.

It is not controversial to state that modern organisational life clearly extends beyond the private confines of the United States Army. The public sector and private industry are good examples of modern day organisation life in which there is a milieu of complex, intricate, social and practical cultural activities, that include both gentle and even humiliating types of rites of passage (Fineman, Gabriel & Sims 2010).

Hence, what is not captured by Bourne's (1967) discrete account of military life is a picture of how modern organisational life works inside a small medium enterprise. Absent from the military example of rites of passage, is an account of how potential new employees are recruited and then incorporated into an existing, fully functioning and successful organisation, like Newland Limited.

When Newland's recruited new personnel, similar patterns of rites of separation, rites of transition and rites of incorporation occurred. I am, therefore, able to use these three subsets behaviours of rites of passage, as a means of comparison (Trice & Beyer 1984). This is what I set out to illustrate and provide in this chapter, using rites of passage, as a way to explain Newland's staff recruitment process. I will begin with an explanation of the cultural activities related with the pre-recruitment phase.

Pre-Recruitment Phase

Intentionally, Newland's director's maintained a focus that safeguarded all the organisational aims and objectives against any undesirable commercial risk taking. The directors were aware that the infiltration of poorly fitting personalities could threaten Newland's stable fiscal materiality, economically fundamental to ongoing commercial success. The board were especially vigilant about the recruitment, induction and internalisation of new personnel.

Obviously, Newland's economic success was dependent upon a professional workforce made up of managerially, financially and technically competent individuals who could work together (Kutz 2000). Experience and knowledge had proven that Newland's collective workforce were willing to operate in accordance with an internal organisational infrastructure, external compliance demands and varying engineering client requirements (Collin 2006, Hrebiniak 2006).

Even though Newland's three directors were the main decision makers when it came to the recruitment of new employees, each one took personal responsibility to ensure that the existing workforce were kept informed and involved in the recruitment process. Equally, all three director's considered the reciprocal feedback given by Newland's organisational members on any new potential employee, as each was scrutinised in the recruitment event.

In essence, affordability of new employees was the key fundamental factor in Newland's recruitment drive. The recruitment event, however, was always regarded as a positive experience. After the news broke that the recruitment event was to take place, an air of anticipation and expectancy was consistently demonstrated in Newland's workforce.

Significantly, anticipation generated a level of excitement about how Newland's financial position was sufficiently robust enough to justify the recruitment of new employees. What had arisen as a result of good commercial fortune, was the opportunity to increase the workforce, turnover, profit and Newland's economic future. Expectations existed around the potential of the new potential employee and a measure of their suitable quality, values and what type of person could meet Newland's organisational standards.

Also evident, was a forward looking sense of hope that sprung up in Newland's workforce. From the possibility of bringing in new employees came topics of conversations related directly to how such new employees could have a long term positive effect. Consequently, all of Newland's good news, linked to the recruitment event, was spread through rites of enhancement type optimism as members augmented the concept of being involved in an organisation that engendered potential (Andersson, Giacalone & Jurkiewicz 2007, Trice & Beyer 1984).

Illustrated in the following data extract, the concept of the existence of a future organisational time was given in a statement made by a Newland's director, who placed a more objective status upon the potential organisational member:

A resource for supporting development opportunities on (named) projects.

Dialogue about the recruitment event centred around the proviso and terms of how Newland's and the existing workforce would determine the first and foremost criteria for the new additions to the community. Becoming the main focus, the interview event was also discussed in detail. Dates and times were perused so that existing plans could be modified, as and when necessary. Questions were specifically raised about interview planning and especially if the possibility existed for all Newland's engineering staff to be present and involved in meeting and greeting the interviewees.

In-depth discussions focused on the fit of the person i.e. the type of person that was required. Obviously, Newland's existing community workforce didn't just need or want an extremely competent Robinson Crusoe (Wolfensberger 2007) as shown in the data extract that follows. It is evident that two main priorities existed for determining the qualities and capabilities of the desired individual as being able to:

Fit in with the rest of us;

and equally as important:

Being able to cope with the technical side of things.

Undoubtedly, each new employee would need to have the capacity to 'fit in' to the existing group structures and hold the right kind of technical expertise to conduct the detailed complexity of working with 3-D engineering data. The ideal balance would be a fifty/fifty weighting, coupling technical ability with a subjective quality of the right kind of person type. Akin with rites of passage, the right type of person would minimise changes and quickly restore organisational equilibrium disturbed by the incorporation of a new member (Trice & Beyer 1984).

One further priority emerged in contrast to the need to 'fit in' and 'technical coping'. Nevertheless, even though the technical weighting of fifty/fifty would be a recruitment preference, some Newland's members dismissed technical ability as being an option and more of a necessity in order to maintain equilibrium (Trice & Beyer 1984):

Technical expertise should be taken as read, assumed, for a company such as ours.

'Fitting in', 'technical coping', 'technical expertise—a necessity' and recognition of 'the group itself' were obvious factors of Newland's unique organisational culture. Yet, without spending some time in the presence of the interviewees, what would be more difficult to determine would be their personal qualities and attitude, which would form the real basis for fitting in.

Consistently, Newland's workforce built complex and diverse teams in order to successfully conduct the 3-D engineering work (Brotheridge & Lee 2006, Ringer 2007). Without fail, it was a clear organisational expectation that all team members were meant to carry out the assigned detailed tasking arrangements within these teams and remain comfortable and effective within them (Kutz 2000).

Consequently, team members set up production expectations that had to be equally met by all team members. Again, it was evident that prolonged delays of work output would not be tolerated by Newland's highly specialised engineering clients, who also had to rigidly meet their own operational offshore and onshore schedules. Work accuracy was specifically aimed to meet client agreed engineering tolerances. Any mistakes could affect project assigned budgets and more importantly, plant safety.

Keeping constantly in touch, in order to share and impart knowledge, were cultural activities in Newland's teams that kept vital project tasks in progress and work equilibrium maintained (Ambrosini, Bowman & Burton-Taylor 2007, Collin 2006, Trice & Beyer 1984). Likewise, these actions affirmed Joshi, Sarker & Sarker (2007) observation that frequent communication helps to build and maintain a team's social capital. Any person who could not genuinely act to perform assigned tasks would be disruptively incapable of building successful team relationships and hence, fail to enhance Newland's organisational objectives (Jeske 2001, Lightsey 2006, Trice & Beyer 1984).

In direct contrast, some allowances were actually made for interviewees favourably received. For those with potential, if technical competence was proven to be adequate, some individual characteristics perceived as shyness, lack of confidence and quietness would be tolerated. Integrating for the common good, however, was always the main priority (Trice & Beyer 1984).

Faith was placed in the belief that becoming a part of an active team could promote new staff to overcome certain difficulties, provided that the potential team member was willing to help to solve situations, learn through mistakes and be a willing worker who was able to interact with other team members (Collin 2006, Kutz 2000).

Consequently, some personality traits were immediately rebuffed. Dominance, over confidence or over assertiveness would not be tolerated. These traits, regarded as 'negative' could threaten the teaming constructs and organisational stability (Trice & Beyer 1984). The need to dominate other team members could block communication. Over confidence and forcefulness had the potential to create or cover up mistakes and therefore, seriously inhibit the tasking work in progress.

Taking on a completely different perspective to the one given on individual technical ability and its importance to Newland's stability, one employee placed the 'fitting in' emphasis on the integrated common good (Trice & Beyer 1984). This employee argued that a concept of the group, as one single entity, existed in Newland's and that this group had the capacity to make the recruitment 'fitting in' and 'technical coping' decision on behalf of the community:

The group itself would best be making the assessment of the quality of the person if the technical expertise was already taken as read.

Collective involvement in the decision making process was sought by one Newland's employee. This person advocated that once technical expertise had been determined, the 'quality of the person' should be the next consideration to be made by Newland's existing community, identified as 'the group itself'.

Even though Newland's workforce successfully gathered and collected in group formations, it could be argued that group decision making was difficult to achieve, as not all group members were able to totally agree.

Each Newland's member had their point of view of the circumstances being discussed (Jeske 2001). Additionally, organisational members in different positions and roles made their own interpretations of the same organisational events (Stensaker & Falkenberg 2007). Individual members would compete, draw in their supporters and push away non-supporters because each had a vested interest in doing so (Guadagno & Cialdini 2007, Sheard, Kakabadse & Kakabadse 2011).

Because of these complexities, it was not viable that 'the group itself' would actually make any decisions. In order to reduce conflict and its disruptive effects, Newland's directors retained most of the decision making responsibility (Trice & Beyer 1984).

In an organisation like Newland's, when it came to decision making, the directors were the individuals who took the relevant action and also the personal responsibility. No director, however, made a decision without full consideration being given to the feedback received from Newland's employees, as any lack of consultation with the workforce could threaten leadership trust, disturb equilibrium and disrupt stability (Berson & Sosik 2007, Trice & Beyer 1984).

Additionally, in order to maintain ongoing involvement and to prevent management being sidelined through a lack of organisational leadership trust, sufficient autonomy was given by Newland's directors to the workforce. The existing organisational members were given the freedom to determine the desired aspects of potential team members, as long as the existing organisational operational strategy was safeguarded (Belbin 2003, Hackman 1990, Thomson & Hassenkamp 2008, Trice & Beyer 1984).

As Newland's Operations Director and manager, I was close to Newland's owner, who acted as the managing director. I was aware of the owner's concern that in rushing the recruitment event, in order to quickly fill a vacant space, the right type of pragmatic technical person could be found, but the wrong character type of individual brought into the existing community.

Previously, Newland's had experienced organisational disruption and harm by the actions of a technically minded, pragmatic type of company director. The difficult experience and conflict was never to be repeated (Trice & Beyer 1984). So in order to protect the organisation, what also needed to be adequately considered in the recruitment event, was the threat that the attraction of Newland's 3-D technical environment could be a magnet for the more pragmatic dominant type.

What was broadly agreed was that although engineering and technical expertise was a necessity, the character type of the individual who would ideally fit into Newland's, would be a person who was able to complement and harmonise the existing group community. Valid integration would require a good personal attitude towards work and other people, from a person who was also technically competent (Jeske 2001, Kivetz & Tyler 2007, Trice & Beyer 1984).

Adversely, what was not acceptable under any circumstances, was a person who had the potential for creating an adverse impact upon Newland's proven successful processes. There existed inside Newland's an equilibrium, that was often referred to as 'a caring family' and one with which all existing employees were comfortable. Newland's family-like existing social constitution was to be maintained at all costs.

The incorporation of the wrong type of new member could disturb the equilibrium and create unmanageable circumstances that put the caring concept at risk (Brotheridge & Lee 2006, Fischer 2007, Trice & Beyer 1984).

Having outlined Newland's pre-recruitment phase, I will now focus on the actual recruitment event.

Recruitment Event

Newland's attracted new employees by offering the opportunity for each to work in a 3-D engineering environment of a highly technical modern day SME. Like most current day organisations, Newland's used promotion and attraction techniques to appeal to the right type of individual (Kivetz & Tyler 2007). In order to save time, costs and to minimise disruption to Newland's existing workforce however, a shortcut was taken to optimise the recruitment process (Trice & Beyer 1984).

It was unanimously agreed by Newland's three directors that the use of focused specialised interpersonal skills was an essential requirement in the first level of interviewing. The consensus was to use an external recruitment agency to shorten Newland's recruitment event (Ambrosini, Bowman & Burton-Taylor 2007).

At the outset, I arranged a preliminary meeting with the recruitment agency representative and specifically asked the recruitment agent to come to Newland's office. The primary purpose of the meeting was to give this representative an 'insight' into the 3-D engineering services that Newland's provided and also, for this person to obtain a feel for the people and 'our company ethos'. The following data extract demonstrated the start and development of a successful working relationship:

We enjoyed meeting you as well and know that you have gained an insight into our company ethos. I think the best approach is to make up a short list of candidates and then we can spend one to two days doing the interviews (say two to three each day x two days)

Obviously, the recruitment agent found the visit useful. The response gave an indication of the work that had been conducted on behalf of Newland's:

I just wanted to keep you informed on my progress so far...Once again may I thank you for the visit last week, it has proved to be invaluable in assisting me in the selection process.

Newland's integrative needs for technical competence and an ability to fit into an existing organisational community were re-emphasised as the two main points of significance for the new staff (Trice & Beyer 1984). The importance of informality was also raised:

As you know, we intend to review the individuals on two points: their technical competence and the ability to fit into our group structures which will include a candidates introduction to all of the company members on a less than formal basis; as we did with you. We'll hear from you next week?

The interest in the applicant was paramount. Any new person or potentially admirable character entering the office space raised interest in the workforce. The level of curiosity in them depended upon the amount of time the stranger spent in the midst and also, how they were initially received. Placing a smartly dressed visitor into the conference room in preparation for a job interview and closing the door, almost brought the whole of Newland's workforce to an immediate standstill. These types of applicants were commonly referred to as:

Suited and booted.

In a tribal society, Malinowski (1922) observed something similar ranging from the arrival of the interesting stranger on the shore to frequent uncomplimentary remarks and jocular familiarity. Newland's workforce were no different. A keen eye was kept upon the person until their departure after which, the interviewer was constantly requested to provide information about the kind of person the interviewee was and if there was any potential possibility of that person being employed.

Initial feedback was placed upon the demeanour of the person and their behaviour upon arrival into reception. Good manners were particularly mentioned and held in esteem. A smiling pleasant person created ease at the meeting and greeting. The proactive extension of a hand for shaking was met with equal accord.

Dress sense was particularly criticised, especially if hair looked unwashed. It was not expected, however, that an interviewee would arrive in a business suit, but being overly casual caused discomfort and was interpreted as a lack of respect.

Rites of enhancement give public recognition for accomplishments to individuals in order to motivate others to similar efforts and emphasises the social value of good performance (Trice & Beyer 1984). Obviously, any interviewee that disrespectfully failed to meet Newland's dress standards was regarded as diminishing both organisational and individual accomplishments hence, was to be subjected to degradation in order to wholly dissolve any potential impact made (Trice & Beyer 1984).

This point was particularly interesting as throughout most of their working days, Newland's workforce wore casual clothes.

In the hot summer months, the engineering staff wore shorts and t-shirts and at other times, jeans and t-shirts of various designs and quality, ranging from designer store to feral beach surfer. This was mainly because the office was extremely hot as it lacked air conditioning. The administration staff and directors also bore a smart casual appearance.

The reasons for hiring and acceptance were—'they would be a good fit'; deemed as 'compatible personality'; 'well, we like the look of them'.

During an interview, one young candidate had made a good impression, but was not an exact fit. I summarised what I regarded as the candidates strong points and brought them to the attention of the Software Development Director, who had the final say:

Might not be technically an exact match...he has an assertive character and even though he is young, he is not aggressive...a good asset to the company...depends upon his technical ability.

The reasons for not hiring and for rejection were based upon a 'gut feel' that detected either an immediate or a delayed disapproval of the interviewee. The 'gut feel' did not necessarily have a firm foundation to it, but was usually felt by more than one Newland's employee. The group of individuals involved were observed to communicate this sense of 'gut feel' to each other as a generalised dislike, discomfort about certain traits and worries about working with such a person. In doing so, all gained joint support to combine the verbal statements of degradation and consolidate the reasons for rejection (Trice & Beyer 1984).

A strong sense of rejection accompanied the 'gut feel'. For some Newland employees, the need to reject formed so quickly, that it could not be ignored or overlooked. Other members of Newland's workforce sensed disharmony with the interviewee. What followed was a motivating compulsion, by Newland's collective group members, to jointly agree and pursue the action of rejection.

That need for rejection was vocalised sometimes by a spokesperson or jointly in the group.

Prejudices emerged and politically incorrect statements were made to reduce the status of the incumbent (Trice & Beyer 1984). Such statements were never made in the presence of the potential incumbent, only within the confines of Newland's organisational walls. Rejection usually followed quickly.

Other reasons for rejection of candidates were less vague. Discomfort, suspicion and a lack of tolerance was raised when a candidate was late for an interview and the decision for rejection was clearly articulated:

My feeling with (name) is that his lateness for the interview was not a good start. I know that at times, fate intervenes, but at an interview, one has only chance to present yourself and get it right for the day.

Acceptance of the successful candidates emerged within a two to three day period after completion of the interview process. Second interviews were sometimes conducted to reassess the decision of acceptance, but not always. Rarely was a candidate that was brought back for a second interview rejected. First impressions did count and later, considerations for 'personality side' as well as 'fit' came to the fore to justify the second round of interview:

Purely on my first impression, I'd have to agree with you on the suitable candidates. I didn't get a real chance to have a chat but on my first impressions, these two stood out.

As decision time approached, one director moved position when a major realisation occurred. An enduring tolerance for hazardous site conditions was an important integrating quality for both the individual and other team members (Trice & Beyer 1984):

If we need to choose between the two then we need to decide what is most important to us—personality or proficiency…My preference would be to conduct a follow up meeting with both candidates before making a final decision; if pushed, I would probably favour (name) at this stage but I appreciate that extended periods of working together in hostile environments may put a greater emphasis on the personality side of the balance.

For Newland's 3-D engineering work, a particular type of skill was most often required.

Longer term thinking came to the fore when one interviewee became an attractive proposition:

This will give (name) some insight into what (the actual company name) is doing and this will keep him interested in us, especially if we are still interested in his mathematical ability at the start of the new year. We can then make the approach to him when we have a firmed up commitment for the work.

Only because both were young and had just finished university, I re-evaluated two new potential organisational members in order to:

Give them a chance.

I raised one final point of concern before the decision was made to make a written offer of employment and:

It would best be said that both would have to learn to settle into the work environment with us because I feel that they both had a sense of freedom lately and this will take some managing to get them to work quietly at a desk for a working day without causing too many distractions.

Once the recruitment process decision making was completed, a written offer of employment was sent to a successful interviewee.

The most salient point of the written offer of employment was the invoking of a ninety day probationary period that protected Newland's against any threat of liability under current employment law. Even though the probationary period was initially a provisional arrangement, but with permanent intention, Newland's still invested time and training into new staff through the induction and introduction processes.

In the previous section, I have intentionally set the organisational scene in relation to Newland's pre-recruitment phase and demonstrated the activities directly associated with the recruitment event, using data extracts where applicable.

I can now use the subset of behaviours of rites of passage, i.e. rites of separation, rites of transition and rites of incorporation to illustrate the process for new staff who began employment with Newland Limited (Trice & Beyer 1984).

Induction Process – Rites of Separation and then Transition

The first subset of behaviours of rites of passage is rites of separation (Bourne 1967, Trice & Beyer 1984). Although, the focus was primarily military, what was still observed in Trice & Beyer's (1984) account of rites of separation, were the assortment of symbols and organisational processing activities that awaited the arrival of the first day recruits.

In any organisational set up, the strange physical surroundings, the movement of people, equipment, noise, voices, faces and attitudes all meet newcomers head-on. It is highly likely, therefore, that apprehension, tension and anxiety immediately disturb equilibrium, as each new arrival confronts the unfamiliar mix of activities going on inside the organisation they have joined.

Trice & Beyer's (1984) account permits me to raise my own observation about rites of passage. If the rites re-establish equilibrium, then that equilibrium has to have been disturbed prior to re-establishment taking place. Such disturbance manifests in the rites of separation and extends therefore, to both the newcomer's equilibrium and in the case of Newland's, the equilibrium of the existing workforce.

Both public and private enterprises make adequate preparation for the arrival of new employees. Newland's, as an SME example of modern day organisational life, was no exception.

According to Trice & Beyer (1984) rites of separation began when new recruits reported on their first day to an induction centre. Similarly for Newland's new staff, rites of separation began when each reported for their first day at the office. More importantly though, disruption to Newland's workforce equilibrium associated with rites of separation, became obvious prior to the first day of arrival of the newcomer.

Disturbance of equilibrium in Newland's existing workforce manifested in inaccurate assumptions being made about the incoming new staff (Trice & Beyer 1984). Subtle questions were asked about the newcomer's pay, bonus and holiday entitlement.

Doubt revealed questions about whether the right person had been chosen and also, would this person stand the test of time. All of these concerns became distractions as the time between the written offer of employment being sent and the impending arrival of the newcomer lessened.

One specific leadership practice adopted by Newland's directors was to advise the existing workforce when the employment contract offers had been sent out to the successful candidates with a detailed clarification of the position offered. If it was a senior position, then details such as pay, holiday entitlement and bonus were kept confidential but, the role responsibilities would be defined.

Contrary to this practice, if the position was of equivalent status or junior, the starting employment conditions could be made public. This type of information was always well received by Newland's workforce. Consequently, informing Newland's community helped to minimise any distractions or disturbances (Trice & Beyer 1984).

Rites of passage move an individual from one social role to another therefore, status is most often changed (Trice & Beyer 1984). Accordingly, such rites are part of the unwritten laws of organisational life as established members initiate and socialise newcomers into the existing culture (Fineman, Gabriel & Sims 2010). It would not be an unreasonable assessment therefore, to focus some attention upon Newland's existing members, in relation to status, as they participated in the recruitment event (Trice & Beyer 1984).

The potential outcome of the status placed upon a newcomer could be a threat to an existing organisational member. The consequence of placing a higher status upon a newcomer would mean a reduction in status of an existing organisational member. The possibility of a loss of prestige associated with the newcomer, caused anxiety and disruption to Newland's workforce equilibrium, even though the newcomer was still absent (Trice & Beyer 1984). In order to maintain workforce equilibrium, unanimously, Newland's directors set out to keep the existing workforce sufficiently involved and continuously informed.

Whilst the recruitment event progressed, communications regularly centred around the arrival of and preparations for the newcomers. Newland's then conveniently became the main focus, as enhancing organisational good news helped to relieve tension (Trice & Beyer 1984).

Genuinely, it was unanimously agreed that a lack of preparation and organisational readiness would be an unacceptable profile for a modern day SME employer, like Newland's. In order to reduce anxiety for the newcomer, lessen the impact of being introduced into a strange environment and minimise any disturbances for everyone involved, the directors made it clear to the workforce that it was their wish, that all of Newland's new employees should have a ‘smooth integration experience’ into the organisational fold (Trice & Beyer 1984):

My thoughts are simply that if you feel you can handle what we all agreed will need to be a "smooth integration experience" now for (names) then I would suggest that they should be asked to start sooner. (Name) told me that (names) are keen to start as soon as possible. I am for this, but want you and them to feel that their first day is not a "strained activity". In terms of employment contracts, I can issue an amended to the contract with an earlier start date. No problem on that side. I would say go for it now so, just give me the nod and I'll jump to it...

A ‘smooth integration experience’ was sought but unfortunately, this had not always been the case. In the past, a demonstration poor leadership skills, a lack of direct involvement and a deficiency of readiness had made a particularly new employee’s transition period difficult. Not surprisingly, the intake became a ‘strained activity’ for both the newcomer and the workforce (Berson & Sosik 2007, Clair & Dufresne 2007, Espedal 2007, Sosik & Jung 2003).

One positive aspect to the disturbance of Newland’s workforce equilibrium, however, was the opportunity for each member to review and reflect upon the condition and status of their existing organisational possessions, such as desking, seating, bookcases and laptops (Trice & Beyer 1984, Whitty & Carr 2006).

Obviously, new desking would be purchased. Status manifested in a promptly surfacing hierarchy. Inevitably, the new desking would usually be allocated to an existing organisational member, as this person, mainly through ingratiation, praise, flattery or sometimes dominance, had been able to successfully bid to place their precedence above the newcomer and existing members (Berson & Sosik 2007, Pfeffer 2010). Consequently, the new employee would inherit the old desking. Newland’s directors never got involved in the discussions but were aware of their existence.

Additionally, new chairs were viewed with covetous eyes. What determined the legacy, however, was the actual condition of the desking and the chair. Uncomfortable, soiled or wobbly chairs were ignored, discarded and replaced.

In direct contrast to furniture negotiations, a brand new laptop was nearly always given to the new employee. It was an unusual event if a new employee had to inherit someone else’s old laptop but, occasionally, it happened. Reliability of computer equipment was an important factor for Newland’s employees. Also at this time, Newland’s existing members took the opportunity to review the condition, reliability and suitability of their own computer equipment.

Furthermore, status also surfaced as Newland's existing members closely monitored the allocation of brand new laptops. Equilibrium was disturbed enough to make justifications for new computer equipment an immediate priority (Trice & Beyer 1984). Envy of the newcomer's potential receipt of a new laptop manifested in Newland's existing members. Demonstrations of **self-pity**, irony and sarcasm accompanied shabby and woeful descriptions of the states of their own laptop aired primarily, in the presence of Newland's directors.

Associated with a single act of rites of conflict reduction, the hints were never ignored by Newland's directors (Trice & Beyer 1984). The need for some level of arbitration became apparent. Depending upon the condition of the existing computer equipment and the state of the company purse, where possible, equilibrium was restored when Newland's directors voluntarily agreed to replace laptops for other organisational members at the same time.

Consequently, team spirit was lifted and cohesion affirmed as the promise of new equipment mediated any disharmony linked with the arrival of the newcomer (Trice & Beyer 1984, Whitty & Carr 2006).

Rites of separation introduced the new employees to the office based familiarisation and handling of Newland's work equipment. Later, the rites of transition would cover the actual training and the utilisation of the equipment for real-time production work. For the moment, however, I will continue with the concept of separation and acquaintance (Trice & Beyer 1984).

On the first day, the new employee was shown to their desking area where they could place their belongings and make their claim to the space. A short company introduction, payroll, health and safety briefing was conducted by the Operations Director who then accompanied the new employee back to their relevant section.

Organisational specific attire has been shown by Trice & Beyer (1984) to be one element of rites of separation. Likewise, Newland's employees placed significant emphasis upon office dress code.

Part of Newland's induction process was the adjustment of dress sense, prominently down. Even though it was expected that interviewees would arrive smart, new staff were quickly introduced to the style of clothing worn by the Newland's workforce, which was of a more casual nature.

Dressing down, sometimes in shorts, most often in jeans, was the uniform of Newland's organisational culture. Each were expected to comply. For the newcomer who was slow to comply, their equilibrium was deliberately disturbed by the existing members through gentle teasing, similar to the discrediting influences of rites of degradation (Trice & Beyer 1984). A degree of humiliation and personal discomfort quickly brought about an acceptable change (Trice & Beyer 1984).

Additionally, during rites of separation, this was the time when organisational specific material objects, associated with assigned new roles, were handed out (Trice & Beyer 1984). Similarly, the handing out of work equipment was the next part of Newland's induction process.

A fully configured laptop, loaded with Newland's modelling analysis software, was ready and waiting to be given to the new engineering staff member. This laptop was handed over by the senior engineer, who would be acting as an early supervisor and assistor, as the new staff member gained familiarisation with the software.

Later, a more comprehensive programme of training in the use of the analysis software would be given. Initially though, the new member was expected to develop some familiarity with the basic functioning of the programme and get accustomed with the display and output. The new member could work alone with the laptop, but the individual was always seated in the presence of a more experienced engineer, who would willingly provide assistance when necessary.

Sometime later on in the first week, the new employee would be introduced and given access to Newland's site equipment which comprised of a theodolite, cameras and all of the ancillary surveying equipment. This activity of intended technical consequence, was the new staff member's first introduction to the equipment packing and unpacking procedure, a Newland's ritual of practical importance, vital for the mobilisation of the site teams (Trice 1984, Trice & Beyer 1984).

A very important part of the equipment familiarisation and association process was to teach the new engineering member how to use Newland's surveying equipment in an outdoor space (Trice & Beyer 1984). In this phase, the outside space was the building's car park. The first duty of the engineering newcomer was to learn how to safely move Newland's bulky surveying equipment from the storage space to the outside space. Once the set piece had been undertaken, the engineers returned to the office, packed the equipment into storage boxes and returned the equipment to the storage room.

Trice & Beyer (1984) say that rites of passage have manifest consequences for individuals who are helped through a change in role and status. Additionally, rites of renewal have similar consequences for groups or whole organisations. In the case of Newland's, the purpose of familiarisation and association with the surveying and camera equipment for the new staff member was to build confidence in actually moving the equipment and handling it in different locations.

Simulating the movement of the equipment from the storage room, unpacking it, moving it from one surveying position to the next in an outside space, replicated the ritualised mobilisation process necessary for beginning all of Newland's engineering projects, that would eventually economically benefit the whole organisation (Trice & Beyer 1984).

It was the familiarisation, association and acquaintance processes of the rites of separation that helped each of Newland's new members to settle into their new job. Once this period had been completed, each new staff member moved onto a more formal type of training in the use of Newland's site surveying equipment and 3-D modelling software.

The intensity of the involvement of the new staff member into Newland's organisational processes was augmented. Consequently, this movement from the familiarisation and association process invoked a Newland's type rites of transition (Trice & Beyer 1984).

In Trice & Beyer's (1984) account of rites of transition, no time schedule or time based programme of events has been given. In contrast, Newland's new members were expected to be able to demonstrate basic proficiency skills in site procedures and the use of the 3-D modelling software, during and after completion of their ninety day probationary period.

At the outset, weekly, then fortnightly, then monthly progression steps were undertaken to ensure that each new engineering member had learned the basic skills of Newland's 3-D modelling techniques correctly. This monitoring of progress would ensure that each new member had started to build sufficient confidence to produce the contract specific engineering accuracies and percentage content of the work scopes. At this stage, speed of work was handled sensitively and tentatively.

Trice & Beyer's (1984) reference to the skills learning phase of rites of transition does not identify what early expectations were placed upon new recruits, or if there were any at all. In the case of Newland's, there existed an expectation that after completion of the probationary period, all new engineering members would have developed an ability to be able to produce the right accuracy of work content, within an agreed period of production time.

This timely production of work was paramount to Newland's financial stability and survival (Trice & Beyer 1984). Keeping project costs limited and preventing delays in order to produce a margin of profit was a crucial part of Newland's financial commitment to each shareholder.

Exposure to organisationally specific activities that are directly associated with role status, as a way of learning, is given in Trice & Beyer's account of rites of transition. Using an existing accurate 3-D model of a plant or platform to model from Newland's project archive, each new engineering member began to learn to use Newland's 3-D modelling software. Each were taught how to analyse a surveyed structure, pipe, vessel or piece of plant equipment, from a digital photograph and build a 3-D virtual model representation of the same plant element.

Efforts were made to ensure that efficiency and competence in the use of Newland's surveying equipment was built up by mentoring and practice (Trice & Beyer 1984).

It would be reasonable to make two assumptions about the processes described for the new recruits by Trice & Beyer (1984) in rites of transition. First, these newcomers would not be functioning in isolation. Second, the multiple activities associated with rites of separation and transition, as described (Trice & Beyer 1984) would require ample time, planning and manpower in order to handle the many related diverse and practical events.

Training, learning and repeated testing, therefore, would require the full cooperation of other competent organisational members. Adequate supervision, therefore, was an important aspect of Newland's transition period (Trice & Beyer 1984).

Similarly, Newland's rites of transition was always a difficult balance of maintaining ongoing business commitments, coupled with the necessity for the continuance of training of new employees, who required exposure to and support from experienced engineers.

It was not the altering influences of rites of transition that kept the focus of Newland's existing members on revenue generating work in progress, it was moreover, rites of integration that assisted Newland's organisational survival throughout the distractions and interruptions associated with the induction and training period. One major consequence of rites of integration is that disparate groups are brought together in common concern for the continuity of the organisation involved (Trice & Beyer 1984).

Newland's induction process was not a structured contingent event. The progression of the newcomers required organisational and personal flexibility from Newland's planning directors and supervising engineers, if the objective of the 'smooth integration experience' was to be achieved.

All of Newland's existing contract work still had to be implemented, even though cultural attention had been turned to the presence of new employees in the midst. Hence, Newland's organisational survival was preserved by harmonising existing business commitments, with new employee start and especially training dates and utilising organisational resources, time, planning, manpower and equipment, as and when necessary (Trice & Beyer 1984).

Contrary to idyllic project needs, however, work in progress and client demands sometimes entailed the supervising engineer to be absent from the office.

I know we planned to start (names) in (date) but I think we could possibly get them started sooner:

1. *To work on Angel.*
2. *Snohvit equipment.*

We seem to be running round trying to cover two or three jobs each and wondered what your thoughts on this idea are?

A genuine anxiety was raised when an allocated supervisor discovered a newly planned absence in their work schedule. This person was to be deployed elsewhere, for the first three weeks of the employment of the new person, who was extremely keen to start with Newland's.

An email conversation between the Operations Director and the Software Development Director indicated that the planned absence was worrying. My own concern was based around the risk of losing a talented software writer to another company. If this potential new employee had been deemed as ideal for writing Newland's type engineering software and was kept waiting too long, this person might go elsewhere:

...could use that time to familiarise himself within the company and bring himself up to date on some of the technical information that he will need for the work. Even if he spent the first week reading, he will be fairly prepared for your return after about (date). You could leave him a summarised sheet of what you need him to start researching perhaps even thinking about refreshing himself on some of the theory that he has obviously learned, but was at the back of his mind at the interview.

In response, the Software Development Director reiterated the same position so obviously, my offer of a short term alternative solution had lacked any impact or influence:

I am concerned that starting (name) too early and leaving him to undertake reading exercises could be demotivating to him (having taken on board his comments at interview).

Right or wrong in my assumption, I felt strongly that the Software Development Director was demonstrating an inability to comprehend that Newland's might lose a potentially talented software writer with good mathematical ability. Empathy had given me with impression that the interviewee was genuinely interested in Newland's employment offer and would 'jump at the chance'. Acquiescence did not come easily so again, I reiterated my point of view. Addressing directly the interviewee's concern about being left to work completely alone, unsupervised, in a previous job, I offered an alternative suggestion:

I think (name) was sufficiently aware that we wouldn't leave him to work alone, unsupervised and without relevant guidance in his work. I think he would jump at the chance to start with us.

Intentionally, I set out to highlight the interviewees eagerness to start work with Newland's at the earliest opportunity. My emphasis, however, was akin with rites of enhancement type prospects and the social values associated with the potential performance of a newcomer that consequently, could enhance Newland's long term prospects (Trice & Beyer 1984). Salient though my observations were, I failed to win the argument.

Once the ninety day probationary period had culminated and subject to the supervising engineers determining that the new staff members had become competent in their skills, each newcomer was offered a permanent position with Newland's. Adequate supervision of Newland's new staff members had brought them from their first day experience, through familiarisation, acquaintance and association to become a fully trained surveying and 3-D modelling engineer (Trice & Beyer 1984).

When the ninety day probationary period had been divested from and each newcomer had accepted a permanent position with Newland's, all became more accepted by the existing workforce. Each seemed to be referred to more directly by their name and ignored less. Consequently, each were regarded no longer the newcomer. Newland's newly trained engineers became part of the organisational culture and began their more in-depth relationship and association with the existing workforce through similar rites of incorporation (Trice & Beyer 1984).

Socialisation Through Incorporation

Rites of incorporation seem to be both an ending and a new beginning. The temporary induction and training periods of new recruits culminate into the beginning of a relatively permanent assignment to the organisation involved (Trice & Beyer 1984).

Likewise inside Newland's, incorporation was a moment in time when each new engineer simply phased into the existing processes and no delineation or marked event took place. Acceptance was simply a matter of course, if one had proven an ability to stand the test of training, time and social interaction, after which integration would follow naturally.

These individuals were the latest additions to Newland's workforce. Each were still unfamiliar and strange to the working environment and were sometimes younger. Reality would dictate that the true test of their authenticity, ability, competence, endurance and commitment would come when each were mobilised to a site and were expected to work in the hazardous conditions of a fully operational plant or offshore platform.

Additionally and equally as important were the office based analysis and 3-D modelling techniques. If in training each newcomer had demonstrated an ability to produce the right accuracy of work analysis content, within an agreed period of production time, then initial expectations of the probationary period would have been fulfilled. Likewise with the site surveying techniques, reality would determine the true analysis ability of the newcomer, when 3-D modelling production programmes and client deliverable dates had to be timely met.

For the moment though, by being willing and cooperative in training, competent in newly acquired technical skills, collaborative and mutually supportive, through accomplishment, all had enhanced their social value and influence and demonstrated integrative qualities that were accepting to existing group members (Williams, Parker & Turner 2007, Trice & Beyer 1984).

Risking themselves in the process helped each to fuse and combine their social skills into the existing community, feel less intimidated and become integrated through participation and sharing (Brotheridge & Lee 2006, Neri 2006, Trice & Beyer 1984). For the new, social distinction was gained by being a good worker in general (Malinowski 1922). 'Technical ability' and 'fitting in' had been proven.

In rites of passage, the individual, existing members and the organisation in which the individuals are involved, collectively respond, as employees facilitate their transition from newcomer to incorporated organisational member (Trice & Beyer 1984).

Organisations like Newland's are social systems and communities of practice in which status changing activity, transitional learning and incorporating adjustment takes place (Schutz 2005, Trice & Beyer 1984). For Newland's community, incorporation was aided and socialisation increased through collective participation in two of Newland's group structures, the Group of Uncertain Diversity and the Morning Coffee Group.

The group of 'Uncertain Diversity' was a planned weekly group, an event held each Monday morning, up to a maximum of one hour. The group meeting was held in a formal setting, Newland's conference room. It was led by the Operations Director and all staff were expected to attend. Two underlying principles gave the group its name.

The first rationale was topic related. The purpose of the group was to discuss Newland's generalised work content such as, the status of project work and its progress, site conditions, timetables, pay, working hours and holidays.

The second group characteristic was less ordered. Distractions easily disturbed the group focus from these main topics, to unrelated diverse uncertainties like the unrelated contents of conversations recently held with clients, opinions made about specific client requests and any other information that had arisen during the working week.

Newland's employees more often referred to this meeting as:

The usual Monday morning meeting.

Though one Newland's member called it:

The GUD group

What was salient to the GUD group was that neither an agenda nor minutes were prepared before or after the meeting. The lack of preparation of a meeting agenda, that forced topic discussion or written down recordings of what any person had said, was a deliberate management action on my part. An unstructured approach to the GUD group, however, determined that the weekly event was regularly a combination of part order, part disorder and difficult to conduct (Barnes, Ernst & Hyde 1999).

Consequently, the lack of structure, free-for-all environment, meant that the group space retained the potential to be utilised for any discussion topics. Even disgruntlements with management or other work colleagues were raised (Barnes, Ernst & Hyde 1999, Friedman 2007, Neri 2006).

The main aim of the meeting was the reduction of conflict by drawing attention to and discussing any critical matters that could impact upon the day-to-day functioning processes of Newland's commercial activities and hence, organisational survival (Trice & Beyer 1984). Subsequently, when problems arose, Newland's management already had a flexible forum in which to reassure organisational members that something was being done about predicaments.

For any new staff member, introduction into the GUD group gave each an insight into the functioning of Newland's whole workforce and the potential and capabilities of what could happen. Communication and the lack of it, cohesiveness and non-obliging behaviours were displayed. Unhelpful sarcastic comments, making an established member the point of a joke, face pulling and the deliberate withholding of relevant information were regularly demonstrated. No social veneer existed in Newland's GUD group behind which was hidden workforce anger and frustration (Barnes, Ernst & Hyde 1999).

A calm and relaxed attitude was encouraged by the leader, but this was usually diminished by distracting conversations and unnecessary verbal interruptions that constantly took place within it. The politeness that was most often sought was not always achieved (Berson & Sosik 2007).

Spontaneous unrelated chit-chat and unconnected cliche type conversations most often took place that at times, kept others out and specific fellow supporters in (Guadagno & Cialdini 2007, Stensaker & Falkenberg 2007). These on-off type interactions seemed to be part of the group and were not discouraged unless they really started to take the meeting truly of its main core purpose and a concern emerged, in the leader, that shambolic chaos was beginning to reign.

In the GUD group, sometimes the newcomer became the focus of lightweight verbal prodding. The group was a testing ground for the new employee and the expectation was that the newcomer would retaliate, stand ground or wittingly even the score. Bullying never took place, both the leadership and the wider group community positively ensured that. Bantering, jocular attention and joviality aimed directly at the new member encouraged that person to become more at ease with the tumultuous activity of the GUD group.

Smiling faces lessened any threat. Voicing a contribution as organisational needs and commercial demands were aired, reviewed, discussed and agreed, created respect and ensured the newcomers further integration into Newland's organisational community (Trice & Beyer 1984).

More cordial, socially active group interactions happened for the newcomer each working day. Being of fifteen to thirty minute duration, the Morning Coffee Group was a social group that took place each working morning. The group was a place in time where Newland's employees would re-join and reconnect with each other, each morning, when coffee and tea would be consumed. In direct contrast to the GUD group, Newland's Morning Coffee Group was more courteous, offering its participants an amenable, genteel, relaxed, and hospitable atmosphere.

Unlike the GUD group, the Morning Coffee Group was held in an informal setting, Newland's reception area, where only seating for four persons was available. Some of Newland's workforce, therefore, sat and others had to stand.

Another characteristic of the Morning Coffee Group was that only limited reference was made to the work content and extensive reference was made to social events and activities. It was a place where social events were comprehensively discussed such as television programmes, sport activities, interesting and/or odd news stories and the weather. Work related matters were lightly addressed, such as timetables, targets, tidying the workplace and working practicalities in hot and cold environments. The atmosphere always remained orderly and polite.

Newland's directors also participated in the morning coffee ritual. The operations director, a female, was always invited to sit but the managing director, a male, was always left to stand. Organisational roles were not actively played out by the directors. Still, the hierarchy still manifested through a show of respect, compliance and the reinforcement of Newland's family type, reciprocal relations.

Sometimes even compliance demands could be made explicit by Newland's management knowing that in relaxed conversation, held over coffee in an informal social atmosphere, important implicit and explicit social and organisational knowledge could be easily shared community wide (Ambrosini, Bowman & Burton-Taylor 2007, Hrebiniak 2006, Kessler 2006). Mostly though, this was the venue where Newland's organisational enhancing good news was spread (Trice & Beyer 1984).

There was a ritual associated with the Morning Coffee Group (Trice 1984). One group member, a female, would consistently make the tea and coffee—the 'first cup of the day'. Other group members accepted and permitted this action. Only when this lady was absent did another one step forward to make the 'first cup of the day'. This was usually the same group member, a male.

It was noted, however, that sometimes the new employees voluntarily stepped forward to offer to make the 'first cup of the day'. Despite the offer from the newcomer, the member who regularly stepped in as a replacement, would take ultimate charge of the situation. Sometimes though, this male would allow the newcomer to proceed and make 'the first cup of the day', and at other times, would not (Pfeffer 2010).

At the same time that knowledge was being shared, gossip seemed to elude the social environment of the Morning Coffee Group. It was always considered by the directors this was because the gossip was undertaken elsewhere.

Previously in this chapter, I have mentioned how Newland's workforce built complex and diverse teams in order to successfully conduct the 3-D engineering work, in office and site based locations (Brotheridge & Lee 2006, Ringer 2007). One of these teams was called the Virtual Team, which was permanently located overseas. Similarly to the UK based teams, the Virtual Team also conducted site and analysis work on behalf of Newland's. I expand upon these work activities in a later chapter.

Practically, the time zone differences between Greenwich Mean Time (GMT) and Malaysia Standard Time (MST) meant that the Virtual Team could not participate in either the UK based recruitment event, the GUD group or the Morning Coffee Group.

Significant efforts were continuously made to aid participation in all of Newland's work activities by the use of modern day technology however, the time differences meant that the social interactions associated and regularly conducted within the GUD group and the Morning Coffee Group, did not place. Likewise, face-to-face involvement in the recruitment event was not feasible (Dixon & Panteli 2010).

Newland's Virtual Team remotely coordinated the activities of their own project work and recruitment events, as and when necessary:

I have mailed (name) about a request from our agent here to train some people on (software name) but I think the priority goes to this (software name) job. I will email (name) about this and hopefully I can offer my help for this job.

Therefore, the real possibility exists that Newland's Virtual Team members may have held their own similar yet, cultural type groups (Hardin, Fuller & Davison 2007).

Newland's induction process, like rites of separation, manifested in the handing out of work equipment such as desking, seating and a laptop. Familiarisation, acquaintance and association were evident. Rites of transition facilitated the movement of Newland's new recruits, from their first encounter with the organisation, to a more intense training regime. Socialisation was reinforced through an engaged interface in the GUD group and the daily, less formal, interaction of a social based group, the Morning Coffee Group.

Later, the roles of story-telling, food and the celebration of special occasions would increasingly embed the socialisation of both the new employees and the existing community. The integrating effects of story-telling, food and celebrations made an important contribution to how Newland's vital work activities were kept in motion.

These roles, however, did not exclusively reinforce the discrete activity of incorporating new staff. Because of their integrative significance, the roles are featured in a chapter on how Newland's work was undertaken as rites of integration.

Rites of passage fill vacant organisational roles with new recruits who have the capacity to transform into organisational compatible occupants, who then emulate the existing members (Trice & Beyer 1984). Likewise, Newland's empty positions were filled with individuals who had the capacity to transform into a Newland's type staff member.

An ability to demonstrate sufficient technical skills and to become a socially accepted member of staff, within a set period of induction, caused minimum disruption to Newland's ongoing revenue generating project work and therefore, organisational survival was aided by 'technical ability', a 'smooth integration process' and 'fitting in' (Trice & Beyer 1984).

In this chapter, I have given a detailed outline of the interactions that took place within Newland's prior to the recruitment event taking place. I have then covered Newland's recruitment event and given data examples of the interactions between organisational members and the recruitment agent. Newland's induction process has been compared to the rites of separation and transition. The socialisation of newcomers has been compared with the rites of incorporation.

In the next chapter, I will explain how Newland's work was done.

Chapter 5
Results: How the Work was Done

Comparable models emerged in Newland's that were complementary to the assimilating effects of rites of integration (Trice & Beyer 1984). In this chapter, I will demonstrate how Newland's sustained an organisational culture that maintained types of rites of integration. Internal to this culture were five subsystems that got Newland's work undertaken. The first two subsystems were contingent activities i.e. scoping and pricing followed by the necessary team activities to undertake the work.

Following on, three social based activities of story-telling, the role of food and Crystal Celebrations helped to reinforce integration. I will begin with a short explanation of the rites of integration after which Newland's subsystems are explained.

Rites of Integration

Participation in the rites of integration encourages the interaction of diverse subsystems (Trice & Beyer 1984). Bonding occurs through mutuality, cohesiveness and cooperation. Different kinds of subsystems thrive in complex organisations or other collectivities. The integrative effect of these subsystems, however, only benefit the involved members. Rites of integration therefore, are disparately exclusive.

According to Trice & Beyer (1984) the major consequence of the rites of integration is that disparate groups are brought together in common concern for the continuity of the organisations involved. The rites of integration unifies differences and coordinates the involved organisational whole, so that organisational perpetuity is maintained and therefore, continuity is more assured (Trice & Beyer 1984).

Although rites of integration would be unique and exclusive to every organisation, for Newland's, integration and ultimately organisational perpetuity was made certain by the undertaking of revenue generating operational activities.

When conducting Newland's work, the workforce had to sufficiently maintain robust internal processes of production based upon proficiency, time and accuracy. These reciprocal arrangements got work orders processed, duties assigned and tasks completed in organisational compliance with client's wants, desires, engineering standards, project specifications, the fulfilment of organisational duty and the protection of the company's interests.

Simultaneously, there was also a need to maintain the intellectual confidentiality of how all of these processes worked so that Newland's was never placed into a position of commercial vulnerability by the leakage of organisational secret ingredients.

Alvesson (2002) says that organisational culture is as significant and complex as it is difficult to understand. Senses and feelings can only be gained by being an inside member influenced by inherent social patterns that require interpreting and deciphering (Alvesson 2002, Fineman, Gabriel & Sims 2010, Schein 2010, Trice & Beyer 1984).

Likewise, Newland's employees adopted certain attitudes and approaches in order to fulfil their work obligations that manifested in the organisational culture (Jeske 2001, Smith 2007, Trice & Beyer 1984). Furthermore, Newland's was completely reliant upon employees goodwill, attitudes, direct efforts and commitment to duty, all set inside the infrastructure of an organisational SME, where these culturally expressive activities were undertaken (Trice & Beyer 1984).

I will now turn to Newland's five divergent subsystems (Trice & Beyer 1984). Starting with scoping and pricing, I will use data extracts from one project to give examples of how Newland's work was done. Conversely, I will occasionally illustrate relevant points using data extract from other projects, in order to emphasise those salient, but important points.

Pricing and Scoping Work

The first Newland's subsystem that promoted the common good and helped to perpetuate organisational survival would be an obvious one for any trading establishment, the generation of money (Trice & Beyer 1984). Newland's scoping and pricing subsystem began with the financial evaluation of potential engineering work.

Continuously, Newland's had to maintain sufficient working capital to fund the payroll and operating expenses of large engineering contracts that could extend over many months, even years. Undoubtedly, money was vital to sustain Newland's continued development of innovation, economical and commercial success (Jorgensen & Ulhoi 2010).

Newland's potential project work was priced upon an invitation from a prospective client who had a budget approved engineering project that was required to be undertaken. Obviously, Newland's had a vested interest in doing the work (Jorgensen & Ulhoi 2010, Russell 2008, Yuanmeng 2011, Zimmerman, Barksy & Brouthers 2009). Even though exclusiveness was a dimension of rites of integration, common participation immediately bridged engineering client and Newland's, linked by project specific scoping and pricing responsibilities (Trice & Beyer 1984).

Clearly, the joint objective between client and Newland's for scoping and pricing was to place an agreed financial value upon the potential project work, after which approval would be sought and then, the project implemented. Subsequently, disparate client and Newland's pricing engineer became temporarily linked by this joint objective, their intentions being, to get the engineering work scoped, priced and undertaken (Trice & Beyer 1984).

Different personal objectives, however, manifested in the background of these reciprocal discussions. Both client and Newland's pricing engineer would evaluate, scope and price the job according to their desire or need to obtain the best deal available. Unquestionably, each would safeguard the perpetuity of their own organisations (Trice & Beyer 1984). A motivated client intended to keep the project cost as low as possible. Newland's pricing engineer wanted to generate as much revenue as could be obtained from doing the work.

Newland's had a complex way of pricing work. Quotations to scope and price always had to meet a client specific buying and order approval system. Consequently, pricing was different for every client project specification and scope of work. Getting the process wrong meant upsetting a valued client, losing the market position to a competitor, loss of revenue and the longer term consequences of a reduced trading capability. Pricing was based upon work scope, cost of mobilisation, surveying, analysis and the transfer of the 3-D model deliverable into a 3-D design software package.

Included in the detailed narrative of rites of integration, is an account of how some influential organisational members annually discussed and negotiated their intentions (Trice & Beyer 1984). Through tough and even embarrassing questioning, boundaries were renegotiated, redefined and reinforced in common concern for the continuity of the organisations involved. Comparably, Newland's scoping and pricing process entailed three similar distinguishable characteristics.

First came the obvious negotiations of scoping and pricing, followed by the more subtle renegotiation of the pricing by the client. Then last of all, akin with rites of enhancement, the good news of 'we've got that work' would be conveyed to Newland's workforce.

Obviously, scoping and pricing entailed knowing where the plant was located because Newland's site teams would have to travel there. Sometimes the marketing engineer could visit the plant, usually if it was conveniently located. For overseas plants and especially offshore platforms, where access had to be systematically planned, work was scoped and priced using engineering drawings, photographic visual aids and/or internet based mapping.

As the plant location indicated in the following data extract was overseas, Newland's potential client sent the pricing engineer the plant's geographical location to view from a laptop:

1) *Google Earth KMZ file showing location and area covered*
2) *Gif file showing aerial shot of plant from the south side*
3) *Gif files showing elevation views of some of the plant*

Subsequently, the quotation document could be prepared by Newland's pricing engineer. The scoping and pricing document would start with a detailed understanding of the purpose or reason why the project was to be undertaken. Next, would be the details of the survey coverage and a proposal on the methods used. The quotation document would then detail the teaming requirements, travel, manpower, costs of the work, budget assumptions for contingencies, invoicing terms, terms and conditions of the sale and a detailed programme of work that included start, finishing and delivery dates.

Making arrangements for an event is an activity of rites of integration (Trice & Beyer 1984). Likewise, through the joint cooperation of two disparate yet linked representatives, each from separate companies, a scope of work was designed and a price agreed by the collaborative interactions of client and Newland's pricing engineer.

Newland's client had an initial perception of which areas in their plants or platforms the acquisition of 3-D data could be useful for. Primarily, the cost of the service was a strong determinant factor. Initially, the first approach usually indicated that the scoping and pricing given was not firm but was simply, an estimation of what potentially could be done. The following data extracts is given as an example of early negotiations:

I have put together a draft Excel quote for the (project name) area you sent to (name). I have given you the calculations for this as well so you can see how we have worked up the costs. I hope this is what you want to see cost and different approaches for this type of work. This is just to give you ideas of cost, etc.

Considering the legacy of 3-D engineering data was always an evaluating factor for Newland's clients, i.e., how useful the data would instantly be to their project and the longer term benefits that the client could receive. Hence, Newland's work history and project experience also counted. Although, the data extract given here is related to a different client in a different location, it is a good example of how a Newland's client considered legacy and the longer term benefits of acquiring 3-D engineering data for asset management:

Good to talk to you this afternoon about building a proposal to capture and model the (unit name) at our refinery in Germany. We would be interested in exploring the costs and timescales in two areas:

- *Creating a 3-D model with at least 2" resolution*
- *Creating a 2-D image set that could be hosted on an (hosting name) platform for asset management purposes.*
- *We aren't quite sure what the benefits of this would be but would like to discuss this further with you as to how some of your customers are using this method.*

I have attached a number of files that will help you understand the location, size and complexity of the area that we want captured. Please indicate when you might be able to schedule this work. Let me know if you require any further information to enable you to make a proposal.

Predictably, Newland's client would attempt to obtain a price reduction through tough, but open negotiations. Common good continuity for the two organisations involved in the pricing process was maintained by renegotiating the price of the work by the linked relevant representatives (Trice & Beyer 1984).

Revising a quotation to fit into client project funding, therefore, was a common practice for Newland's. Cutting the price of the work was part of the negotiation process.

Decreasing the price of the work, however, also determined a reduction in the work scope. The following two data extracts demonstrated how the pricing revisions were managed to meet the limits of project funding available to do the work:

I have asked (name) to send through the (project name) Microstation files so you can fine tune your quote. I knew that we had added some extra work for the trees but hadn't expected it to be nearly double the value of the P/O again even at cost (am I reading this correctly?). If so, I will need to ask you to stop work until the budget holder (name) approves the variation as this exceeds our normal contingency.

After the client had held a discussion with the budget holder, Newland's received an update on the procurement process and the potential of being issued with a purchase order (PO) for the work:

Thanks for the revised quote which I have summarised as follows:

Sub sea Isolation Valve Assembly Skid	*$ Dollar Amount*
Receiver Assembly Skid	*$ Dollar Amount*
Valve Protection Frame	*$ Dollar Amount*
Total	*$ Dollar Amount*

If this is OK, then I will raise a P/O request for (name) to approve. I did take the time to catch up with (name) and indicated we need to raise a P/O for the above work and also outlined to him our overrun on the subsea xmas tree work. We didn't discuss specific cost but he did indicate that up to 20% contingency was acceptable, however anything further would need to be further investigated. If you are happy to run with the 20% more for this order then great, it not I can engaged (name) to look at this further.

Let me know. I still have to summarise the discussion I had with (name) and provide the photos but hopefully will get that sorted before today's meeting.

Predominantly, scoping was a manifestation of obvious negotiation, subtle renegotiation and the constant revision of job content and pricing between two interested and temporarily integrated company representatives. Almost like a ritualistic display of will versus capitulation, both acted to perpetuate and protect the financial interests of their own organisations (Trice & Beyer 1984).

As would be expected, backwards and forwards interactions were all deliberately undertaken in order to meet client acceptable scopes of work and available project funding. Differences relating with pricing levels, project coverage and model content were unified in accordance with available client resources.

Obviously, the aim was to win the work, but not at any cost. There had to be sufficient money in the project to contribute to Newland's annual operating expenses. In monetary terms, organisational survival and perpetuity was a simple equation for both Newland's and the client, annual income had to exceed annual operating expenses (Trice & Beyer 1984).

Newland's pricing engineer was also the managing director who had the authority to decide what could be capitulated to win the work, either by reducing the work scope or offering a discount. This willingness to move to meet client budget limitations was indicated in the following data extract:

I have held back giving you this until I received the micro station files of the skids. I hope you are OK with the Excel sheet as this is my approx. cost with the information I have. Please discuss this with me if you are worried about the costing as they are not cast in stone.

Rites of enhancement provide the opportunity for a manager to spread good news about their organisations (Trice & Beyer 1984). Addressing each member of the workforce, sometimes individually, Newland's managing director spread the news that the client had accepted Newland's quotation for the work, but with certain conditions.

Subsequently, acceptance in Newland's wider community stemmed from a **non-questioning** of the managing directors decision making coupled with mutual recognition for the accomplishment of obtaining work. Undoubtedly, a worthwhile enterprise would perpetuate Newland's organisational survival (Kets De Vries 2007, Trice & Beyer 1984).

Pragmatically, Newland's engineers had a vested interest in the scoping final solution as their teams would later be tasked with doing the work. Consequently, an early warning system came into play. Geographically, the location of the site Newland's engineers could discover for themselves, but questions arose on project size, client conditions, coverage, the model accuracy required and project supervision.

From these preliminary conversations, a determination could be made on how many days at site the teams would be absent from the office and more importantly, from home. Later, comprehensive project information would be obtained from the engineering specification documents received from the client.

Because the emphasis was placed upon economic survival, Newland's managing director could flexibly and successfully integrate the contractually defined client requirements into an informed and prepared organisational culture in order to get the work undertaken. Acceptance was reinforced through the recognition that the generation of money would follow from the enterprise. Hence, disparate groups were brought together in one common cause, the need for Newland's organisational perpetuity (Trice & Beyer 1984).

Money was perceived by Newland's workforce as a valuable commodity, contributable to organisational survival, which needed to be accumulated and preserved. In harmonising and synchronising all of Newland's awarded project activities, in accordance with client defined terms of business, the workforce could also provide for personal and family existence (Brotheridge & Lee 2006, Neri 2006).

Once the negotiated scoping and pricing had been accepted, Newland's would receive a purchase order to do the work. Newland's work was undertaken in teams activities triggered by the commercial obligation that Newland's had made with the client.

Team Activities

Rites of integration places the integrative emphasis on groups of individuals who, through interactions, bind together common shared beliefs and commit them to a larger system. In doing so, different groups are united in that common concern. For an organisation, the sought after aim is the perpetuity and continuity of that involved organisation (Trice & Beyer 1984).

Obviously, in order for rites of integration to manifest, there has to be a gathering of people in which these rites would become apparent. Logically, teams that unite in order to undertake work on behalf of an organisation are therefore, gatherings in which rites of integration could consequently manifest (Trice & Beyer 1984).

Newland's team activity of mobilisation triggered the impermanent movement of Newland's engineers and their equipment from the office base, to a remotely located site, in order to carry out the first part of an agreed project scope, the site survey.

Later, upon completion of the site survey, Newland's engineers would make the return journey back to the office and begin the process of the next new phase of the project scope, the analysis of the data captured at site.

In order to illustrate how mobilisation manifested in the undertaking of Newland's project work, I think it is important to give an explanation of the diverse structures of the teams and team objectives.

Newland's team structures were called the Cold Team, Pairs, the Hot Team and the Virtual Team. Commercially important site surveys and analysis work were discrete functions that were undertaken in these teams. I will start with the first team that formed to accomplish project work called the Cold Team and Pairs.

Uniquely named, the Cold Team was derived from the term *coordinated in a localised destination*. It was made up of pairs of individuals, jointly working and functioning in order to carry out the assigned site survey work, together with all of the equipment required to conduct the site survey. Geographically, the Cold Team would be temporarily located nationally, overseas, onshore or offshore away from the office and also, more importantly, from home. Newland's site work was conducted in as many Cold Teams that the work volume demanded. One team member would be allocated as the team leader.

Pairs were a subordinate element of the Cold Team and only existed in that context. Pairs were the couple of individuals that formed the site teams and the site teams always worked in pairs. There could, however, be a number of pairs undertaking the survey scope i.e., two site teams would comprise of two engineers in each site team and there could be two or more located site teams. Whilst meeting the Cold Team set objectives, these pairings worked in hazardous heavy engineering industrial type environments under difficult and uncomfortable conditions.

When the site survey had been completed, the Cold Team would leave the site and return. Once settled back in the office, a subsequent and different team was required to accommodate the next phase of the project work, the analysis of the site data. Subsequently, the team that manifested was called the Hot Team.

Distinctive to Newland's, the Hot Team was derived from the term *in-house organised together*. This team was formed to carry out the minutely detailed analysis of the site data that had been collected in the Cold Team and Pairing structures. Office based, the Hot Team was made up of three or more individuals. One senior engineer was nominated as team leader. Sensible micro grouping of three individuals meant that the process of work would be internally visible to all the team members.

Consequently, the team leader could closely manage the team activity.

Exclusively, the objective of the Hot Team was to produce an as-built 3-D model of a remotely located client property, that had previously been surveyed by the Cold Team. Clear technical emphasis was placed upon the tasking responsibilities associated with the aim of analysing large volumes of complex site data. Meticulous analysis work would be carried out, in a specified amount of time, in order produce a project deliverable that would later be sent to the client. Commercially stressed, it was a Newland's team structure that was always pressurised by the external influences of time and money.

Newland's Virtual Team was permanently located overseas. In the delegation and allocation of tasking schedules and activities, daily face-to-face contact was not always possible for the Virtual Team members (Hambley, O'Neill & Kline 2007, Potter Balthazard & Cooke 2000). Consequently, for most of the time, the Virtual Team members were reliant upon web-based communications.

Dual responsibilities were placed upon the Virtual Team that manifested in both Cold Team and Hot Team duties. Sometimes, Virtual Team members would travel to site, mostly overseas and conduct the survey work. At other times, the Virtual Team members would receive an allocated set piece of modelling work sent from the UK office.

An explanation of Newland's team structures has now been given. The specific purpose of each team was to get Newland's work undertaken, so I can now begin to illustrate the complexities of these team activities. Using data extracts as examples, from the same overseas project as given before, I can demonstrate how these diverse team gatherings, worked jointly, reciprocally and in a unified way so that Newland's organisational survival was perpetuated (Trice & Beyer 1984).

Rites of integration promote organisational survival because enabling interactions take place in gatherings that have set objectives (Trice & Beyer 1984). 'Doing' therefore, is the key factor.

Newland's tasking arrangements took place within three divergent group structures, where all of the concentrated tasking functions were focused upon and detailed work was undertaken. Substantially, Newland's tasking arrangements embraced common practices and methods of work that ensured the tasking function remained comprehensively consistent throughout the process.

According to Trice & Beyer (1984) divergent subsystems interact with each other and bind, then commit shared feelings to a larger system. In doing so, different groups are joined together, in a common concern, for the continuity of the organisation involved. If subsystems of this type interact and integrate, then activity must also be taking place.

Three contingent subsets of behaviour manifested in Newland's, so that different, but related team activities could be coordinated and the essential revenue generating work undertaken (Trice & Beyer 1984). These three subset activities were the Pre-Booking System, Equipment Packing and Sequencing. I will begin with an explanation of the pre-booking system of which team participation was a critical ingredient.

Interrelated peer cohesion is built when leaders take some time to plan, organise and coordinate tasking arrangements, according to Brotheridge & Lee (2006). Conversely, Hanson (2006) states that regardless of the method used, the key is having teams clearly identify roles for each team member. Unfavourably, poor performance could adversely affect other team members and the team objective (Tagger & Neubert 2004). However, when team leaders take responsibility for making the right kinds of impressions to influence team members to achieve team objectives, teams do function well (Yukl 2002).

Mobilisation of the site teams was an economically important organisational activity for Newland's (Trice & Beyer 1984). As the impending activity to depart from the usual place of work and travel elsewhere was contemplated, the need for the Cold Team leader would manifest. Proportionately, the position of team leader was taken up by a member who would be travelling. In anticipation of the imminent departure, the Cold Team members would prepare for travel by the practical organisation of themselves and their site equipment.

In order to coordinate activities, Newland's pre-booking system was utilised by designated team members to ensure that as each member picked up and began their duties of mobilisation, other undesignated team members would play a supportive role. Consequently, Newland's pre-booking system was the procedure used to invoke team help into manifestation by communicating intended actions and the expectation of supporting resources, upon demand.

Support was required to assist the Cold Team in two ways. Precedence was to invoke practical help with all of the immediate travelling arrangements so that the mobilising objectives were timely met. Subsequent support was future-oriented that brought to the fore, the forward planning for the essential Hot Team configurations.

Essentially, Newland's pre-booking system made certain that resources would be available for two purposes, the movement of the Cold Team from one location to another and the Hot Team analysis configurations required later in the work schedules. Resource needs extended to sufficient manpower, relevant engineering skill, 3-D modelling expertise, computer hardware, the use of in-house 3-D modelling software and the use of external third party design software licences.

Combined, these coordinated support activities and available resources, synchronised through the pre-booking system, ensured that Newland's economical commitments were met hence, organisational survival was maintained (Trice & Beyer 1984).

Constant vocalisations ensued as mobilisation got under way. Travelling arrangements, client interfacing, conducting the site survey, equipment needs, personal and family requirements were all discussed. Administration was asked by the mobilising engineers to send flowers, birthday cards or baby gifts to meet family obligations for those engineers who would be absent from home on these special occasions. Newland's was rarely reimbursed for these costs.

Whilst either packing the equipment or supervising others doing the packing, the Cold Team nominated leader would directly address the team members who were not travelling. An authoritative attitude of the Cold Team leader ensured that support was offered, unquestionably, loyally and efficiently. This vocal address would be firm and herald the upcoming support requirement, by pre-informing the non-travelling engineers of future needs, in relation to the project work schedule and tasking. This pre-informing was demonstrated in the following data extract from a conversation between travelling and non-travelling engineers:

I'm going to need all of you on this job or when I get back!

Productively, the pre-booking system was initiated and put into operation ensuring that the returning teams would have the relevant support and resources available in a state of readiness. Although functioning in the present, supervising or doing the packing, a focused Cold Team leader was able to refer to a future-oriented organisational tasking function and time. This was the data analysis work that would have to be completed to attain the consolidated project objective of surveying, 3-D model build and later, a client deliverable.

Immediately to hand, there was a laying out of the path ahead to ensure that the two impending tasking assignments, site surveying and data analysis, had a chance of successful intervention. Consequently, Newland's commercial obligations would later become a successfully met objective for which payment would be received (Trice & Beyer 1984).

In response to the Pre-Booking System, a unison was formed by all team members and preparations made for both the imminent and future events. Project related knowledge and information was circulated through conversations that stemmed from instructions, directions and guidance from a team leader.

Private family matters were not aired in public yet, were still addressed during this time, but more on a one-to-one basis. Possibly, the integrative effects of rites of integration permitted the private venting of emotion in relation to personal difficulties associated with engineers who were required to travel and temporarily leave their families (Trice & Beyer 1984).

As with rites of integration, disparate organisational members were consolidated to ensure that the usual norms of commercially focused tasking activity would not be placed at risk, thus preserving Newland's commercial integrity and ongoing financial existence (Trice & Beyer 1984).

Another dimension existed to the pre-booking system. This dimension was focused on the human beings who were addressed during the ritualistic display of the pre-informing requests for support. In one of my field notes, I made particular reference to this:

The group member who is nominated with the tasking arrangements seems to have some sense of "Badge-ing" notated to them because they are regarded as being a tool for the survival of the group as a whole. Whoever holds the "Badge", holds the position as leader when they describe their tasking arrangement to the group and put the "pre-booking system" into some form of action or a pre-determined knowledge that the action will be deferred to sometime later, but will be put into operation at some point in time in the future.

This is spread across the teaming arrangement which is made up of two members; however, the team leader seems to hold the "Badge".

Whichever team leader was nominated with the responsibility for invoking the mobilisation activities seemed to have a sense of 'badge' notated to them. Accordingly, this member was regarded as a valuable human implement or resource. Becoming primarily the implementer of the team objectives, the 'badge holder' put the mobilising activity into practice by setting the pre-booking system into action.

Again, seen in the same field note entry that follows, was the emergence of the voice of the implementer. Notably, needs and expectations were conveyed by that person in relation to mobilisation activities:

The mobilisation that was due to take place this week seemed to be of relevant importance to the group. It was noted by the researcher that the member who was looked upon by the group as the leader who opened the meeting, was not the leader at the end of the group because the position of the leader changed. The position of the leader changed because of an event that was related to time and a tasking arrangement that was to be carried out.

One group member M-35, who was one of the two members who would be travelling, was particularly vocal and informed the whole of the meeting of his travelling arrangements, the planning and the tasking arrangements that would be required for the project.

It seemed, by the researcher, that because this person is personally and immediately affected by the events such as travel and working abroad, he was really efficient and coherent in passing on relevant and important information and also, his feelings and opinions around what might happen once he returns and the requirement for support from the group in order to fulfil the further tasking arrangements that would be required in the future. M-35 was bringing important news to the group as a whole and did this with ease and with clarity.

Primarily, whoever held the badge of the human implementer also held the leadership position at the same time that the badge was held. Even though the team leader was regarded as a person with leadership responsibilities, the focus was not on the team leader as a person, but on what significance that badge holder represented.

Consequently, the badge holder was the voice and hand of the team objectives.

Newland's team leader would become an implementer, that would gauge, facilitate and manage the tasking content to meet the mobilisation objectives. In doing so, the team leader would act, dispense, coordinate and consolidate the necessary resources that were required to move the site teams and equipment from one location to another and conduct work vital to Newland's organisational survival (Trice & Beyer 1984).

In response to mobilisation needs and requests made by the badge holder, the following data extract, a field note entry, demonstrated how one member determined priorities in direct relation to giving mobilisation support:

One employee, D-37, was present at the meeting who had not been able to attend the training because he had needed to test some new equipment and prepare himself for a project.

By pre-determining specific facts and communicating that to the assisting engineers, the badge holder ensured that action would be either taken up immediately or deferred to a later time. Influentially, the badge holder was instrumental in facilitating the needs of the immediate moment and setting the future in a way that would permit action to defer and manifest later. Principally, successful intervention of the pre-booking system was a simple concept. Indisputably, it ensured that the need for organisational members to respond and do work now or support later, was set in the memory of others.

Evidently, the Pre-Booking subsystem of mobilisation was ideal as long as the willing others in Newland's communal labour force would comply. The rites of integration assisted this process (Trice & Beyer 1984). What was set in motion by the mobilisation activity was the manifest consequence that disparate organisational members were brought together in one common concern. Consequently, meeting the contractual economic promise made by Newland's would bring forth a subsequent financial gain generated from a successful enterprise (Trice & Beyer 1984).

The next contingent subset of behaviour, inclusive to Newland's types of rites of integration, was equipment packing, a ritualised procedure primarily adopted to mobilise site equipment, without which the site survey could not be conducted (Trice 1984, Trice & Beyer 1984).

Despite Trice's (1984) observation that rituals seldom produce intended technical consequences of practical importance, Newland's equipment packing ritual productively moved vital site equipment, alongside the travelling engineers, from the office premises to a remote site location.

Being an important step of a potentially successful commercial endeavour, without the ritual equipment packing, Newland's would fail to meet the first stage of the agreed contract work (Trice & Beyer 1984). I will now provide an explanation of equipment packing.

Two or three days before the appointed date and time of departure, the nominated Cold Team engineer, assigned for travelling to the project site, removed the right amount of site equipment from the storage room. Meticulously, each piece of equipment was removed from its storage container. Next, a unique ritual inspection of intended technical and practical importance began (Trice 1984, Trice & Beyer 1984).

An allocated number of theodolite were removed from their green storage cases and each one was placed upon a tripod. Test surveys were carried out to check for any equipment inaccuracies. Prisms were checked for damage to the prism casing. Eye pieces were examined. Cameras and lenses were checked for damage to the camera body, loose fittings and breakages of the lens.

Test photographs were taken of survey targets to check calibration accuracy. Photography flash equipment was checked for broken bulbs. Batteries were charged and/or replaced.

Each piece of equipment was then re-packed into a specifically designed foam lined travelling box. The theodolite, or more than one theodolite, was packed into its own green travelling case and sealed. The theodolite tripod and survey targets were packed into a cardboard box and taped up. Cameras were packed into specially designed aluminium travelling cases, locked and sealed. The smaller pieces of survey equipment and camera accessories were packed into a suitcase and locked and sealed.

To satisfy custom requirements, an equipment movement list was prepared. This was referred to as a Notice 756, a shipping list that detailed all of the travelling site equipment as accompanied baggage.

Because of their overseas location, Newland's Virtual Team stored a minimum level of site equipment in their premises. Sometimes the project scope entailed the movement of equipment from the UK office to overseas in order for the Virtual Team to conduct the site survey.

Prior to mobilisation taking place, the Virtual Team member would send a request to Newland's assigned Cold Team leader for a list of surveying equipment to be brought over from the UK, that matched the contractually agreed work scope:

Currently, I have with me one full set of theodolite, one wooden tripod, 1800+ blank target and one office issued dell m70 laptop. For the survey, I will need:

- *One short prism*
- *One long prism*
- *2 short lenses camera*
- *One camera flash*
- *Some 1000 more targets will help although this will need further clarification*

(Name) said that other thing like bag and consumables (battery, etc.) will be provided by him. He also said that he will buy two laptops for site work. He is also thinking to produce the target stickers locally.

As the amount of site equipment used matched the volume of work, pre-notifying an equipment needs list was an important feature in the mobilisation activity. The calculation was detailed methodically and parsimoniously. A glut of equipment on one site and a shortage at another had consequences that could manifest as delays at site and subsequently, financial penalties.

The loss of equipment at site or forgetting to pack a particular piece of equipment was a seriously worrying factor for Newland's Cold Team, as it would always inhibit the site survey.

Though not directly related to the project illustrated in this chapter, the following two data extracts stem from telephone calls to the UK based office, as a site engineer demonstrated the impact of losing or leaving the necessary site equipment behind:

I've dropped the steep sight eye piece into the ocean. Can you rush through and buy another one and ship it out to us, fast! Can we claim on the insurance?

And on another occasion:

I've forgotten to bring the flash unit. Can you drive to the hotel at the motorway junction and bring it with you. We can be there for about six o'clock, but not before because we are working until then.

When earlier addressing the scoping and pricing of work, the importance of money was linked to Newland's organisational survival (Trice & Beyer 1984). Consequently, the pricing of work always met client specific project needs. If equipment was lost, then the financial burden of the loss had to be met by Newland's. In the data extracts, specific reference to an insurance claim helped to ease the engineer of their burden of responsibility. Additionally, the engineer clearly defined the terms of meeting up, using their free time for the equipment handover.

Sheepish confessions, in the form of story-telling, were elaborated upon when the Cold Team returned to Newland's. This was done timely, on the first day back at work, in the days first social gathering, the Morning Coffee Group. Substantial risks to the project work, however, were always minimised whilst the site teams were absent and undertaking work on the site.

Rites of integration assist coordinated efforts, for a common aim, as individuals participate in the rite (Trice & Beyer 1984). Participation in mobilisation synchronised the divergent activities required to begin the first stage implementation of Newland's vital commercial work. Coordinated site teams were activated and began their travel to the site location where, the site survey work would be undertaken.

The final subset of behaviours, covered the actual undertaking of Newland's work in two phases, conducting the site survey and the analysis of the 3-D data.

In the first phase, the Cold Team leader had the main responsibility for the sequencing, undertaking and successful completion of the site survey. Part of that responsibility was communicating with the client representative at the site. One difficulty for the team leader was that sometimes, the client representative would interfere with the surveying process and attempt to make unapproved changes to the agreed scope of work. Hence, the team leader's autonomous decision making was limited by the contractually agreed scope of work, nature of the surroundings and the client interface.

Importantly, the major factor for the Cold Team was that there had to be a coordinated effort, using joint skills, that maintained what had been contractually agreed.

Pre-investigating the area to be surveyed on an overseas offshore drilling platform, the site team had to meet the surveying objectives within a set time frame. Primarily, the tasking objective for the site team was to collect the site located data, for a set period of time and once the task had been completed, return to the office. One of Newland's engineers made observations of the site conditions, linking what was now visible to the work scope that had been arranged in advance:

There was decent access all around the areas of interest, we were going to use the 6m pole and the zoom lens for the difficult areas, there are gantries around the place to shoot from. We didn't have a permit on the Monday, so we spent the afternoon walking around the place. I don't think we're far off with the quote. I will know more when we get into it. The derrick area is out of bounds due to drilling at the moment still a very scary area though…everything else is doable.

It can be seen in the data extract that the site engineer made an assessment directly in relation to the previously agreed scope of work parameters. Reference was also made to 'we', that identified the presence of others. In particular, the site engineer noted the hazards and contemplated accessibility. Uncontrollable circumstances interceded when site restrictions delayed the work by one day. Reference was specifically made to money hence, survival (Trice & Beyer 1984).

During the pre-investigation time, however, realisation occurred. Newland's quotation sufficiently matched the actual scope of work and the volume of work required to complete the task. Up to this point in time and contract phase, Newland's organisational survival had been assured (Trice & Beyer 1984).

After completion of the site survey, the Cold Team would invoke mobilisation and ritually pack up the site equipment (Trice & Beyer 1984, Turner 1969). Upon return, the individuals would bring back stories and tell of the spoils of their experience whilst being away on an expedition (Malinowski 1922). Once relocated to the office, the Cold Team(s) ceased formation and the Hot Team(s) manifested and set up the required analysis configurations.

Similar to the Cold Team leader, in the second and final phase, the Hot Team leader had the main responsibility for the sequencing, undertaking and successful completion of the analysis of the site acquired data.

Depending upon the size of the work scope, the analysis task would be split between a number of Hot Teams, each containing three people. There was often more than one Hot Team working on the data analysis. When this occurred, the Hot Teams cooperated with each other in a softly yet structurally defined type of team setting, a Hot Team Matrix.

Within the Hot Team Matrix, all of the analysis tasking objectives remained the same.

Only the scope of work content that was being analysed was different for each Hot Team. As the analysis work was being undertaken, each Hot Team leader liaised regularly and acted accordingly. The Hot Team Matrix was held together by the sharing of relevant information. In talking and sharing, knowledge was moved between the teams. During each review, the team leader would be responsible for the monitoring of progress, informing others, supervising, supporting and cooperating with others.

Specific detailed analysis work content, client influences and team leadership overview feedback was identifiable in the following data extract:

(Name) is working on the (Client Project, Job Number, Site Location) job, no order for further work at the moment, but there is a need to produce some demo material to proof the as-built against as-design concept. I am working on (Client Project, Project Name). The (Name) deliverable is an ongoing issue with (Client) and hopefully be sign off fairly soon, we just need (Client Engineer) and his cohorts to verify and QA what we have sent out to them. As an addition to this, we have the skid work to do. A P/O is going through (Client) system at the moment, but work is ongoing with it.

Unlike the (Client Project) we are well up in the time for this one (so far). I think this will be an ongoing deliverable with (Client) as they seem to like to keep involved with what is going on. (Engineer's Names) will be starting to analyse (Module No. Name) as of next Monday as part of the ongoing training and development, this will also be used for demo work. (Engineers' Names are assigned to Project). With (Engineer's Name) training as he goes, when finished, (Engineer's Name) should be working on another module of (Project) unless anything else comes up.

Newland's analysis work was a complex activity that had many components to the process. Communications with the client were regularly undertaken to keep the tasking activity in motion. Chasing up relevant engineering information was part of the process:

1. Still waiting on the information/models of (project module names) we had a reply from (client) regarding this on Tuesday. The person responsible for this is (name) who is currently away on business in Singapore.

2. Also waiting on the extra piece of model that was sent a couple of weeks ago, this came via an email from (name) but the.dgn sent was incomplete.

3. Information is still required regarding the format of the tags for use in (project name) (name) emailed (name) regarding this matter on Thursday last week.

(Name) sent me an email yesterday regarding the format of the tags we used, it looks like there is some rework to do on this. We've also just received another email from (name) regarding the tagging in (project name) he is trying to get us annotated drawing so we can update the model in Microstation.

Because of commercial pressure, sometimes the patience and goodwill of Newland's engineers got stretched too far by increasing client demands, that could place Newland's at financial risk. In the following data extract, the tone of the message is clear:

It seems to me that we are still being asked to run new functions on the project—this is not part of the work order as far as I can see and I think that we have been far too accommodating in accepting such requests already on this project. I've voiced my thoughts on this previously; that running these kind of functions on a live project involves an unacceptable risk on our part as we cannot be expected to take responsibility for any changes that these functions make to work that we have already cleared.

The amount of time that we are burning on these additional activities cannot continue free of charge—presumably you want us to use the additional contract to record these extra costs?"

Additionally, the state of the S2 sign-off is becoming laughable; I have been advised this morning that (name) is now on vacation and that the S2 milestone is still not signed off—how long are we expected to wait? We have delivered all of our milestones on time as well as performing additional work on the project that is beyond the scope of the work order. We have been extremely understanding and compassionate about (name's) accident but we have not been advised of any timetable for the sign-off of S2.

As we approach the year end, we need to ensure that all invoices for completed work are posted and I, therefore, request your approval to issue the invoice for the S1 and S2 milestone.

In order for Newland's site and analysis work to be undertaken successfully, boundary lines were always set by the commercial and financial constraints of the project awarded. Although, rites of integration permit the venting of emotion through the loosening of various norms, a constructive client relationship had to be successfully maintained in order to perpetuate Newland's commercial survival, so usual norms had to be both reasserted and reaffirmed by sometimes reiterating contractual boundaries (Trice & Beyer 1984).

Significant to Newland's commercial survival, important boundaries had to be manifested in the management of client relationships, travelling arrangements, hazardous environments, geographical distance and most often, inconvenient technology failures (Hardin, Fuller & Davison 2007, Trice & Beyer 1984).

As Newland's Virtual Team was permanently located overseas and dependent upon web-based interactions, the successful operation of technology was what made the undertaking of analysis work feasible (Collin 2006, Dias 2007, Hansen 2006).

One of the two ways in which Newland's Virtual Team worked successfully and effectively facilitating the analysis work remotely, was first through the use of modern day web-based technology, using emails backed up with live chat and conference calling. Newland's Virtual Teams therefore, were integrated via the virtual world (Trice & Beyer 1984).

The second way that virtual world integration was maintained was a Newland's wide strategy of maintaining communications in the teaming arrangements, by keeping all of the team members regularly informed (Trice & Beyer 1984). This would ensure that the contact process was kept in a state of readiness, constant, fluid and any opportunity to lose information did not arise (Joshi, Sarker & Sarker 2007, Guadagno & Cialdini 2007). Both real world and virtual world communications helped to perpetuate Newland's commercial survival during the undertaking of vital work (Trice & Beyer 1984).

Favourably for Newland's, the Virtual Team members were able to remain comfortable with the remote arrangements, even though face-to-face contact was not possible (Hambley, O'Neill & Kline 2007). Also, the members were able to provide notification of their readiness and willingness to begin the nominated project tasks, as and when required.

Even though the Virtual Team lived and worked overseas, members did not express any concern about the associated remote delegations process connected with the assignment of tasks. Practically, Virtual Team members were removed from the main decision making process for tasking assignments, though each were made aware that these actions were taken in teams and the GUD group. This remote assigned process was demonstrated in the two extracts that follow:

In the Monday morning meetings, we usually use the meeting space as an opportunity to discuss work priorities. We are aware that unfortunately, you do not have an opportunity to be present, but we are now in the process of ordering a new telephone system and this will provide us with the right kind of technology to include you as well. You will be aware that in (date) I discussed with you that at times, we need to make a decision here about how you will be nominated work which may not always include you in the decision making process. This has happened in connection with the (project name) contract.

Clearly, the response from the Virtual Team member offered a sense of realism about the remote allocation of analysis work. Undoubtedly, a degree of trust, doubt and time projection was demonstrated, when the ramifications of third party decision making came into effect:

Clearly, I only have the benefit of your communication in terms of everyone else's input—though I did talk to (names) about it on Friday and didn't hear any objections. A smooth welcome would certainly be ideal but can we guarantee that there won't be any firefighting to do come July?

In order to feel a vital part of Newland's teaming arrangements, the Virtual Team members wanted to have a sense of involvement, not just 'left aside' and not regarded as 'just a helper'. A level of commitment is clearly demonstrated in the following data extract, which is a response from the Virtual Team's head in relation to the management of the undertaking of Newland's work:

Staying in the other part of the world practising 'Virtual Team' concept is not a real problem. I valued much the trust that the company giving me...However, there are some tasks that are too complicated for me but I can always pick up the telephone and ask for assistance. The fact that the office makes day-to-day decision without consulting me doesn't affect me much...I respected Mr (name) but I always have the trouble to do anything as Mr (name) will object one's idea because he thinks the other way and he will get mad if one's doesn't inform him first...I'm not feeling left aside anymore and feel that I'm really a vital part of the team and not just a helper.

Critically, the Virtual Team members wanted integration coupled with a sense of social acknowledgement inside Newland's. In response, the directors, manager and team members took personal responsibility to maintain that commercially vital integration through good communications (Trice & Beyer 1984).

By maintaining this level of involvement, the remotely connected working relationships were not impeded by the distant, third party decision making of Newland's UK based managers, allowing inter-organisational trust to thrive and integration to be maintained (Ashleigh & Nandhakumar 2007, Clair & Dufresne 2007, Trice & Beyer 1984).

Consequently, regular contact kept Virtual Team members in the minds of Newland's UK based team members and hence, integrated (Trice & Beyer 1984). The processes of undertaking the assigned task maintained involvement and sustained connections, making the ongoing supervision of the work output manageable, even when technology problems arose (Hardin, Fuller & Davison 2007).

If limitations did exist in Newland's Virtual Teams, it was only because of this team's dependence upon technology and the internet. Subsequently, these limitations were considered only directly related to the reliability and endurance of the technology and the time needed to put the technology right. Once a technology and tools failure had impeded the Virtual Team, then other team members could divert the tasking assignment elsewhere.

Keeping all of the project processes in movement would easily avert any tasking failures and subsequent project delays that had potential to place Newland's at commercial risk (Trice & Beyer 1984).

Newland's evaluation process of pricing and scoping, followed by the undertaking of team activities, were interrelated to rites of integration, because the main consequence of these diverse activities was participation in reciprocal, unified actions that perpetuated organisational survival through the generation of revenue (Trice & Beyer 1984).

Scoping and pricing opened up the opportunity for Newland's to obtain work from a client who was willing to temporarily integrate and jointly participate in negotiations over the work scope and price. Pragmatically, the ritual endeavours of Newland's mobilisation got specific tasking assignments underway and kept them in motion. Subsequently, continuity was reinforced by employee behaviours, doing and communication.

Customarily, the habitual pre-booking system brought together the people and objects required to undertake vital commercial work without which, Newland's could not survive (Trice & Beyer 1984). Consistently, the ceremonial ritual of equipment packing prompted the successful movement of people and objects to diverse locations.

As a consequence, Trice's (1984) definition of rituals can be disregarded as Newland's own messy ritual successfully produced intended technical consequences for the teams and equipment that were mobilising. Specifically, this Newland's ritual manifested in certain behaviours (Trice 1984, Trice & Beyer 1984).

Apart from constant vocalisations taking place, packing boxes and suitcases lay opened on the office floor, for a minimum of two to three days before departure, their contents visibly on display. Throughout the whole of the office space, battery chargers were plugged into wall sockets. Theodolites, surveying equipment and their travelling cases sat on the sofas. Paperwork, drawings and the quotation document were left on the coffee tables. It was usual for rolls of packing tape and a large roll of Bubblepak to be seen.

Engineers went shopping in office time to buy any equipment, safety gear, bags and even new clothes. Generally, what was usually a **well-kept** space became cluttered, untidy and most often abandoned. What appeared to be disorganised however, was in fact an orderly method of preparing person and equipment to travel overseas. Equally, as conditions permitted, the same ritual brought them all back.

In common participation akin with rites of integration, the Cold Team, the Hot Team and the Virtual Team manifested for the specific purpose of undertaking Newland's revenue generating project work (Trice & Beyer 1984).

Numbers of Cold Teams sprung from the office base and temporarily relocated in different places, nationally, overseas and offshore. Back in the office, The Hot Teams meticulously analysed site data and produced an accurate 3-D model of a clients plant or platform. Equally, the permanently based overseas Virtual Team, through virtual world integration, played a vital role. All of these combined team efforts therefore, ensured Newland's economic success (Trice & Beyer 1984).

The data extracts given in the chapter demonstrated these activities and also, the attitudes of Newland's workforce. It was the joint effort of both activity and attitude that prevented the possibility of any commercial or financial vulnerability surfacing that would inhibit Newland's organisational perpetuity (Trice & Beyer 1984).

Inside Newland's, some organisational activities that also helped to maintain perpetuity were socially focused events, that were focused on enjoyment and amusement rather than work (Tews, Michel & Bartlett 2012, Trice & Beyer 1984).

Through relaxed and unifying interactions, these activities created pleasure in the workplace. Hence, a formal, dutiful work focused attitude was lessened, temporarily set side, by the affirmation of expressive interaction and informal conversation (Tews, Michel & Bartlett 2012). Consequently, Newland's organisational performance was enhanced through unified, reciprocal sharing of pleasurable activity, e.g., exchanging narratives through stories, the satiable consumption of food and the celebration of special occasions (Trice & Beyer 1984).

Advocacy, association and socialisation were dimensions of these activities. By relaxing the working day, making the required allowances and creating the right kind of atmosphere, Newland's members could participate in the activity without any conflict arising (Trice & Beyer 1984).

These Newland's activities were three discrete ceremonial subsets of behaviour, story-telling, the role of food and Crystal Celebrations.

Story-Telling

Newland's employees were able to conduct work intelligently through personal endeavour, reliable integrity and plausible credibility (Kivetz & Tyler 2007, Kets De Vries 2007, Russell 2008). As a result, organisational knowledge was a payoff from the product creation of diverse procedures, work methods and protocols, that existed solely for the provision of vital revenue creating activities (Trice & Beyer 1984).

Like all other office settings, Newland's employees were confined within organisational walls. As a result, there was no escaping the social influences of the morning get together over coffee, the formalities of the GUD group, the messy on and off setups of teams that moved people and objects from one place to the next, the frustrations of the modelling production teams and the array of client and administrative disturbances throughout the working day. Through these diverse activities, knowledge was regularly circulated and shared (Ambrosini, Bowman & Burton-Taylor 2007, Franklin 2007).

Realistically, Newland's walls contained more precious knowledge than could be accounted for. Generated knowledge, the building, merging and consolidation of it, Newland's accountants could not ultimately calculate, measure or factor, in the same numerate ways that production and output could be. Although it was not accounted for, Newland's shareholders and directors regarded all types of knowledge as being of great value and of composite worth, thus making it a creditable soft asset worthy of recognition and protection.

Even though vital task specific engineering knowledge was obviously shared in Newland's Cold, Hot and Virtual teams, this type of knowledge sharing was not exclusive to these teams. Knowledge, arcane lore, was also shared in the wider community by Newland's story-telling activity (Trice & Beyer 1984).

There were three dimensions to Newland's story-telling. The first dimension was the actual telling of the story. The second was the assessment and interpretation of those stories (Espedal 2007). The third way was by observing, watching and listening to the story-teller.

Akin with rites of integration (Trice & Beyer 1984) the importance of Newland's organisational survival was reinforced through common participation in story-telling as diverse groups combined to listen and participate in story-telling.

Inside Newland's, story-telling was about the bringing of news from one dimension to another, protecting the knowledge that was in transit. Story-telling came primarily from the individuals who had travelled to see clients both overseas and locally or, who had simply just been away and returned to regale of their experiences. Such comings and goings were regarded as Newland's everyday commercial events, yet story-telling was a way in which important information was shared and it was regarded as vital to organisational survival (Trice & Beyer 1984).

Each time that the opportunity to tell a story arose, like when an absent employee had returned from being away, the story-teller was carefully and quietly listened to without interruption. The story-teller was given the opportunity to speak with clarity and deliberation to an attentive audience.

There was a chronological element associated with the story-telling event. The story was always told in the present, but was about historical events that the story-teller had just participated in. Sometimes the story extended to the perceptions of a similar event, that could take place at a future time.

Story-telling was also an event that helped other organisational members who also travelled on behalf of Newland's. Newland's recently returned travellers brought back important knowledge and shared their experiences about situations and places that other members might encounter, when their Cold Team was mobilised later.

Newland's members integrated themselves into the storyline (Trice & Beyer 1984). Eccentric elaborations of events were significant in Newland's story-telling and these idiosyncrasies were never questioned. In fact, the opposite applied. Stretching the truth about the event or the external people associated with the event, in a humorous light-hearted way, encouraged laughter from an attentive and amused audience.

Trice's (1984) definition of story says that it is narrative based on true events, often a combination of truth and fiction (Trice & Beyer 1984). Also, latent consequences of rites of degradation provide a way for members to acknowledge that problems existed and to discuss their details. Group boundaries are then defended by redefining who belongs and who does not. Consequently, the importance and social value of the role involved is reaffirmed.

Embellishments about the travelling arrangements, the client, their employees or site conditions were the storyline that made the story-teller the centre of attention.

Possibly, their story-telling abilities reaffirmed their social status upon return into the group, as the story-teller role permitted the transparent and amusing diminishment of situations and strangers, who were not part of the Newland audience (Trice & Beyer 1984). Additionally, embellishments and equally diminishments, made difficult circumstances appear real but less daunting to an audience member who may later, be the person in the same circumstances.

Story-telling was the Newland's forum where latent consequences of rites of integration permitted the venting of emotions, as usual norms were temporarily set aside. Consequently, Newland's engineers could let off steam over difficult site encounters without the fear of any managerial conflict arising (Trice & Beyer 1984).

Integrated by the storyline, perusing all of the knowledge, whether truth or fiction, was an aspect of story-telling (Trice & Beyer 1984). Perusing, was the well paid attentiveness to stories, that emanated from the spoken word of the story-teller, who contained the story experiences within their hearts and minds.

When Newland's employees returned to the UK based office, each were expected to tell their story and the story-teller would give interesting accounts of past adventures akin with rites of integration—the passing on of arcane lore from and to each other (Trice & Beyer 1984). This was the role of the story-teller.

Newland's story-teller was a persona that emerged only when the story needed to be told. The telling of the story was conveyed from an individual who had come and gone or a person who was visiting Newland's for a particular reason. The wax role was one that appeared within any of Newland's group structures, at any time, for the purpose of the story-telling, then waned when the story was told. The role of the story-teller did not relate to the person who played that role, as it was the role that encouraged the persona to emerge.

Interesting and appealing story tellers in Newland's would temporarily manifest into character, provisionally integrate into the community and successfully act out the said function, which was to tell a story of personal experiencing, one based upon fact and at times, embellished by fiction (Trice 1984, Trice & Beyer 1984).

More importantly for Newland's organisational existence, the story-telling role was an informative one, a sharer of knowledge, expertise and capacity. The role manifested when an individual, or team, divulged useful or helpful information to others.

Interpretations of events and rules were provided to members, upon request and fruitfully, when members were prepared to listen and receive the information.

This sharing of knowledge was also important to the revenue generating activities. There was always the possibility that in the team activities, gaps could exist, through which important information would fall, be lost, be lapsed, ignored or not paid sufficient attention to, in the right kind of way, which in turn, could disable organisational survival (Hrebiniak 2006, Kessler 2006, Trice & Beyer 1984).

Group members listened intently when knowledge was being shared. There was a gain from being quietly present in the group and by having an ability to listen and take note. The knowledge, arcane lore, in transit was secured in the minds of relevant others (Trice & Beyer 1984). For Newland's, therefore, the role of the story-teller was constructive in protecting organisational perpetuity by successfully passing on important and relevant knowledge and arcane lore.

Additionally, the role of the story-teller was an organisationally useful one, as it also encompassed practical and flexible facilitative facets.

Fittingly, the role of the story-teller could be a knowledgeable internal resource or a trusted external resource that could be procured and engaged, as demonstrated in the following data extract:

There will obviously be an input from (company name) in this, (providing images and project summary) but the bulk of the work will need to be done by the external designer...From my perspective, technical content seems what we need and I place my trust in their ability to understand what we as a client might need.

Additionally, the role could be a strategist, who could identify needs in relation to negotiation, time, technology and economic opportunities or an effective, intuitive operator, who had the ability to turn strategic plans into action:

You're right, (name) is a good friend; this is a good and bad thing. As you say, it may be difficult to negotiate/haggle pricing but conversely I would expect that the friendship will ensure a good commitment from (name).

Significantly, the story-teller was the flexible provider of knowledge and the wise person, who both touched the organisational environment and reinforced it, by connecting groups through story-telling. Consequently, because of their integrative qualities, coupled with the social ability to hold the attention of the collective workforce, in one place at one particular time, both the story-teller and the storylines were important factors for Newland's ultimate common good (Trice & Beyer 1984).

The next dimension to Newland's type rites of integration was a ceremonial one (Trice & Beyer 1984). Successfully, the ceremonial ritualising of the birthday cake produced intended consequences of practical importance to Newland's community promoting more social value than technical. In this cultural ritual, food played an important role.

The Role of Food

According to Thomson & Hassenkamp (2008) food is significant in many ritual ceremonies. They cite Turner's (1969) definition of rituals as a social phenomenon in which persons of a particular culture must interact to create any kind of social life. It is social and periodic.

Equally, Newland's ritual of the birthday cake was social and periodic. Organisational members gathered socially in the reception area, integrated and interacted, in anticipation of ceremoniously eating cake to celebrate Newland's special occasions.

Analogous to rites of enhancement, this was also a moment in time when Newland's success and perpetuity could be recognised and individual achievements acknowledged in a celebratory style (Trice & Beyer 1984).

A Chocolate Caterpillar Cake, called Colin, purchased from a well-known high street food and clothing store, was a cake icon in Newland's organisational culture. To mark the celebration of a birthday and regarded as a tradition by Newland's group community, this cake and only this cake, was purchased and brought into the office by the accountant.

If the cake had been bought earlier than the special day, it was stored in the fridge until the time was right time to eat it, i.e., someone's birthday. As expected, local knowledge of the chocolate caterpillar cake's existence was disseminated quickly and everyone looked forward to eating it. It was taken for granted that the cake would always be in the fridge when it was someone's birthday, because Newland's accountant could be relied upon to purchase it. Inevitably, the accountant was always reimbursed for the cost of the cake.

Between 2.00pm and 3.00pm, the cake was removed from the fridge by the Operations Director and the accountant. Every organisational member of the community, present in the office, would gather in the reception area. Ceremoniously, the cake was placed onto an oblong tray and laid on the reception sideboard with a large carving knife laid next to it. Practically, the knife always pointed towards the wall, as a matter of health and safety at work.

Sometimes *Happy Birthday* would be sung and at other times, it would not. This was not based on whether the member was popular or unpopular, but was more a reflection of Newland's organisational mood at that time.

For instance, if work was progressing well and/or Newland's had received payment for completed project work, then the mood was upbeat. If Newland's was operating under difficult circumstances, i.e., work was not progressing well or the client was unhappy or cash flow was under threat by a delayed or late payment, then the community mood reflected this and singing would not take place.

Even though organisational members were brought together and could sufficiently relax, enjoy the occasion and eat cake, commercial circumstances were laid aside but, survival instincts were not forgotten (Trice & Beyer 1984).

To begin the ritual, the Operations Director was expected to cut the cake. Consequently, I was the person who did this by cutting it into eleven pieces, starting from the tail end and moving towards the head. The accountant would make the tea.

As the Operations Director ceremoniously stepped towards the cake, the same exchange of words always took place. Unambiguously, the Operations Director would ask for someone else to cut the cake because in the cake ritual, equality was more important than seniority. Inevitably, pressure was always brought to bear and the Operations Director acquiesced to the group demand.

Consequently, Newland's hierarchy was levelled by rites of integration (Trice & Beyer 1984). The links between management and workforce were reaffirmed and promoted by temporarily reducing the senior to an equal status, using food as a ritualistic instrument. Additionally, the cake eating event provided a temporary break from strict codes of behaviour that were normally enforced by Newland's organisational rules (Trice & Beyer 1984).

There was a cutting ritual for the cake icon. Prior to the cutting taking place, the Operations Director would warm the knife under the hot water tap. If the knife was warm, it would cut through the chocolate coating cleanly. The group had retained the knowledge that on every cutting of the cake occasion, the knife warming would take place. One of the new members asked what was happening and was told:

Fran is warming the knife because it will cut through the cake cleanly, without wasting it.

The cake was distributed. The managing director usually had the head because it had a white chocolate face on it. The Operations Director always had the tail, because it was the smallest piece, with the most chocolate on it. Other individuals liked the pieces that contained coloured chocolate beans and some, the pieces that had the white chocolate feet attached. The face and tail were always reserved for the managing director and the Operations Director. When one of the new members asked if they could have the tail, they were categorically told:

No! Because Fran always has the tail.

The process of rituals, a prescribed way of performing a series of actions, is the work of Turner (1969) who then expanded his thought processes to include Van Gennep's (1960) work on liminal space.

In this Newland's social gathering, every member sat in the reception area and ate their slice of the cake. This points to the idea that Newland's reception area was a liminal space, a sort of no-man's land, that would remain neutral from political and organisational constraints. There was a sense of freedom around the group, when they ate their cake and banter was readily vocalised.

Freedom to let off steam is granted through latent rites of integration (Trice & Beyer 1984). During Newland's cake ritual, there were no boundaries in terms of what subject could be discussed except of course, common decencies were always maintained. Sometimes the closer rugby players talked their coded language and remained in clique, laughing amongst themselves and most often drawing the group attention towards them.

Serious matters were also discussed however, the content was never that dire that it would remove the group from their altruistic spirit, brought on by the sweet indulgence of the cake. It was very rare that work matters were brought up, but if the telephone rang it was answered. Organisational survival instincts even outweighed the cake occasion (Trice & Beyer 1984).

Newland's members enjoyed the break from their desks. The informal atmosphere was something like being at play at work, where humour also brought solidarity through celebration, shared meaning and experience (Goldmintz & Schaefer 2007, Wilkinson, Rees & Knight 2007). It was a time that business pressures could be momentarily set aside and the company of work colleagues enjoyed simply for pleasure, entertainment and fun (Tews, Michel & Bartlett 2012, Trice & Beyer 1984).

When everyone had consumed their cake, if there was any left, in conjunction with the washing up being done, the cake that remained was replaced into its box with a verbalised address:

(Name) can take that bit home for (family name) or the children.

Everyone then returned to their desk and to their work. Predominantly, the outcome of Newland's chocolate cake food ritual was always a successful one. It harmonised a social balance of sustained continuity and a feeling of cohesion amongst the workforce. In doing so, the mood of Newland's community was uplifted and enhanced, even when commercial circumstances were not conducive (Thompson & Hassenkamp 2008, Trice & Beyer 1984).

If any group member was absent from the cake ritual, their name was mentioned as the cake was cut and then consumed. This demonstrated the ability of Newland's workforce, on a social occasion, to consider and acknowledge any absent members, especially those who had mobilised and travelled away on behalf of the organisation.

Through special efforts, rites of integration encourages the social interaction between strangers (Trice & Beyer 1984). Equally, food helped Newland's to receive strangers into the organisational midst. Time permitting, if visitors or outsiders were present in Newland's office when a free lunch was available, all were welcomed to the social occasion.

In direct contrast, however, the cake ritual always remained a closed event. If the cake was in the fridge when a visitor came, it was highly unusual for it to be revealed and shared with a stranger.

No individual, however, was ever isolated from the group when a free lunch was available. Outsiders were invited to partake and share themselves and their experiences with the group. Sometimes visitors and outsiders told their stories as well. No one was ever treated as a stranger and a threat to the group. The group social occasion was both open and inviting towards them.

Although, Newland's was not a family owned firm, family type cohesiveness was always encouraged by Newland's owner and Operations Director. In reality, however, as in any family type environment, divisiveness was also equally as apparent (Brotheridge & Lee 2006, Gibb Dyer Jr 2010, Neri 2006). Sometimes, although the temporary integration of visitors was successful, it was manifested through hush-ups and the inhibiting of impolite behaviour (Trice & Beyer 1984).

Mostly though, like a family is generally polite to visitors and strangers who are invited into the home, Newland's sense of community was successfully widened to bring into the social centre many visiting persons. Temporary integration through this social activity was always successful, in spite of the mood or attitude of some Newland's members (Trice & Beyer 1984).

The next and final social activity helped to generate integrative feelings of accomplishment and community within Newland's (Trice & Beyer 1984). This enhancement ritual was called Crystal Celebrations.

Crystal Celebrations

From the ceremonial and the ritual also came the traditional, which was always important to Newland's (Trice & Beyer 1984). Special occasions were celebrated as they arose.

5 February of each year was Newland's annual anniversary and birthday and it was always recognised as such. This was done in a way that was unique to Newland's called Crystal Celebrations, that also included the ceremonious eating of cake.

For each five years that Newland's had traded, a lead crystal glass was engraved with the company name and the dates—for instance, 1983 to 1988, then 1989 to 1993 and so on. For Newland's twenty-fifth year silver anniversary, a glass was engraved with the dates *1983-2008, 25 years*. The women were given a champagne glass and the men a whisky tumbler. These engraved glasses were crystal icons of Newland's organisational success and achievement for over thirty years.

Newland's managing director and Operations Director had jointly served the company for almost thirty years, having set up Newland's in 1983. Each now has six engraved glasses to display in their homes, highly valued mementoes of their life's work and continued service to Newland's.

Earlier on in this chapter, I demonstrated how Newland's employees celebrated someone's birthday by communally eating chocolate caterpillar cake. Cake was also eaten to celebrate Newland's Crystal Celebrations, other special occasions and project achievements.

When news was received that Newland's had been awarded a high value contract or the successful completion of one, employees would celebrate by eating cake. No chocolate caterpillar cake manifested in the fridge, as for the Newland's special occasion, it was a different type of cake that was purchased from the local bakery.

Purchases from the local bakery were good enough when Newland's received news of an impending new order. Importance was given to the preference of cake that was ordered from the bakery, i.e., cream doughnuts, vanilla slices, custard buns, and chocolate eclairs. Seasonal timing sometimes determined choice. Most wanted favourites were eaten throughout the year, but it was usually a mince pie at Christmas time.

As well as doing their work, Crystal Celebrations became part of Newland's employees organisational life. Through personal endeavour, promoted by and contained within an organisational framework, there was a strong desire to keep and maintain the celebratory and the traditional to crystallise in time, Newland's aim for perpetuity (Trice & Beyer 1984).

In rites of enhancement, public recognition of individual accomplishments, from which all members derive benefit, is acknowledged (Trice & Beyer 1984). Additionally, according to Andersson, Giacalone & Jurkiewitz (2007) employee hope and gratitude can manifest in many ways through the imagination, metaphor and dramatization.

During Crystal Celebrations, Newland's hierarchy emerged and was recognised. Acknowledgement, however, was exclusively aimed at the two directors who jointly set up Newland's in 1983. Without hesitation, gratitude was always offered from the workforce to the directors concerned. Although it was always appreciatively received, it was never asked for or expected. By openly expressing gratitude, this public acknowledgement of Newland's founding directors enabled the rest of the organisation to take some share of the credit for those accomplishments (Trice & Beyer 1984).

In this chapter, I have given a detailed account of how rites of integration manifested in five subsystems that helped Newland's get vital revenue generating project work successfully undertaken, without conflict arising (Trice & Beyer 1984).

Communally, involved members committed themselves to diverse activities with a common aim and blended together organisational resources that activated, progressed and fulfilled commercially focused, set objectives. This was how Newland's work got done.

Integration was affirmed, through unifying interactions, aided by social bonding of Newland's workforce. Committed by organisational involvement and personal ambition, members deliberately advanced organisational aims thus, reinforcing employee relationships on informal ceremonial levels, that helped to facilitate the undertaking of work.

The major consequence of Newland's type rites of integration is that it helped to maintain the continuity of the organisation as it aimed for commercial perpetuity (Trice & Beyer 1984). Rites of integration put important operational project activities into motion and gave provision for less than formal gatherings to form in which directors, managers and workforce would relate upon equal terms, for a short period of time. Newland's organisational longevity was crystallised in time, in icons of success and the ritual of the ceremonial eating of cake, also received and welcomed strangers.

The next chapter is about a different kind of organisational experience, conflict. It is appropriately named Organisational Dysfunction and Resolution.

Chapter 6
Results: Organisational Dysfunction and Resolution

During my employment with Newland's as a director and manager, a pre-research event brought about a significant role change for me. Likewise, there was an adverse impact upon Newland's. To explain this event and the organisational consequences associated with it in greater detail, I will make comparisons with Trice & Beyer's (1984) rites of degradation, rites of conflict reduction and rites of renewal. I will start this chapter, however, with an account of pre-research events.

Pre-Research Events

According to Trice & Beyer (1984) rites of degradation provide a framework in which to publicly acknowledge that problems exist and to discuss their details. Group boundaries are defended by reinforcing who belongs and who does not. Reaffirmation of the importance and social value of the role involved is determined. The intended consequences of the rite is to dissolve the social identity and associated power of the person subject to the degradation.

Trice & Beyer (1984) also make two additional observations about rites of degradation in modern organisations that are relevant to my research. The rites occur fairly infrequently and they seem to be required only for the removal of relatively high status or influential organisational members. The Newland's experience encountered both of these observations.

Evidently, a good denunciation requires the full attention of an audience (Garfinkel 1956). In order to be successful, the denunciator must negatively and effectively redefine the characteristics of the person who is being denunciated, in the eyes of the witnesses, to the denunciation work.

In modern organisations, the forced removal of a high-status member is one element in the general theoretical category of status degradation after which, organisational succession usually follows (Gephart 1978).

Pfeffer (2010) says that some people have power and others do not. Personal change, however, is always possible. First, one has to believe that the change is feasible.

Second, strengths and weaknesses need to be reviewed, as objectively as they can be. Third, there has to be an understanding of the most important qualities for building a power base, so that the focus of limited time and attention, can be given to the goal for change. According to Pfeffer (2010), obtaining and holding onto power is hard work. One needs to be thoughtful, strategic, resilient, alert, and willing to fight when necessary.

Although, the use of rites of degradation to remove high status individuals from office in an organisation may be infrequent (Trice & Beyer 1984) an event of this type happened in Newland's, when the relationship with one of the directors broke down.

Physical humiliation representative of a tribal degradation ceremony did not take place (Trice & Beyer 1984). No credible external consultant emerged to produce data to highlight problems directly associated with the individual concerned (Pfeffer 1981). Organisational humiliation began by one single action being taken by the involved Newland's director. Without any warning, this trusted person invoked Newland's grievance procedure, against the company and the other two directors, after a series of debilitating internal events and disagreements had taken place.

Newland Limited was my place of work, where I was the Operations Director and a manager of the enterprise. It was my responsibility to manage the everyday business activities of Newland's, that included all of the financial and statutory reporting requirements, plus the operational management of the entire workforce.

I will now briefly outline the events that weakened Newland's organisational performance and atmosphere. So much tension was created in the workplace that it culminated in the removal of a long serving, high status officer from the company.

When I outlined my roles as manager and Operations Director in the research methodology chapter, I revealed that intermittent problems existed in the workforce between 2005 and 2006, when Newland's was experiencing management problems.

Behaviours in Newland's workforce clearly indicated that a problem existed. Doors were slammed, there were uncomfortable silences, sarcastic comments, toilet meetings, stand offs, covert discussions and sideways swipes of the eyes as a director or manager passed by. Giggling and whispering occurred as a manager departed the covert discussion zones. Stern faces and worried faces displayed concern.

There existed the constant threat of employees leaving and worst of all, a key senior employee, well under the influence of alcohol, telephoning the office in an attempt to convince the others directors that this person was still working and functioning at home.

Newland's owner was genuinely concerned. Open discussions were initiated with the workforce and a chosen spokesperson put forward their case. Newland's had a director/manager who was not functioning well, organisationally and personally.

Seeing the opportunity for change, the workforce tentatively disclosed that the teams were finding this manager's required level of excellence just too difficult to achieve. First of all and felt organisationally community wide, a drunken boss was unacceptable. Unworkable management perfectionist demands were too unrealistic and as a result, it was felt that failings were being encountered on all levels of production work. Certain individuals feared for losing their jobs.

A lack of discretion, loss of appropriateness, binding to rules, undermining, the lowering of motivation and the constant criticism of individual efforts had severely diminished the leader, in the eyes of the team members, the person was attempting to lead (Einarsen, Aasland & Skogstad 2007, Espedal 2007, Tepper 2000).

Consequently, the audience that the denunciator required, in order to conduct a good denunciation, was already present, watching and waiting inside Newland's organisational walls (Garfinkel 1956).

Degradation, Power and Succession

In the three stages of rites of degradation, the first is to focus attention upon the person, the second is to discredit them and the third is to remove them from office (Garfinkel 1956, Gephart 1978, Trice & Beyer 1984).

As Newland's Operations Director, I expressed my concern about the significance of all of the negative events, in the belief that the workforce's poor performance was not so seriously entrenched that there lacked any capacity for change and modification with the right kind of leadership adaptation (Einarsen, Aasland & Skogstad 2007, Espedal 2007, Tepper 2000). Critical denunciation work had begun (Garfinkel 1956).

Prime administrative duties of Newland's Operations Director were to manage the company's statutory reporting requirements alongside directorship responsibility. As a result, the Operations Director's connection with engineering task production was only initiated when the project work was completed and the time arrived to send out the project deliverable and coordinate the contract agreed billing procedure.

Consequently, Operations Director duties were more removed from the day-to-day processes of the technical needs of the engineering production teams however, to an empathic observing leader and manager, the negative and prohibitive effects became more obvious and worrying.

Subsequently, the significant event of organisational succession began when, at the direct request of Newland's owner, I took over the responsibilities of the technical director/manager (Gephart 1978).

One consequence of the organisational succession was that the director concerned was given long term sick leave and at the same time, referred to a medical examiner. Then, adverse action taken by the director concluded with their removal from office, as one of Newland's long term serving directors, by means of the grievance procedure as an instrument of removal.

I will now outline the process of how the grievance procedure was conducted after which the Newland's director, responsible for organisational diminishment and reduced production output, voluntarily resigned from office.

Unexpectedly, a formal letter, sent in accordance with Newland's grievance policy, arrived from the director concerned, addressed to the Operations Director. Not surprisingly, the content of the letter prompted the need for immediate consultation with the company solicitors. After taking legal advice, the other Newland directors invited the aggrieved party to a review panel to be held at Newland's office.

Less physically humiliating than the removal of sandals, stools and a buttock bouncing reduction to commoner (Trice & Beyer 1984) nevertheless, the ritual symbols to be used in the status of degradation of Newland's director were the main doorway, the conference room table, specifically arranged seating, a questionnaire and a panel of individuals who at the time had taken up positions of authority, influence and detachment (Gephart 1978).

In the knowledge that the panel meeting was to take place, the aggrieved party had to visit the office and pass through the doorway of a business that had been organisational home for over twenty years. Organisational humiliation and the reduction of status had already begun by Newland's highlighting that problems existed, discussing them in detail with the internal workforce and external solicitors and placing the director on long term sick leave (Trice & Beyer 1984).

This person came to the office having already been removed of high level status, but still remaining as an employee director (Garfinkel 1956, Gephart 1978, Pfeffer 2010).

On the day of the panel meeting, the panel consisted of Newland's three remaining directors, managing director, Operations Director and Software Development Director. Specifically, the conference room had been arranged so that the panel sat on one side of the table and the aggrieved party sat on the opposite side.

A questionnaire had been prepared by the Operations Director, which comprised of a list of questions related directly to the accusations made against Newland's in the grievance letter. The answers could only be yes or no.

With planning set in place, the Operations Director had briefed Newland's other directors about how the process would be conducted. Only the Operations Director would speak to the aggrieved party. The panel meeting was to be recorded after which, a full transcript of the tape would be made and retained.

The director was invited to sit at the table on the allocated side. The operations director sat directly opposite the aggrieved party and seated on the left was the software development director and on right, the managing director. The Operations Director asked each question and ticked the relevant yes or no box. The other two directors on the company side did not speak, did not ask any question and were only present in the room acting as witnesses to the procedure.

Once all of the questions had been answered, a letter was given to the director, suspending him from office and from the organisation, until further notice. Newland's organisational denunciation audience watched from a distance as the director left through the door, in which he had entered, now formally removed from status (Garfinkel 1956). The full tape transcript of the panel meeting was made available to each set of solicitors. Shortly afterwards, the director voluntarily resigned. No attempt at reconciliation was made by either party.

In 2006, the full management process of the engineering group became my responsibility as Newland's Operations Director. This role change brought me in closer contact with all of the production team members, who now perceived me as being their first point of contact, in relation to all organisational activities, including engineering production work.

Rites of degradation, although infrequent, became a life changing reality for two of Newland's directors (Trice & Beyer 1984). Newland's workforce, as the denunciation audience, witnessed the reduction in status of one organisationally involved high status member (Garfinkel 1956). Also witnessed, was the organisational succession of another individual, willing to fight when necessary, now tasked to repair the damage done (Pfeffer 2010).

Conflict reduction rites gives organisational leaders and managers a way to fix organisational problems. Arbitration of organisational dysfunctional conflict is made apparent by managers communicating a willingness to cope with existing problems, by keeping a listening disposition in place that pays attention to complaints and ideas of those participating and also, by demonstrating how far authority is willing to go to recognise the claims made (Trice & Beyer 1984).

Consequently, by its very nature, leadership is a human endeavour (Vogelgesang & Lester 2009). Hence, leadership authority stems from the personality and interpersonal style of the leader. Softer leadership styles can influence tactics aimed at making subordinate organisational members like, respect and admire the leader (Yukl 2002). One of the most powerful forms of social influence available to managers and leaders is a self-awareness of their charismatic leadership (Sosik 2001).

Good managers regularly consult with their subordinates and engender trust through being emotionally intelligent (Sosik & Megerian 1999, Berson & Sosik 2007).

Pertinently, leaders who have made a commitment to personal development are better able to encourage others to introduce the emotional aspect of life into their work during and after a crises (Clair & Dufresne 2007).

As a Newland's manager, I strived to keep my self-awareness as a way to influence all of my leadership tactics and to keep the role of manager close to the workforce, amenable, but not too overtly friendly (Berson & Sosik 2007, Sosik & Jung 2003).

To advance my own personal development, during the period of 1998 to 2002, out of work time, I had re-trained as a Rogerian person-centred counsellor. These counselling skills acted as a point of reference and assisted in the management of the organisational duties that I had been assigned (Clair & Dufresne 2007, Rogers 1951, 1980).

My first organisational repair task was to introduce some fresh concepts about working in teams. The purpose of this brief was to bring the workforce back into a more efficient and effective working process and managerially assist in the improvement of the overall morale in the workplace.

The intention was to organisationally and jointly agree how improvements could be made to Newland's management tactics. An ACAS free online training e-course, called Teamworking, was used. A conference room based meeting was the venue for the e-course and the discussions that would follow (Trice & Beyer 1984).

Setting out to make the salient points, I had to rely heavily on personal judgement and management experience, to begin to correct certain attitudes and deliver the message to Newland's workforce that change was necessary.

Appropriately, I addressed the workforce's historical feeling of being unable to be sufficiently open and to act authentically. Additionally, the objective was to alleviate any fears related to historically receiving a bad managerial experience (Espedal 2007, Einarsen, Aasland & Skogstad 2007, Tepper 2000).

Fittingly, the first point of admission was made by Newland's management stating clearly that the problem existed and the resulting bad atmosphere had made a significant contribution to the lack of workforce morale. Each side was able to put their point across, airing complaints and correcting present interpretations of past events. These interactions began to help to reduce the underlying anger and workforce frustration that had been bound up, for a long time, by the impact of a critical and derisory leader (Einarsen, Aasland & Skogstad 2007, Espedal 2007, Tepper 2000, Trice & Beyer 1984).

Using an employee review, I intentionally set out to address the points raised, that were causing workforce anxiety and tension. I raised my point of view in writing, to each employee, with an invitation either to speak directly with me or to write back. Most had their interview discussion with me and then wrote back.

The following extracts are my responses to employee replies, reflecting and paraphrasing the specific points each had raised in their interviews:

Employee 1:

You said that you would like to ensure that the handover of work is more transitional and prolonged than has been happening previously...you said that you have felt "immediately cut off" and this has left you feeling "disconcerted and sidelined".

Employee 2:

I sincerely hope that you have had the opportunity to see and experience that the earlier management style, "the old way of working" such as "criticising" and "limiting another's autonomy" is no longer happening and you are "constantly encouraged and supported" by other team members, including myself.

Employee 3:

My present perception of you is one that is temporarily related to your workload because last year you said at times "you felt concerned that you had delegated more than you were comfortable with"...you have mentioned three main points that are important to you; (1) being proactive (2) establishing ways to keep motivation levels maintained and pooling resources and sharing skills. I was wondering if these three items still remain priorities for you?

Employee 4:

I am glad that we have had a conversation about our relationship and perhaps this is what you and I need to work on in the future, but I need to say that I don't regard it was a problem in any way, but that in this review "we have reached a turning point in understanding each other more" and we should build on this. I did not wish for my review to be "uninspiring" for you and I realise, after this conversation, that perhaps our working relationship was lacking some depth; "that kind of energy" that I felt was missing.

Employee 5:

I am glad that you have raised the matter about wanting to lead projects and take the work through to the deliverable stage, including the work element that is involved with the transfer of the data into the (client named) solution and any other Asset Management solution that (company name) is working with.

Employee 6:

You have a very willing nature; a "giving" kind of temperament which is one of your best assets. You have said that you make every attempt to conduct yourself and your work in an exemplary manner, to take pride in your work, but (directors' names) recognise this effort as something special and meaningful to us.

Plainly and openly, I admitted that as my initial managerial position did not take responsibility for the supervision of the engineering production teams, I was not sufficiently attentive to their daily reality. In contrast, I confirmed that I understood how each team member faced the technical difficulties and complexities of undertaking Newland's project work.

Additionally, and more importantly, I admitted that I was aware of the existence of the negative and critical attitudes of the leadership at that time. These management admissions felt risky, but helped to compartmentalise the conflict so that Newland's organisational equilibrium could be restored (Trice & Beyer 1984).

Open discussions and transparent confessions, jointly conducted by Newland's directors and employees in cooperation, helped to bring out hidden feelings of resentment. Responsibility could be placed in the right areas, on the right people, in a new time framework. Blame was never utilised to rejuvenate the management and employee relationship, as the aim was to engender workforce trust (Sosik & Megerian 1999, Berson & Sosik 2007).

Compromise aided memories of persistent negative situations and denigrating attitudes to be divested to the past. Tacit agreement naturally emerged without hostility (Trice & Beyer 1984). A new era had begun inside Newland's organisational walls.

A New Age

Rites of renewal apply to a variety of elaborate activities intended to refurbish or strengthen existing social structures and thus improve their functioning (Trice & Beyer 1984). One interpretation of Trice & Beyer (1984) version of rites of renewal is the opportunity for organisational restoration, restitution and reinstatement.

Successful organisations are the product of distributive, collective and complementary leadership (Kets De Vries 2007). Measuring the styles of real leaders can determine what styles and behaviours are most effective in actual teams (Hambley, O'Neill & Kline 2007). If rites of renewal are applied to an organisation, the rites would be dependent upon a leaders ability to strengthen the existing social structures and improve their functioning, so leadership styles and behaviours have to become an element of the rites (Trice & Beyer 1984).

Authors French & Bell (1978) and Trice (1984) argue that team building is justified by a myth that a family-like bond exists within work groups that can be nurtured and used for the company's benefit. In the Newland's experience, the family-like bond was not a myth and its existence was evident inside the organisation in the ways in which management related with employees and employees in turn, responded to organisational demands (Brotheridge & Lee 2006, Neri 2006).

The removal of one of Newland's directors offered a new organisational starting point. The pitch for the endorsement of greater confidence in the abilities of Newland's engineering staff had resulted in organisational succession (Gephart 1978). This was thought of as a new era however, Newland's employees were genuinely anxious about all of the changes and how these changes would impact upon job reliance, themselves and their families. A long term serving employee and director had resigned and it would take some time for the organisation to settle.

Newland's had encountered some attitude and communication difficulties because uncertainty existed in how to respond and to whom. Each employee was encouraged to talk through any situation, if that person wished to do so. The intention was for employees to come to terms with all of the organisational changes and how such changes would affect them and their future employment (Gatongi 2007, Hannabuss 1997).

As a woman manager in an highly technical engineering environment, there were moments when a kinder and caring attitude was an organisational advantage. I had the ability to empathise with Newland's workforce, as a manager rather than a friend or counsellor. The person-centred counsellor had the opportunity to become organisationally useful (Rogers 1951, 1980, Rogers & Freiberg 1994).

Newland's workforce still remained uncomfortable about the past when unacceptable levels of management attitudes had been aimed at the workforce. The damage needed to be aired (Rogers 1951, 1980). Also, these limitations extended to a lack of being able to open about other organisational important matters such as pay, bonus, holidays and well-being. A management intervention review had frankly addressed most of these issues. Forgiveness took some time coming because it required Newland's workforce to have a change of attitude and resolve any underlying anger (Anderson 2007).

Afterwards, trying to please facades and incongruent responses were hesitantly surrendered. Pressures for organisational conformity were immediately reduced to a more autonomous level by Newland's management. Independence in tasking arrangements was offered. Mistakes were not regarded as a major organisational crises, but opportunities to recognise where changes had to be made.

One phenomena that emerged was that the discussions were not always solely related to the removal of one of Newland's directors. The opportunity to be more open manifested in other subjects being aired.

Creating a deeper level of contact, the joint experiencing of difficulties and understanding the need for organisational preservation and dependability, helped the workforce to address frankly and speak more openly with Newland's management.

Concerns were most often related with Newland's ability to win new work, the financial longevity of the existing work and the pressures of balancing work and family life, especially when the engineers were away (Greenhaus & Powell 2003). Organisational perpetuity was always at Newland's core (Trice & Beyer 1984).

Myths aside, Newland's family-like activities, in particular the morning gathering for coffee and the eating of cake, helped to reinforce existing social connections and ease the burden of the recent organisational loss (Brotheridge & Lee 2006, Neri 2006, Thomson & Hassenkamp 2008).

Also, the more frequent rites of enhancement helped each member to equally participate in making organisational reparation, regardless of status and influence (Trice & Beyer 1984). In these moments of equality, the desires and wishes for new things were openly expressed. Dreams and nightmares were also mentioned.

Through story-telling, Newland's employees consciously or unconsciously, unavoidably involved work colleagues with the events in their lives. Once the story had been told and heard and its knowledge was out there, it could not be unknown (Watzlawick, Beavin Bavelas & Jackson 1967). Participation in the telling of stories, sharing life experiences and even gossip, helped Newland's community to reinforce who belonged and whose influences and memories could be divested to the past (Trice & Beyer 1984).

In discussions, Newland's workforce openly voiced justification for the removal of the director, even in the presence of the remaining directors. Some Newland employees expressed absolute relief that this particular person had gone. The action was endorsed when several of Newland's members said in the presence of more than one person:

Anyway…well rid of!
It was time…
I'm glad (name) has gone.

Others clearly demonstrated happiness, ambivalently coupled with sadness, because of the loss of a person, who at one point in time, had been a well-established Newland's member. Generally, each person admitted the changes were necessary for the sake of Newland's organisational perpetuity (Trice & Beyer 1984). Eventually, the social identity of Newland's resigned director slowly dissipated as the workforce began to reintegrate and build closer working relationship with the remaining directors.

Organisational succession did not come easily and the struggle for victory was hard work (Pfeffer 2010). After legal consultation, the directors of Newland's formally ended an employee's contract, but it was a shallow victory. The person lost was a long serving employee who had been popular in the past and made a major contribution towards Newland's success, but unfortunately was unable to remain as an organisational member.

Building the power base that would necessitate organisational change came from a manager who was central to the organisation (Pfeffer 2010). This manager was able to utilise humanistic ideologies, such as the use of person-centred counselling skills, empathic communication, a congruent authentic approach, a regard for organisational impurities and sufficient managerial objectivity to facilitate change (Rogers 1951, 1980, Trice & Beyer 1984).

Strength of character and business acumen came also from the same manager. Being financially in control of the purse strings and continuously aware of Newland's viability, sufficient pressure could be brought to bear to demonstrate management inadequacy, marketing threats and commercial risk when project work had to be repeated.

Even being able to masquerade behind my position as Operation Director, the loss of the director concerned did have a personal impact upon me. I felt very sad, tinged with regret however, I was able to place myself into an adequate level of professional detachment for the sake of Newland's ongoing commercial activities, including the well-being of employees.

My initial response to the director's attack was disbelief. I did not encounter any difficulty in being aware of what the whole episode would mean for the person who had left Newland's and what their future might entail. Because this person had served Newland's for a significant number of years, I was actually afraid for them. Here was an ex-employee, that had worked in a particular habitual way for Newland's, that had also provided long term benefits for the enterprise.

More importantly for them, I wondered if this person could, at such a late stage in life, develop the capacity to re-adapt to a new situation.

After the resignation, my reaction was both anger and despondency. Three points resonated with me and I openly addressed my feelings with the other directors. I didn't hide my disappointment:

How dare (name) do this to us?
What did we actually do wrong?
Where do you think it all went wrong?

I associated this with the loss of a significant person who had been present in my organisational working life and also, in the presence of Newland's group community for a long period of time. My questions were never answered.

As Newland's Operations Director, I was also worried about how I had been perceived by my work colleagues as I conducted the uncomfortable process of removing a company director from their high status office and more personally, an employee from their job. I felt like an actor on a stage, somewhat exposed, tasked with portraying the whole of that role to the watching public and my public was Newland's employees who depended upon me and could judge me.

Although, it was a painful course of events for the whole of Newland's organisational community, a more confident workforce believed that the right action had been taken. I personally felt the ambivalence of being polarised between guilt and the necessity for the preservation of Newland's and the safeguarding of the employees who depended upon its success, commercial integrity and perpetuity (Trice & Beyer 1984).

In the whole of Newland's organisational history, this was one particular significant moment in time, when the directors did act with strength of leadership directly from the top however, the consequences of that action did affect the whole of Newland's community (Gallos 2006). This action by Newland's directors did, however, legitimate and reinforce existing systems of power and authority that are associated with rites of renewal (Trice & Beyer 1984).

Modification to Newland's existing social arrangements eventually came as employees recognised and accepted the need for organisational change to occur, in order to preserve, safeguard and perpetuate the organisation (Trice & Beyer 1984).

In terms of individual responses to me, empathy was reciprocated and kindness was demonstrated. Jointly combined, Newland's workforce had all painfully, yet successfully, and more important equally, come through what was socially regarded as a rite of degradation, entering a new organisational era, a phase of enhancement, reintegration and renewal (Trice & Beyer 1984).

In this era, to freshen up the face of the company, both in the eyes of the watching client public and employees, Newland's directors jointly agreed to redesign the company logo. This fresh start helped to leave behind a tired representation of Newland's, giving it a modernised, fresher, up-to-date image.

Each employee was consulted with the various designs and colour schemes.

Newland's employees wanted to agree to the use of a concept in the design after which, 'the concept of collaboration' and 'connectivity' became the joint themes for the logo. Clearly, both concepts represented the concept of integration (Trice & Beyer 1984).

Consequently, Newland's organisational logo colours changed from red, black and white to green and silver. The new company logo eventually agreed by all, became affectionately known as:

The parachuting poodle.

In Newland's organisational lifetime, there was a rare appearance of rites of degradation, that later removed a high status official from office.

Rites of renewal provide an invitation and the framework to create elaborate socially refurbishing and strengthening activities (Trice & Beyer 1984). Using the management skills available to hand, Newland's management were able to positively intervene when threats emerged. Organisational conflict was reduced by a director level invitation to discuss openly that problems existed and a managerial promise that something would be done about it.

A commitment to change helped to set into motion restoration of management integrity, restitution of the right type of organisational command and reinstatement of workforce trust.

Organisational renewal dealt with workforce emotional difficulties that had been encountered by the existence of poor leadership and later, the witnessing of the manifestation of rites of degradation. Exposed by the rites of degradation, what was also determined later by the manifestation of the rites of renewal, was the obvious reinforcement of who belonged and who did not (Trice & Beyer 1984). This uncovered the concealed latent organisational difficulties that were embedded in Newland's culture as management mistrust, lack of confidence in leadership protection, tension and hidden resentment.

Newland's organisational dysfunction was addressed through the joint consent of the directors and management intervention, aided by person-centred counselling skills in the workplace. Getting the relationships repaired was a challenge for Newland's management that required courage, but the opportunity was readily available for the taking (Manzoni & Barsoux 2009). Hence, the taboo and shadow side of Newland's organisational culture began to diminish, as the workforce built trust and confidence in the management's fresh approach.

The equalising effects of rites of enhancement also helped to integrate change (Trice & Beyer 1984). Continued relationship building lightened and relaxed the atmosphere and communications improved. The gateway to a happier organisational age opened up (Manzoni & Barsoux 2009).

In changing the company logo and colours, a material object artifact, helped Newland's organisational community to leave behind a pictorial representation of a difficult organisational era (Trice 1984, Trice & Beyer 1984). Revitalising the organisational logo raised employee demonstrative attitudes towards it, when the logo was given an affectionate nickname. By adopting attributes of positive expression towards the company's new image, Newland's employees demonstrated a general enhancement in a change of attitude and acceptance of radically modified internal organisational management arrangements.

In this chapter, I have been able to compare significant Newland's organisational events with rites of degradation, rites of conflict reduction and rites of renewal. The next chapter demonstrates my management role in terms of rites of creation and rites of integration.

Chapter 7
Results: Manager in Rites of Creation and Rights of Integration

Using Trice & Beyer's (1984) rites of creation as a means of comparison, in this chapter, I will give an explanation of my successive relationship with Newland's workforce, as post rites of degradation Operations Director and manager. To start, I will briefly outline rites of creation. Then, I will compare my own management interventions with rites of creation. I also have the opportunity to use rites of integration again to explain some management interventions. Last of all, in line with Trice & Beyer's (1984) request, I will also give an account of a new rite.

Rites of Creation

Studying organisational cultures in terms of rites of creation is a real opportunity for any organisational researcher. Trice & Beyer (1984) state undeniably, that no examples have emerged of what might be called rites of creation—rites for establishing new roles and embedding them in ongoing social arrangements.

Additionally, no rites have been documented that have a manifest intent of dissolving existing structural arrangements without degrading the occupants. Similarly, no rites or ceremonials have been found for establishing new organisational structures or radically altered ones.

Trice & Beyer (1984) believe in the possibility that rites and ceremonials, conducive to change, already have been invented and are being practiced in some modern day organisations. This type of information is valuable to other organisations. How these rites work is worthy of research. The opportunity, therefore, has arisen for such rites to be documented because Trice & Beyer

(1984) say that if they do not exist, perhaps someone should try inventing and establishing them.

In this chapter, I will use rites of creation to explain how I worked as Newland's Operations Director and manager within an organisational role significantly changed by rites of degradation (Trice & Beyer 1984).

Management traits, skills and subsequent employee responses will be compared within the framework of rites of creation, especially in relation to establishing my new role and embedding that role in Newland's ongoing social arrangements.

When explaining one particularly useful management trait and skill that I adopted, I also have the opportunity to re-use Trice & Beyer's (1984) rites of integration. Later, an account of a new rite is given.

Manager in Rites of Creation

Simply, if managers are to embed established new roles into ongoing organisational social arrangements, then there has to be interaction between manager and organisational members. Consequently, the sights of rites of creation are placed upon managers, making them responsible for both effectively using the rites and also for inventing new ones (Trice & Beyer 1984).

Clearly, managers and leaders are aspects of organisational life. Managers in organisations place traditional authority upon a workforce, by formal governance intervention, in accordance with conformance and compliance demands and the commercial aims and objectives of an involved organisation. Accordingly, the influences and manipulations made by management upon the workforce, directly and indirectly, enforce organisational authority.

Markedly in organisations like Newland's, leadership is an integral part of effective team work (Hambley, O'Neill & Kline 2007). This integral role makes leaders responsible for making the right kind of impressions, through influence and persuasion, to achieve organisational aims and objectives (Yukl 2002).

Already laid out in the current body of literature, are the strong constructive points of managers. In order to do their work, managers require discretion, freedom and mandate (Espedal 2007) charismatic influence (Sosik 2001, Friedman 2006) emotional intelligence (Sosik & Megerian 1999) and strength of character (Hrebiniak 2006).

According to Sosik & Jung (2003), self-awareness also manifests in a good manager. Understandably, a commitment to personal development makes managers more comfortable about raising and discussing emotion in the workplace. As a result, the empathic manager can help to turn a toxic situation and subsequent damage into organisational learning (Clair & Dufresne 2007, Hatch, Kostera & Kozminski 2006). A congruent manager has less discrepancies between their authenticity and how others evaluate them (Sosik & Jung 2003).

However, it is a unpalatable reality that inside organisations, there are leaders that have the capacity and motivation to be "destructive" (Tierney & Tepper 2007, Schaubroeck et al 2007). These kinds of leaders reduce organisational performance, increase tension, constrain action and erode motivation (Manzoni & Barsoux 2009). Particularly notable is that these individuals have also been identified as having strong technical skills (Einarsen, Aasland & Skogstad 2007).

As I worked as Newland's organisational manager, I never questioned if I was charismatic or emotionally intelligent. Neither did I ever wonder about how integral I was to Newland's teams. Confidently, I knew I had strength of character because I had already shown an ability to put the needs of Newland's above those of a long serving director. Undeniably, I had made a commitment to personal development when I trained as a Rogerian person-centred counsellor between 1998 and 2002 (Rogers 1951, 1980).

Although, I would enjoy taking the strong constructive points highlighted in the literature and making them my own, I know from experience that in order to be an effective organisational manager, one also has to retain a degree of humility.

When Newland's experienced the loss of a director, it was a significantly disrupting organisational event. Post event, it was my main responsibility, with the help of Newland's other directors, to improve the organisation.

Early on in this chapter, I said that managers take responsibility in rites of creation as they set out to embed change into existing organisational arrangements through interaction. In the next section, therefore, I will demonstrate management traits and characteristics to balance power and authority with popularity and propose for them to be defined as dimensions of rites of creation.

Apart from using my person-centred skills as a point of reference, I also had management interventions that helped to facilitate the responsibilities of both my director and management roles. I saw myself as an invoker of Newland's organisational needs, an interpreter of events and members attitudes and an integrator of all three, organisational needs, events and members attitudes.

Like any other organisation, there were times in Newland's when management interventions needed to be invoked. Invoking took place, not necessarily to intercede too quickly, assert the management position or attempt to avert a crises, but to offer a different viewpoint and bring to light other available employee choices, if timescales permitted such choices.

Thus, I propose that one manifest, expressive social consequence of rites of creation is the imposition of necessary change, without creating too much disruption at the organisational level, through unambiguous invoking or rites of invocation. Rites of invocation become therefore, a subsystem of rites of creation.

Invoking did not have a diminishing effect on Newland's workforce, but changed the course of events to fit the existing commercial circumstances, without creating too much organisational disruption. At Newland's organisational level, therefore, the latent expressive consequence of unambiguous invoking became acceptable change (Trice & Beyer 1984).

Being consistent in providing relevant organisational information, through managerial guidance and supervision, was a Newland's managerial objective. Reciprocally, this would encourage the invoking of team practical thinking in relation to tasking arrangements, short term or long term planning and the impact of any future business opportunities that had already been identified through marketing.

Invoking had a particular usefulness. It helped to put into place decisions that could be both administratively and technically unpopular. Work priorities sometimes meant suspending some actions in preference to others, even when all of the activities were important features of Newland's ongoing project work that perpetuated organisational survival, akin with rites of integration (Trice & Beyer 1984).

Intermittent contractual changes would modify and interfere with the already established production of revenue generating work in Newland's Cold, Hot and Virtual Teams. Undoubtedly, there was always a commercial consequence as either additional work had to be done for the same price or alternatively, the client would reduce the work scope. Either way, Newland's potential for the generation of revenue was affected (Trice & Beyer 1984).

These types of unpopular decisions were assisted through invoking. It did however, require managerial invocation courage when related to the technical and production elements of Newland's ongoing work, because both the focus and the course of the work were changed.

Invoking heralded the management call for change. Ultimately, this change became a direct leading of the teams that subsequently moved the team processes away from an already established natural progression, linked with the client determined specification for the production event. As a direct consequence, the work volume either increased or decreased. Additionally, the effects of these ramifications changed the pace and direction of the teams which in turn, stalled the communications.

The leadership intention of invoking was to illuminate the proposed new action rather than aggravate the immediate state of operational activity or degrade members at Newland's organisational level undertaking the work (Lipgar 2006, Trice & Beyer 1984). Additionally, it did not mean simply binding to rules in order to get the work done thus, forcing rather than facilitating desired change (Espedal 2007).

Interference was, however, the downside to invoking. This type of invoking also had the potential to inhibit and even stop Newland's engineering output. The ramping up of monitoring can obviously do more harm than good (Ferrin, Bligh & Kohles 2007).

Consequently, a form of leadership dependence would surface. There would be a looking towards the leader in expectation that something should or would happen thereby, turning productive teams into leadership dependent states. Simultaneously, stalling would slow down or even stop communications.

Frustration would be demonstrated by production team members at what was perceived as inconsistencies and/or unwelcomed change. Tension in the workplace would increase between Newland's management and workforce, if the demand for change became prolonged or vague.

Disturbances created through invoking were able to be tolerated as long as it was clear that the changes were directly related to the client needs and were not necessarily, subtle options or the preferences of Newland's management.

Invoking could assist rites of creation because in order to embed necessary change, the reasons for and the importance of the change had to be recognised at the organisational level within the workforce. In the Newland's experience, if the change was client based then embedding such change was easy. If it was more a case of Newland's subtle management option or desires, then change was absorbed less freely and subtle resistance would be experienced.

Perceived reactions to change would create resistance in Newland's workforce. Perceptions of change had to be managed truthfully and honestly. Even if the changes were subtle options taken up by Newland's management, then that had to be communicated to the workforce.

The purpose of rites of creation is not to degrade the occupants as change is enforced at the organisational level (Trice & Beyer 1984). Before setting out to impose change, if Newland's management desires were not congruently exposed to the workforce, then the opportunity for organisational mistrust could arise. The contrary of desire is doubt and this in turn, could threaten the relationship between Newland's management and organisational members. Consequently, organisational survival could be placed at risk (Lapp & Carr 2006, Trice & Beyer 1984).

Notably, hope played a part when change was either necessary or desired by Newland's management (Andersson, Giacalone & Jurkiewicz 2007). What was desired by Newland's management was member recognition that certain decisions were made for the greater organisational good (Lagos 2007). In spite of the discomfort, frustration and unsettling effects that the micro managerial demands brought with them, necessary and even desired change aided organisational survival (Trice & Beyer 1984).

One further element of rites of creation is therefore, the need for management to authentically communicate the reasons why any change, necessary or desired, subtle or significant is being adopted. Subsequently, only the congruent manager can successfully manifest the rites of creation at the organisational level, without disrupting or diminishing the existing members (Trice & Beyer 1984).

Portrayed in the literature, the constructive manager commits to personal development (Clair & Dufresne 2007, Hatch, Kostera & Kozminski 2006, Sosik & Jung 2003). Perhaps some training in person-centred skills for use in the workplace, could help managers and leaders to enhance skills that help to unambiguously invoke all kinds of organisational change (Rogers 1951, 1980).

As a way to balance power and authority with popularity, some rites of 'authenticity' or rites of 'invocation' could answer Trice & Beyer (1984) call for organisational managers to invent and establish some new pertinent rites, that these managers could call their own.

As congruence is a way of being, rites of authenticity should emanate from the person who is acting as the organisational manager (Rogers 1951, 1980). Perceived as authentic by the workforce, this manager could empathically recognise and utilise any emerging cooperation. By encountering resistance through compromise, rites of authenticity could help this manager to facilitate all organisational requirements and consequently, reduce conflict (Trice & Beyer 1984).

Rites of invocation should help managers to express the emotions that affect their leadership facilitation, especially during difficult circumstances. Invocation in Newland's required the authentic display of courage, hope, belief, desire and anticipation by a congruent manager.

Perhaps other organisational managers could use rites of invocation as a way to prepare for difficult planned events that require the facilitation and integration of significant change, like downsizing, redundancies, shutdowns or the removal of high status members. Rites of invocation could help to reduce organisational conflict for those managers and employees who remain in-situ (Trice & Beyer 1984).

Balancing popularity with power and authority is facilitated not by simply invoking rules, but also by a manager being able to interpret member attitudes and behaviours that become a consequence of invoking. Interpretation, therefore, is a dimension of rites of invocation.

Sometimes as Newland's manager, I both desired and needed to take a neutral stance and consider the contributions and values placed upon a particular situation by other members. Taking no action was as important as taking action, as time, function and work processes dictated consequences. Additionally, as both a manager and an individual, I also needed some 'thinking space' so that I could arrive at my own interpretations of the events. Consequently, I encouraged members to think for themselves (Franklin 2007).

Interpreter, as a skill, will successfully facilitate management interventions by surrendering the need for constant and uninterrupted supervision. Management popularity could be aided by maintaining a style akin with a 'hands-off approach'.

According to Hatch, Kostera & Kozminski (2006), the infiltration of chaos and creative forces constantly challenge technically ordered organisations so that they do not stagnate or fail to adapt to circumstances. Pertinently, sufficient freedom for decision making enabled Newland's teams to make the applicable and relevant choices in order to successfully achieve the team objectives.

Offering such a level of team freedom did however, require some element of management control. Too much freedom was controlled by Newland's management by making each team member take personal responsibility for their decision making. Even though the taking of personal responsibility was expected, it did not relinquish Newland's management from theirs. The liability of management remained for the sake of the well-being of both organisation and members together with the anticipated success of Newland's commercial endeavours (Trice & Beyer 1984).

When work undertaking became intangible or difficulties occurred, the interpretative element of rites of invocation helped to increase the communication within the workplace.

When participatory communications were directly increased, the ability to discuss difficult circumstances or members traits were encouraged to be aired jointly, transparently and not secretly within a clique or Newland's outside groups. This openness changed group behaviour as members became more able to confront the difficulties and confidently air feelings.

Even low levels of transparency helped mutual trust to manifest and for the 'no go' areas to begin to diminish. When trust was exhibited by one party towards a member, it subsequently helped to influence the level of trust between both parties (Ferrin, Bligh & Kohles 2007).

Timescales were set for making difficult, uncomfortable and unpopular decisions. If tension arose, it could be eased by difficult decisions being deferred to a later time, but only if timescales and work undertaking processes permitted such deferments.

It is achievable for organisational managers to draw a line between what a person does and who they are, so that it becomes possible to show warmth, at the same time as setting boundaries and expressing different opinions and wishes (Gatongi 2007). Interpreter was an exponent management intervention of rites of invocation that aimed to balance popularity with power and authority. Interpreter, however, did not always have an impact, especially if perceived as just being a 'personal opinion' of the manager.

At these times, blatant indifference could be encountered. Deliberate procrastinations became evident when management interpretative representations were perceived as having limited or little meaning, or were just unpopular with members. This is demonstrated in one data extract, a neutral statement that made little contribution to the conversation:

...that was an interesting statement.

I knew that an 'organisational grapevine' existed in Newland's and the existence of outside groups often proved my point. Because I always aimed for openness and transparency in my own interpretative managerial intervention, I did discourage the grapevine approach because I regarded it as being indirect. More importantly though, I did not dismiss it because I knew that it was an important part of Newland's social functioning that helped to implement work that aided organisational survival (Hrebiniak 2006, Trice & Beyer 1984).

I regarded direct feedback as being simply idealistic, but more preferred. I did, however, mostly adopt a 'hands-off approach'. Consequently, maintaining a style of not over monitoring the self-managing, task-oriented aspects of Newland's teams, promoted team autonomy, altruism and confidence inside those teams.

As an example of entrenching rites of creation, rites of invocation manifested as an unambiguous invoker of Newland's organisational needs and an interpreter of events and members attitudes that enabled the imposition of change, without creating too much disruption at the organisational level.

Hence, Newland's teams would respond to management interventions that were transparent towards them and delivered by a congruent managerial approach. As long as the changes were perceived as derived from client wishes and not simply the desires of an out of touch manager, frustration and procrastination could be limited but, not totally avoided.

Rites of creation balance managerial power and authority by congruent responsive managers who take the right kind of approach, especially when dealing with teams that have intense working programmes in operation (Trice & Beyer 1984). This will, however, call for managers to be aware of their own intervention style, timing, and the impact of the delivery of the organisational requirements that such managers place upon the workforce (Wageman, Fisher & Hackman 2009). A commitment to personal development could aid both intervention style, management delivery and impact.

As a payoff, rites of conflict resolution are also assisted by rites of creation and now its extended subsystem, rites of invocation (Trice & Beyer 1984).

If managers are more aware of their approach towards the workforce, less tension is created and it is likely that organisational demands will be met with more cooperation rather than resistance. Consequently, as collaboration is built through the right approach, good timing and humility, there would be little opportunity for the diminishment of either the manager or the workforce (Trice & Beyer 1984).

One other aim and objective of my own management approach was to encourage and maintain a constructive and humanistic style of administrative, technical and social supervising guidance and remain effective in the process. These qualities were the aspects of the management intervention style that I often referred to as the integrant, that can now be compared with rites of integration (Trice & Beyer 1984).

Manager in Rites of Integration

Although, rites of integration primarily bind members together and commit them to a larger social system aiming for the common good, the rites also permit venting of emotion and the temporary loosening of various norms. Another consequence is the reassertion and reaffirmation, by contrast, of the moral rightness of the usual norms. The opportunity to relax organisational constraints is not exclusively applied to discrete parts of the organisation involved. All temporary emotional venting, loosening and reinstatements can be applied to all organisational members (Trice & Beyer 1984).

As a Newland's manager and trained person-centred counsellor, I always considered empathy as an interpersonal management skill that had a vital role in the integrating process of passing on instructions and ideas into the workforce. Consequently, empathy underpinned my leadership approach, offered me privileged access, set realistic priorities, recognised workforce cohesiveness, valued pragmatism, promoted altruism and assisted positive assertion. Wilhelmson (2006) sees leaders in a similar way placing emphases upon common values, deeply rooted in a humanistic outlook on persons, being non-prestigious, mutually trusting, loyal and generous towards one another.

Certainly, there are differences between being a manager and being a leader. As a manager, I always had a 'managerial place to lean' because Newland's organisational requirements were not wishes and desires that stemmed from nothing. The demands were derived from the organisational compliance requirements that had to be commercially met.

As a leader, it was different. Leadership exposes the person in terms of one's own personal capabilities and competencies and how one acts as that leader. Consequently, being a leader is an 'exposure of the self' to the witness of the involved organisational audience.

Constantly, my integrator leadership skill was tested by external requirements and forces that impacted upon Newland's commercial and economic factors. Creative and flexible approaches towards the workforce were undoubtedly required in order to integrate Newland's ever changing client demands. Integrator leadership therefore, would be the foundation upon which all managers and members reciprocal working relationships could have safe passage through all of the versions of their tension creating organisational events (Hatch, Kostera & Kozminski 2006, Trice & Beyer 1984, Wilhelmson 2006).

Mainly, integrator aims and objectives helped to keep communications current yet remained a litmus test of the interpersonal skills and style of the leadership in command. Strength of leadership had the opportunity to emerge in talking and listening relationships that helped to keep incorrect perceptions, anxiety creating situations or the potential for conflict in perspective (Trice & Beyer 1984).

Consequently, gossip was discouraged and kept to a minimum by the continuity of that style of contact. Management popularity was also made good by such genuine contact and a reliable relationship.

Routinely, as I functioned as Newland's organisational manager, there was an element of counsellor within me, from which I could not be removed. Certainly, talking and listening relationships helped to vent pent up emotion and temporarily loosen Newland's organisational norms, when integrating client unexpected changes or when management interventions had unwittingly created tension and conflict (Rogers 1951, 1980, Trice & Beyer 1984).

Although, Newland's members talking and listening sessions were not therapeutic relationships, they were popular interventions. These sessions were encountered in the organisational working space between manager and member, so appropriate boundaries were kept in place.

Notably, as a woman manager, I considered that management gender could also be making a contribution towards the talking and listening sessions. Their moderate success, therefore, may not have been solely related to the counsellor or the use of counselling skills in the workplace (Koch 2005, Rogers 1951, 1980).

After some time had passed since the rites of degradation event, in order to primarily restore members confidence and popularity in Newland's leadership, I intentionally set out to obtain a viewpoint on what qualities Newland's workforce expected of a leader. Using informal conversation, my intervention was successful.

Emotions were able to be vented and there was sufficient loosening of organisational norms for Newland's members to be able to express, reassert and reaffirm, in a constructive way, their honest expectations of their leadership (Trice & Beyer 1984). The following data extracts were those examples of expectations:

A leader should not be a headless chicken, running around.
One that has a calm, composed temperament.
Has interpersonal skills.
Is moderate in their approach to others.
Is fair in their decision making, especially if done alone.
Has an awareness of their own behaviour in the workspace.
Is perceived by others as having such qualities.

Realistically, leadership skills, such as those defined by Newland's members, are attainable by the aspiring leader who sets out to gain a full perception of themselves within their management roles. Within Newland's, the management intervention, integrator, would be successful as long as attitudes, behaviours and the impact of decision making towards members was constantly regarded as 'potentially disrupting', and therefore, always approached tentatively and handled sensitively.

Realistically, popularity was not guaranteed by integrator management and leadership skills. Being a Newland's leader meant also remaining distant as part of the management echelon by maintaining rank of office. In the case of team working, however, a balance had to be struck between the engaged work undertaking requirements of the teams and the wider social aspects of community of which, both manager and leader were members.

Although, integrator aided popularity and ultimately, helped to balance power and authority for the manager and leader, ambivalence and conflict were emotional consequences that regularly disturbed that manager/leader's equilibrium (Trice & Beyer 1984).

This ambivalence and conflict, sitting betwixt and between the positions of decisive manager/leader and popular community member, would come to fruition when the leader was 'put on the decision making spot' or placed into Van Gennep (1960) type liminal space. Managerial confidence and knowledge would be immediately tested. Reputations were put at risk when expectations from the workforce placed responsibility upon the leadership to make the right choice, at the right time (Ambrosini, Bowman & Burton-Taylor 2007).

Certainly, Newland's team functions would generate potential for conflict arising. Polarised positions could inhibit Newland's inter-team coordinated activities and hence, organisational perpetuity. Consequently for Newland's, addressing issues that had the potential for conflict arising constantly required management attention to acknowledge the existence of conflict and provide the opportunity to discuss the details (Trice & Beyer 1984).

In order to give some examples of where conflict could arise as work was undertaken in Newlands, data examples are now provided. Also given, are the resolutions suggested for balancing and integrating a potential solution:

Handling distractions that were not necessarily related to technical change.

Distractions that stemmed from administrative disturbances were more easily resolved by offering an alternative solution and encouraging team members to seek out support from each other, excluding management.

Handling delays that could have a sense of weakening the team.

Delays surfaced that could weaken the teams when client imposed changes became imminent or when the client quickly changed the scope of work. Such delays were resolved and integrated by developing increased communication skills within the teams and encouraging proactive responses to the proposed or actual client changes.

Developing a team ethos that could help to reduce the sense of conflict.

Encouraging team thinking in order to develop closer client engagement with teams to integrate the renegotiated work priorities and thereby, reduce team anxiety and deflect any conflict arising.

Increasing communications with the client and ensuring all client needs were met when changes impacted upon project content.

Promoting and encouraging members to develop perceptions of how to deal with the changed work adequately integrated disturbance creating client changes. Integration of the client changes also manifested the need to communicate with the client, in order to comprehend the changed client requirements.

Realistically, even with the best of management intentions, Newland's teams would slump into a parental dependent state (Bion 1962, 1965). Placing management popularity at risk, on several occasions, I addressed the lethargic attitude with Newland's community. I raised my concern and a possible solution. How popular this decision was remained a mystery, but my popularity did not decline:

I have been the person working through the project charts to summarise what I consider to be the position of each project status. Each team and/or group members agrees or updates me with the information. I don't think that this is the best way for me to lead the meeting because basically, I am doing all the work and "still tying shoelaces". I am not the person closest to the projects and I feel that at times, I could be missing important information that has not been passed on in the working week therefore, my picture is sometimes incomplete.

From (date), there will be a change in the format. In the first half, the team leader will give me an update on their project status and I then have the opportunity to make the necessary notes according to the changes. This means that some preparation work will be required by each team leader. In the second half, what can then follow is a round-the-table discussion about any changes that need to be made in relation to allocation of resources.

On the contrary, however, although there were some decisions that always had to remain with Newland's management, there were also decisions that could be left with employees, either in consultation with management or without it. Integration therefore, helped Newland's managerial popularity through surrendering some employee 'indicators of choice' (Trice & Beyer 1984). These were the slightly awkward areas where compromising management influences would be deemed as being 'on your back' type of unwanted pressure.

The loosening of various norms meant that Newland's employee could retain the possession of their defined 'indicators of choice' (Trice & Beyer 1984). Like the interpreter manager that required 'thinking space', Newland's employees also needed time, space and elbow room for themselves, so each could work effectively on behalf of Newland's, meeting commercial aims and objectives (Trice & Beyer 1984).

For an empathic manager, an employee review can reveal hidden gems of organisational member realities. Newland's employees 'indicators of choice' were given in their responses to the annual review assessment. I have shown my empathic response in brackets ( ):

What we already have, we wish to retain (retention)

We wish to learn by choice (training)
Information will be held close if needs be (disclosure)
We will use this time as we wish (freedom)
Acceptance and recognition (tolerance)
We will take to the heart (age and stature)

Retention, training, disclosure, freedom, tolerance, age, and stature were all employee responses that required the loosening of various norms, i.e., certain employee choices, in order to reaffirm and reassert the usual norms, i.e., organisational project aims and commercial objectives (Trice & Beyer 1984).

In order to provide clarity, each conflict reducing 'indicator of choice' requires further explanation (Trice & Beyer 1984).

Retention emerged in relation to the delegation of work. Autonomy was to remain with the teaming structures, when the conditions and boundaries of the scope of work permitted and promoted autonomy.

Autonomy surfaced and became prevalent when an employee was leaving Newland's and there was a sense of urgency about how and to whom, the leaving employees work would be delegated. Obligingly, the employee who was leaving made an offer to conduct the work, at home, temporarily employed by Newland's, until completion of their earlier allocated tasking scope had been achieved. In this way, support could be given to Newland's teams during a difficult transition in order to 'maintain the continuity of work'.

Although, consultation did take place with Newland's management, this employees offer was taken up by the team supervisors. Newland's management were deliberately left out of the decision making process.

Irregular disparate working conditions did not fail the project objectives. By not obstructing Newland's employee wishes to retain autonomous control of the undertaking of project work, perceived as already being in their possession, this work could continue without disruption, stalling or conflict arising (Trice & Beyer 1984).

In terms of continuity for the sake of Newland's organisational existence, sometimes indistinct management practice could be placed above the principle of risk (Trice & Beyer 1984).

Training of Newland's staff was either mandatory or a form of continual personal and professional development. Mandatory training such as site or offshore medicals, client site access training and plant related health and safety training were unanimously accepted as being part of getting Newland's work undertaken. When health and safety training was governed by law, no obstructions were ever encountered, though the following data extracts gives the indication that sometimes, even mandatory training was an imposition:

Something we have to put up with.

For Newland's employees, however, continual personal and professional development was regarded as being a choice and these choices would always ideally remain an employee option.

Predictably, Newland's employees never made any requests to management about any participating in any personal or professional development training that was not either task specific or directly applicable to the undertaking of work.

Unless training was absolutely fine-tuned to Newland's organisational needs and detailed work content, then there was 'no enjoyment' in the training exercise. The thought of training was quickly dismissed as it was regarded as 'not a worthwhile training experience'.

As Newland's manager, I never created conflict by forcing any training that had not been dictated by either the government or the health and safety executive (Trice & Beyer 1984).

Unsurprisingly, Newland's employees often required privacy in their working life, but did dictate privacy around their private lives. Occasionally, however, there was an overlap and private lives intruded upon working life. At these times, some Newland's employees did not wish to divulge the cause of their distress created by external factors.

Conversely, there were also times when Newland's employees did aspire to holding open discussions about the events within their private lives. Where possible and practical, as Newland's manager, I encouraged these congenial discussions as long as appropriate boundaries could be maintained. If the right kind of boundaries could not be maintained, I would offer help to make the relevant type of referral.

Some of Newland's insightful employees were able to disclose feelings or their 'states of being', akin with taking a personal measurement and/or the temperature of one's own work-life balance (Smith & Gardner 2007). The following data extracts demonstrate what feelings could affect Newland's organisational members:

...sometimes feeling overtired

fatigued

bored

demotivated

...had a sense of being overlooked

Choices to disclose private information always remained with the individual concerned. As Newland's manager, I was willing to listen, take time to participate in the discussion and pay attention to the feelings being disclosed. Loosely addressing the problem, without too much interference, helped to reduce any arising conflict (Trice & Beyer 1984).

Loosening of various norms, through listening and attentiveness, aided the creation of the right kind of boundaries in which to manage the softer side of organisational life. Subsequently, most feelings were not necessarily 'dealt with', but the emotional disharmony did not create disruption at the organisational level (Trice & Beyer 1984). Mostly though, the right kind of managerial listening was the key and person-centred skills helped to arbitrate for the sake of Newland's commercial endeavours (Rogers 1951, 1980, Trice & Beyer 1984).

Freedom, was the next Newland's employee indicator of choice. Primarily, self-determination applied to how Newland's employees could use time that each had freed up for themselves, once their tasking assignments had been completed.

Self-determining freedom was facilitated during the tasking function phase that coordinated and synchronised the segregated 3-D model outputs. Primary responsibility rested with each team to liaise and develop the additional processes that were required to integrate all of the completed tasking elements into one completed 3-D model.

Freedom and self-determination, linked directly with the work processes, enabled the creative elements of the work to be matched to the more rigid project specification requirements. Obviously, Newland's team members indicated that the use of the freed up time available for this type of work should always remain an employee choice.

Indeed, experience, empathy and unconditional positive regard helped me to comprehend that any management interference in the freed up time could discourage autonomy and stultify the creativity that obviously emerged during the consolidation phase of the 3-D modelling work (Hatch, Kostera & Kozminski 2006, Rogers 1951, 1980).

Delivering a complete and accurate 3-D model of their plant, to the client, was a vital process in Newland's commercial commitment. It was the consolidated 3-D model 'deliverable' that gave Newland's the opportunity to be paid for the work. Employee freedom and self-determination, during the consolidation phase of work, was not inhibited by any Newland's manager, as it could interfere with the continuity of the work, the organisation involved and therefore, threaten Newland's commercial existence (Trice & Beyer 1984).

According to Newland's members, tolerance of others would always remain an indicator of employee choice. There was little or no room for compromise and any form of intolerance of others in the group community was not acceptable.

A 'put-down' was regarded as any ways, verbal or physically, in which another individual was made to feel diminished by another, when their recognition and worth could be damaged by the put-down. Such comments also had the potential to diminish organisational wide compromise and cooperation (Trice & Beyer 1984).

Any kind of diminishment of others, Newland's members regarded as unacceptable behaviour, in any of the group or teaming structures. Some unacceptable put-downs were described by Newland's group community as:

A feeling (of an individual) of not being able to speak out
Stifling
A sense of not being able to ask for needs and wants
Silencing

Realistically, however, some 'put-downs' did occur and conflict, as a result of the 'put-down' did arise (Trice & Beyer 1984). As Newland's manager, I knew it was important for Newland's ongoing success, that existing members stayed motivated to remain in the employment of Newland's, especially for the engineers who were specifically trained to undertake the work. Any disruption therefore, at organisational level, could threaten Newland's commercial existence.

Although, I could not prevent the 'put-downs' taking place, either seriously or humorously, as Newland's manager, I quickly discouraged and refused to accept any 'put-downs', even if they did have cultural value (Trice & Beyer 1984).

Despite the promotion of a relaxed organisational atmosphere by Newland's management, age and stature did apply, because Newland's hosted a type of 'command status'. Age and stature, therefore, is the final indicator of choice.

Usually the managing director, the oldest male of the group community, was the person with whom Newland's members discussed most matters. The exception was when the oldest female of the group community, myself, was either asked a direct question, when I voluntarily offered information or more notably, when the oldest male of the group community was absent.

The absence of the oldest male transcended myself, the oldest female, into the position of ultimate command, usually occupied by the eldest male, when my authority was recognised and unquestioned.

There were, however, different rules in Newland's social settings which were especially prevalent at social dinners. When dining occasions took place, leadership positions were related more with good manners, age, as well as stature.

Particular reference is given to social dining occasions by Trice & Beyer (1984).

Specifically, the organisational cultural phenomena linked with eating and drinking at Christmas parties, award or retirement ceremonies and annual dinners have not been accounted for in any literature and is worthy of research.

Within any of Newland's social dinner or lunch restaurant occasions, although I remained as Newland's manager, I was often given the personal experience of simply enjoying the organisational community moment and being allowed to be a women manager of some stature.

On these special occasions, both inside and outside Newland's organisational walls, both myself and the managing director were invited to join in and were always encouraged to sit central amongst Newland's members.

Obligingly, both the managing director and myself sat where the group invited us to do so, in a safe place, that had been specifically chosen by Newland's joint community. The relaxing of usual organisational norms meant that Newland's managers could be securely 'taken to the heart' of the group, tactically and deliberately moving each director within a new social order (Trice & Beyer 1984). There was no suppressing of this integrating request.

Installed into a new position by group demand, each director could then be deemed as being situated in a protected position and strategically placed, in order to be guarded from unknown outside forces. Like having a bodyguard, Newland's managers were most often flanked by younger, larger and stronger group members.

Markedly, in the middle of the group were also placed the other members that temporarily were suffering from a physical injury or who were deemed to be, at that time, in the need of more protection from the community. These individuals were also 'taken to the heart' of the group into a protective zone.

Also, strategically placed and well seated at the end of the table was Newland's youngest director, a tall, athletic type with some stature, that had been deliberately placed by the group community and would be referred to as:

A flanker

Cordially, Newland's members did not solely offer stature in relation to group leader age because even younger members, in positions of authority, gained some degree of importance.

Notably, however, Newland's younger director was strategically placed away from the central position, in the wings, to the side of the whole group. Their placement and position could have been deemed as an acceptable one because there was no remonstration nor any request to change position.

Although temporary, the invention of a new social order, based on age and stature, helped to preserve and maintain a special part of Newland's organisational social life, the celebratory aspect. Undoubtedly, a pleasant setting, ambience, food, champagne, wine or beer helped to reinforce the organisational common aim, which was to ensure that Newland's continuity was preserved in order for the company to be a provider to an involved workforce (Trice & Beyer 1984).

Having outlined the finer details of the indicators of choice, ending with age and stature, it is important to now situate them in a broader context. I propose, therefore, that the broader context be thought of in terms of new rites (Trice & Beyer 1984).

Although, Trice & Beyer's (1984) rites of conflict reduction arbitrate to reduce conflict and aggression, I have identified an opportunity to invent new rites, rites of concession, that prevent the conflict arising in the first place.

Importantly, rites of concession aid to pre-empt the consequences that can create conflict and aggression by where possible and practical, surrendering the indicators of choice that have been exclusively identified by employees.

In the experience of Newland's employees, rites of concession identified certain indicators of choice which were retention, training, disclosure, freedom, tolerance, age and stature.

In the case of Newland's, when the indicators of choice retention and freedom were surrendered, work autonomy and independence was perceived by the workforce.

Rites of concession manifested through the satisfying perception that acceptable working conditions existed for organisational members.

When training was offered as an indicator of choice, Newland's employees perceived the training as a worthwhile experience. Unfortunately, if training was mandatory by law, it was sometimes deemed as unnecessary time wasting, especially if production levels were high and tension was increased.

At this time, the indicator of choice, training, helped Newland's employees to express their real opinions about the training, when their choice was removed by the governing aspects of law. In this instance, rites of concession manifested through the expression of frustration of a tolerable intrusion.

The indicator of choice disclosure kept privacy in place. Boundaries were maintained when employees expressed a desire to remain silent about personal issues that were not to be made organisationally public. Rites of concession transpired through a managers ability to observe with care, but not necessarily intrude or interfere and act if and when invited to do so.

Understandably, Newland's employees indicator of choice, acceptance and recognition, were always expected to be tolerated by Newland's management. In the Newland's experience, this placing of trust helped the workforce to believe that a level of autonomy existed. Sensing also, that sufficient freedom existed for the use of personal judgement in production, Newland's members were able to highlight any concerns and bring those concerns to the attention of management.

Rites of concession could aid management tolerance by organisational managers surrendering their need to control more. By placing trust in the abilities of their workforce, ultimately, managers could govern constructively through conviction, **self-assurance** and belief.

Respect for age and stature stemmed from rites of concession when Newland's managers were able to demonstrate a willingness to let their status be influenced and manipulated by others. On Newland's celebratory occasions, consent allowed a different social order to manifest that determined how well each manager's status was perceived by the workforce.

Rites of concession permitted the workforce to situate managers into pre-determined central positions, places where the workforce deemed each manager should go.

Acceptance and tolerance of the situation by Newland's managers demonstrated that each were able to temporarily surrender age and stature according to the social etiquette that manifested at the time. Also manifesting was recognition that sufficient freedom and independence existed for Newland's workforce to be able to place their influence and facilitation upon their management.

Straightforwardly, Trice & Beyer (1984) specifically call for managers to invent or document any new rites that have helped them to facilitate organisational level requirements, especially in relation to rites of creation.

Using rites of concession as a means of determination, other managers working in different organisations, could identify the workforce's indicators of choice that management were able to surrender. In doing so, workforce tension and difficult situations at the organisational levels, that require high levels of time and concentration to reform, could be pre-empted and thus, prevented (Trice & Beyer 1984).

In this chapter, I have disclosed the fundamental elements of my Newland's management role in terms of rites of creation and additionally, rites of integration.

I have also been able to invent a new set of rites, called rites of concession, the manifest consequence of which is the pre-empting of conflict, rather than the resolution of conflict (Trice & Beyer 1984).

The key points that have been addressed in management interventions, as valued ways of management and leadership, were invoking, interpreting and integrant.

Invoking was the management push for a different viewpoint that raised the opportunity to bring diverse choices to light. Interpreting was a neutral stance for considering further management options that were hidden or unrecognised.

Integrating was to consolidate and incorporate management instructions and ideas with creating conflict (Trice & Beyer 1984).

Giving up the element of control over Newland's employees indicators of choice did not create disruption at the organisational level. Conversely, in the manifestation of the new rites, rites of concession, the opposite applied.

Rites of concession aided Newland's managers and workforce to be able to work jointly, reciprocally for the common good and in doing so, perpetuate the commercial existence of Newland's as a successful small medium enterprise (Trice & Beyer 1984).

Having reviewed my managerial role in terms of rites of creation, rites of integration and rites of concession, I will utilise the next chapter to examine my role as Manager in New Rites of Creation.

Chapter 8
Results: Manager in New Rites of Creation

Simply, I will start this chapter with an explanation of Trice & Beyer's (1984) rites of creation. Then, using a new set of rites as a subsystem of rites of creation, I will explain the management style and techniques that I adopted in my organisational roles within Newland's. The context in which the rites manifested at the organisational level, employee interactions and once again, the role of food, will also be addressed.

Justification for New Rites of Creation

By admission, Trice & Beyer (1984) say that their typology is logically incomplete. Evidently, some gaps in the list of manifest, expressive functions are apparent and if such rites do not exist, then some managers should try inventing and establishing them.

In line with Trice & Beyer's (1984), evaluation for managers who recognise that rites and ceremonials exist within their organisations, there are three salient points that all managers could seriously consider.

First, practicing managers could profit from learning how to evaluate their rites and ceremonials in order to determine the degree to which these managers are achieving both desired and other related organisational consequences.

Second, truly effective managers are those who are good at making assessments and using personal judgement to continue, modify or discontinue any ceremonial activities.

Third, Trice & Beyer (1984) invite practicing managers, working at the organisational level, to invent new rites that provide information on how structural arrangements are working within their organisations. Rites of creation are predominantly mentioned for establishing new roles and embedding them in ongoing social arrangements (Trice & Beyer 1984).

As I have documented in a previous chapter, resolving Newland's organisational dysfunction, culminated in the removal of a high status, long serving technical director from office. Consequently, as Newland's Operations Director, I inherited most of the significant duties of that director. Primarily, the first objective of my new task assignment was in the short term, to improve employee relationships and in the long term, organisational performance.

In rites of conflict reduction and rites of integration respectively, disruptive effects are compartmentalised, after which encouragement is promoted to revive common feelings in order to enhance the whole organisational good (Trice & Beyer 1984).

Whether tension is created or not, a motivated and active workforce can naturally feed the already proven helpful rites of conflict reduction and rites of integration. As daily production activities are accomplished without disruption, organisational equilibrium stays undisturbed therefore, the perpetuity of the organisation remains settled and thus, secure (Trice & Beyer 1984).

Pragmatically though, in order for these two rites to reduce conflict and aggression and facilitate restoration, managers have to adopt pre-cursor means to conduct and accomplish the antecedent organisational actions that are required to aid and assist problem solving and restitution.

Trice & Beyer's (1984) call for new rites of creation, therefore, provides managers with the opportunity to elucidate their diverse pioneering management styles and techniques that motivate the workforce. A new subsystem of rites of creation that I will use to explain my management style and techniques is called rites of intercession.

I propose that rites of intercession have potential to help the individual member, groups and also, the involved organisation through moderate management intervention and receptive employee common interaction. Principally, the manifest expressive functions of the rites is to build, maintain and perpetuate the relationship between management and workforce, regarded as an ongoing inter-reliant affiliation, upon which the organisation can become and remain co-dependent.

Moderating rites of intercession are the pre-cursor rites that help managers, through style, technique and intervention, place traditional authority upon a workforce, in accordance with governance conformance and compliance demands and the commercial aims and objectives of an involved organisation. Commercial perpetuity is maintained through mutually beneficial working relationships that function principally and exclusively in the interests of the organisation involved (Trice & Beyer 1984).

Consequently, in the facilitation of rites of intercession, management styles, techniques and interventions, directly or indirectly, provide sufficient influence to enforce organisational authority upon the workforce. Subsequently, Trice & Beyer's (1984) call for managers to continue, modify or discontinue any ceremonial activities can be aided and assisted through the moderating effects of rites of intercession.

Generally, rites of intercession broaden other organisational rites that have already been revealed in Trice & Beyer's (1984) comprehensive typology of rites.

Spearhead rites of intercession, when facilitated by management, initiate, progress and propagate the three subsystems of rites of passage. Consequently, through rites of intercession, new members are helped to smoothly integrate and incorporate by an integrative management style that purposely sets out to avoid rites of degradation type problems (Trice & Beyer 1984).

By observing a functioning workforce that emanates cultural indicators, authoritative leadership remains balanced and constructive in rites of intercession because influence, guidance and supervision stems from a manager that pays attention to all of the aspects of organisational life (Trice & Beyer 1984). Hence, by addressing problems openly, the need for rites of conflict reduction is commonly avoided as peace-making rites of intercession avoid conflict (Trice & Beyer 1984).

Utilising the communication and interpersonal skills of a manager that complements the workforce, rites of intercession are able to broadly divulge good news about the organisation, at the organisational level. In doing so, both the organisation and the committed workforce are enhanced as hope and optimism, linked with rites of renewal, restores workforce confidence in organisational perpetuity (Trice & Beyer 1984).

Finally, rites of intercession widen rites of integration. Commercially successful functioning relationships at the organisational level are both the aim and the product of rites of intercession. By recognising and responding to signs at the organisational level, the moderating effects of rites of intercession acknowledges workforce intentions and aids productivity through autonomy. A responsive manager, therefore, in touch at the organisational level, does not inhibit the venting of pent up emotion, a latent expressive consequence of rites of integration (Trice & Beyer 1984).

Consequently, moderate management influence manifested through rites of intercession, provides the opportunity and environment for the workforce to effectively correspond to organisational demands placed upon them by a managerial representative (Trice & Beyer 1984).

More importantly, the right kind of environment created and promoted by managerial attitudes allows the workforce to relax as well as exert. This is the time when the workforce are granted the opportunity to enjoy traditional ceremonial activities and rituals that are analogous to their organisation (Trice & Beyer 1984).

I will now begin to explain my Newland's role as a manager in rites of intercession.

Manager in Rites of Intercession

Arguably, by being employed as Newland's director, manager and member of the workforce, I held a governing, supervising and participating role. Newland's other organisational members saw me in certain terms and subsequently, each member developed an ability to successfully relate with me on all levels.

From this close exposure and vantage point, I too had developed a perception that a model existing in the ways in which Newland's workforce community grouped together and interacted with each other. In this background, like all other members, I was an integral component. From this contact, I derived the knowing and knowledge of the reciprocal undertaking of work and more importantly, 'intelligence' of which I could not become unaware or ignorant of. As an ethnographic researcher, I could only continuously question my interpretation of it (Silverman 2005, 2011).

For managers like myself though, if rites of intercession are the means by which traditional authority is placed upon a workforce, inevitably, there has to be an organisational level context in which those managerial instructions are conveyed and received. In the case of Newland's, this context was the concept of family.

This family type concept was the primary basis of relationship upon which Newland's members cooperatively and collectively functioned, for the

Newland's common good and how organisational boundaries were kept in place that perpetuated economic survival (Trice & Beyer 1984):

For this employee, the practice of sub-grouping into more focused, condensed working arrangements is not necessarily the key to the success of the group as a whole, so the concept of the group as a whole, "the caring family" is the centre in which successful tasking arrangements are fulfilled.

Analogous to this type of caring concept, like the one that existed in Newland's, Brotheridge & Lee (2006) have emphasised the similarities between organisations and families, where members propose that these organisations function just like families. Caution, however, is required when defining an organisation as being like a family. Like a parent that controls a child's every move, managers can also micromanage hence, moderating rites of intercession lost their effectiveness through dominance.

Additionally in the concept of family, a caring spirit and altruistic pattern for leaders has been recognised by Brotheridge & Lee (2006) as being a necessary characteristic of management skills. Consequently, in order to develop a favourable climate for both families and work units, leaders must pay attention to both the task and relationship dimensions of their groups.

Characteristically, Newland's was never considered as a typical family firm because not all members of one family, or the extended family, were employed. There existed, however, a successful family type role, a shielding state, that ensured the protection and safeguarding of all involved members.

This involved protection and consideration also extended to Newland's workforce connected families, especially the relatives of absent engineers who had temporarily travelled overseas. A short phone call or an email helped these family type links to thrive so through Newland's organisational wider integration, commercial functionality in progress could remain undisturbed and hence, economic perpetuity ensured (Trice & Beyer 1984).

Furthermore, regular altruistic patterns were demonstrated inside Newland's by members who wished to deepen their involvement during the undertaking of work. Even though these members were not a team member or a team leader, the need to be more involved was observed, when these members felt it was helpful for them to have a more integral approach to the tasking arrangements. These members pressed for a continual review of work progress, coupled with a strong desire to be of assistance and help, in order to pre-empt and/or alleviate any rising concerns for themselves and for others (Trice & Beyer 1984).

An example of Newland's type altruism was demonstrated when a popular member was leaving the company. For an agreed handover period, using their own personal time, this member offered help to support ex-work colleagues during a critical phase of the project.

Specifically, this type of altruism was a way in which Newland's departing employee could demonstrate extended loyalty to an old employer, concurrent with the caring concept of family (Brotheridge & Lee 2006, Neri 2006). By offering extensive and continued support to a large ongoing project, this volunteer member would remain temporarily integrated. Consequently, completion of the project could be ensured and hence, organisational success mostly associated with rites of integration assured (Trice & Beyer 1984).

One last demonstration of altruism and helpfulness was when a leaving employee would make a recommendation of a friend or an associate with a relevant background. Subsequently, the usual recruitment event could be by-passed, thus making a significant financial saving and eliminating any risk of disappointment linked with time consuming rites of passage (Trice & Beyer 1984).

Even at the director level, rites of intercession management styles became evident in Newland's concept of family.

Only in the consumption of the cake icon and the celebration ritual did I exhibit a parenting style of mother or father type leadership (Trice & Beyer 1984). Interactive behaviours associated with 'fair sharing' were demonstrated that promoted and ensured that each 'child in the family' was treated in the same way and each received an identically sized 'piece of cake' (Bass & Avolio 1993).

In direct contrast with the parenting style, Newland's had a director whose interactive approach promoted the perception that over-protectiveness was just 'organisational pampering', deemed as being 'too hands on'. This point of view is adequately defended by Hambley, O'Neill & Kline (2007) and Koch (2005) who say that managers who are too protecting could stifle creativity and autonomous thinking, creating a dependent conditional relationship and the need to constantly maintain comfort, with that need being persistently defended.

Thankfully, I was never a Newland's mother or a father, nor did I set out to be either. Neither did I 'organisationally pamper' any member, however I did not fear nor reject a closer type of employee contact, when the opportunity arose (Rogers 1951, 1980). Continuously, at Newland's organisational level, I was able to utilise my skills to aid and assist my managerial status and Newland's organisational events, helping to keep any arising conflict in check (Trice & Beyer 1984).

Proactive rites of intercession contradict less than successful management styles that can inhibit and reduce organisational performance, which I have previously referred to as "destructive" (Einarsen, Aasland & Skogstad 2007, Ferrin, Bligh & Kohles 2007, Tepper 2000).

The data extract that follows is a Virtual Team member's congruent response to an employee annual review that I conducted. This employee illustrates the need for less restrained rites of concession and rites of intercession type freedom, autonomy and 'elbow room' in order to assertively conduct their work activities:

It is true that I have improved since last year. This is mainly because I have the confidence to do what is normal and necessary for a job to be successful and not worrying whether my action will need extensive consideration by the company...the work approach by (Name) and the office has changed that and the fact that (Name) has left the company and is not in the position of complaining any more helps a lot in parting with that work style...I'm not feeling left aside anymore and feel that I'm really a vital part of the team and not just a helper.

Rather than hindering myself by insensitivity and inattentiveness to member's situations during the undertaking of work, vital to survival, I made a point of addressing even the uncomfortable and risky situations (Trice & Beyer 1984):

I agree that "continuity" of work is an important aspect of what we do, especially in relation to the site content of your work which will impact upon the analysis work as well. I remember when you were moved from one site visit to be mobilised to another and that this unsettled you.

A high turnover of staff was never experienced by Newland's, so these incidents almost immediately manifested a 'sense of loss', because losing a popular organisational member was unfamiliar territory. Unaccustomed to the impact of the unpleasantness of losing a member, brought feelings that often went straight to the core our Newland's organisational heart:

It is interesting to note that the news that D-37 is leaving the company appears to have had an impact on the group. If it is regarded that the company is run on "the concept of family", it appears that there is a "sense of loss" associated with the news that D-37 is leaving. The manager, Me feels that D-

37's leaving can be constructive because it will bring change and it is a change that is associated with the decision of another person and not the management, so there really is no choice about the change, it is "imposed change" that has to be managed and come to terms with.

One employee, L-49 was in tears when she heard the news and apologised for not being "constructive and objective" about the news.

...seems to be having an impact upon D-37 who appears low and reflective at this moment in time. Perhaps he is reflecting upon his position with the company and how this might be different elsewhere. The Company is run on the "concept of family" which offers a caring environment to those people who work within it, but it seems to be a taken for granted attitude by the group that D-37 might not receive this attitude elsewhere and he seems to be responding to that pressure almost as if he believes it already. The purpose of this pressure seems to be to make him aware of what he is giving up by leaving the group.

Each Newland's member took pride in the knowledge that Newland's was a market leader in the supply of 3-D data acquisitions services. Consequently, when work was lost to the competition or a popular member decided to leave and work elsewhere, sometimes for the competition, some members wondered and others clung onto 'what had gone wrong'.

More pertinently, in relation to the leaving member, there was a fear associated with losing a valuable resource. The loss of a like-minded buddy and the loss of a dual technical and creative role was perceived as having a serious impact upon Newland's organisational survival, akin with rites of integration (Trice & Beyer 1984).

Nevertheless, refurbishing rites of renewal improved the functioning of organisational social structures (Trice & Beyer 1984). In taking over the workload of another member, for a Newland's employee, there was learning to be achieved that was linked with refurbishing 'task inheritance'.

'Task inheritance' manifested through interactive negotiations with colleagues. Although, the anticipated departure of a valued member was unexpected, unwelcomed and disrupting for Newland's members, sometimes out of this unforeseen adversity, employees could suddenly find themselves in a creative situation. This transition provided members with an opportunity to learn something new and additionally, contribute to their own personal development and organisational enhancement (Collin 2006, Trice & Beyer 1984).

Although, it was helpful for the 'heir to the work' to spend time and orientate with the member who was leaving, Newland's members said the real learning was actually in doing the task (Collin 2006, Fraley 2007). Newland's members explained that each had experienced a learning curve, identified through self-awareness, aided by 'task inheritance' and subsequently, wrestling adversity into submission.

Despite losses, Newland's familial, shielding state would remain in-situ, unthreatened, but modified by the significance of the events. Newland's members all eventually recovered from the losses. Still remaining at Newland's organisational core, lay the fundamental principle of conducting business events in line with commercial and economic survival, even though personal matters, marriage and relationships were stretched when team members travelled away from home (Trice & Beyer 1984).

Having their significant family member absent from home for a long period of time was not a desirable state for any Newland's connected family. Prolonged absences manifested the potential for work and family to collide and for external conflict to threaten Newland's organisational mobilisation planning (Greenhaus & Powell 2003, Trice & Beyer 1984). Interestingly though, what was pertinent to Newland's was that in their coming and going, Newland's team members vocalised more about missing their children than their spouses.

New rites of intercession provide manager's with the opportunity and pre-cursor means to either take or postpone action, so long as procrastination and/or prolonged indecision does not manifest at the organisational level.

Mainly, in my Newland's manager role, I was a 'watcher and a waiter', confidently knowing that at some point in time, all of Newland's 'intelligence' and the need to pay attention to its influences would arrive at my desk, via the Genius Loci (Neri 2006).

By being predominantly gentle, friendly and helpful, Newland's Genius Loci helped to improve the organisational atmosphere by fostering an integrating effect on all members (Neri 2006, Trice & Beyer 1984).

L-49 observations were that another person's negative behaviour or unsociable behaviour can sometimes affect the "sum of mood" of the group as a whole and if the "sum of mood" of the group as a whole could be deemed as the positive, then one individual's behaviour could change that "sum of mood" to the negative. It is especially relevant when the person who is behaving negatively or demonstrating negative expressions is a superior. This in turn could affect the overall functioning and processing capacity of the group as a whole and ultimately, it's survival.

It is an interesting note to add that at this time, F-53 positively regards L-49 as currently holding the position of "Genius Loci" which relates to the concept of family constructs. As a result, F-53 takes into serious consideration the comments that L-49 has to offer in terms of L-49 being the "thermometer" of the group.

In rites of intercession, managers are proactive, as well as having the means to give themselves time to consider what action can be taken. Some managerial decisions distinctly lack popularity. As Newland's financial decision maker, I didn't always get it right with Newland's 'group thermometer':

I am aware that my decision to place the company's interests above those of the overseas employee have not been well received. They appear not to be well received because I would suggest that my work colleague feels that if I am willing to make this decision for the overseas employee, then the same decision might apply to all other employees and this might impact upon them, either within the present or in the future orientation. My decision also seems to go against the philosophy of the concept of family, where the well-being of employees is a priority.

I feel that the concept of family is being maintained because I am placing the interests of the company's finances as a priority which protects the interests of the company, which in turn, protects the interest of its employees. There is also a question of loyalty here as well because I am feeling that although the directors endeavour to continue to take the well-being of the employees in full and constant consideration, that the employees are not doing so in return.

Before rites of conflict have the opportunity to reduce conflict and aggression, rites of concession aid to pre-empt any conflict arising in the first instance (Trice & Beyer 1984). Rites of intercession, therefore, help a manager to deal with conflict as it is arising and thus, prevent the ramifications of conflict from settling at the organisational level. Recognising emotional responses and interactions as they arise is therefore, a talent for managers to acquire to assist their own types of rites of intercession (Trice & Beyer 1984).

Organisations based upon family type values place emphasis on the welfare of employees and building relationships (Brotheridge & Lee 2006). As in any family, emotional interactions surfaced at Newland's organisational level, that gave an insight into workforce congruence. Consequently, any organisational manager would at best, recognise and deal with the consequences of emotional interactions, as and when they arise.

Assertiveness, or maintaining one's own position of thought and ground, was demonstrated at Newland's organisational level, when alternative arguments were raised that had the potential to weaken or oppose one's own argument.

Inside Newland's, assertion manifested when members had moved beyond the point of rational argument and were at a confrontational apex, shunning the argument, but still not capitulating. Assertion was one way in which Newland's members could redeem a situation by absorbing some elements of another's viewpoint and integrating those salient points into their own argument. 'Saving face' meant that existing convictions could be modified and any confrontation avoided.

Confrontation could not be surrendered under rites of concession. A manager's own type of rites of intercession have to deal directly with every unpleasant interaction, as and when they arise. Luckily, confrontation happened rarely at Newland's organisational level, but sometimes it did manifest between members who were working under pressure.

As Newland's manager I did not quickly dismiss negative employee attitudes of unhelpfulness and diminishment because I considered that confrontational stances, raised voices, sighing, sarcasm, belligerence, gurning and silence were actually congruent behaviours that demonstrated the instant authentic attitudes of Newland's workforce that disclosed real intentions.

Even though these unpleasant behaviours manifested as unsociable and actually diminished the societal relations of Newland's community, these interactions were clear indicators that some organisational matters had gone awry and were in need of managerial reparation. Creative types of rites of intercession were required to alleviate the arising tension and the potential for damaging conflict and aggression (Trice & Beyer 1984).

Conversely, the only area that I immediately confronted was when I became aware that teams undertaking work were excluding others from certain tasking specifics. These actions I regarded as unacceptable unilateral decision making that consequently, could threaten the successful completion of the work and thus, Newland's organisational survival (Trice & Beyer 1984).

Certain Newland's members considered that the workplace was not the environment where any personal feelings should be expressed because such emotional responses were non-conducive to the best interests of the concept of team, professional commercial detachment and the enablement of organisational survival.

Admittedly, each of us has a point of view on the world and each of us responds to that world according to our own psychological set of attitudes (Jeske 2001). Unavoidably though, emotions are invoked when the world around us changes, for the better or for the worse (Robbins & Parlavecchio 2006). Practically, the implementation of tasks is learned in the "school of hard knocks" and the pathways to successful results are likely fraught with mistakes and frustrations (Hrebiniak 2006).

Even outrage can provide structure to a group that is seeking justice (Anderson 2007). Despite the different approaches between myself and Newland's more objective members, I could offer unconditional positive regard to any point of view even when I completely disagreed with it (Rogers 1951, 1980).

At Newland's organisational level, interpretations and misinterpretations could be a breeding ground for both positive and negative responses. If channelled effectively though, resentment linked with misinterpretations could be diverted by a managerial intercession that changed the interpretation of the crisis that was creating tension and conflict (Clair & Dufresne 2007, Trice & Beyer 1984).

In my experience, this was a risky managerial strategy that could have easily backfired, especially when the linked resentment was deep seated and strong. The managerial push for a change of attitude, to a difficult situation, could also become an obstacle to progress if it were not sufficiently managed through adequate rites of intercession (Hrebiniak 2006, Trice & Beyer 1984).

Previously, painful rites of degradation had removed one of Newland's directors from a high status position because that director harboured resentments that had never been effectively processed. Consequently, there was an organisational loss after which rites of renewal, rites of concession and rites of intercession aided Newland's organisational reparation (Trice & Beyer 1984).

To keep that hard won restitution, as a manager, my bleat for communication was actually simple:

...if you've got a problem then say something.

Inevitably, there were times when interpretations and misinterpretations created consequences that required both immediate and deferred managerial attention. Consistently, however, in my own intercession style, I endeavoured to maintain the family peace. By using regular communication and consultation, I ensured that the right knowledge got out at the right time. Subsequently, the manifested incorrect versions of events swayed from inauthentic gossip to authentic information.

Rites of integration permit the venting of emotion through the temporary loosening of various norms (Trice & Beyer 1984). Interpretations and misinterpretations at Newland's organisational level were a way of receiving both right and wrong messages, sometimes based upon truth and knowledge and often upon inaccurate assumptions and gossip. All, however, had the potential to disturb organisational norms (Trice & Beyer 1984).

By constantly remaining in touch with Newland's workforce, I was able to develop and integrate communicating rites of intercession that could later help to reassert and reaffirm the usual organisational norms. Through conversation and listening, by contrasting what knowledge and information was explicitly important, pertinent and valuable and what knowledge could be disregarded as being irrelevant and unimportant, Newland's organisational survival was protected (Ambrosini, Bowman & Burton-Taylor 2007, Joshi, Sarker & Sarker 2007, Trice & Beyer 1984).

Physical distancing and body spacing between Newland's members usually demonstrated that one or more parties were unhappy with an arrangement and were signalling the need for renovation. Rites of degradation dissolve social identities and their power. The rites also defend group boundaries, redefine who belongs and who does not and reaffirms the social importance and value of the roles involved (Trice & Beyer 1984).

In group gatherings and meetings, physical distancing body language was demonstrated by placing oneself away from others or distancing, alienating one's participation in meetings, abdicating to be apart from the decision making, silent withdrawal to avoid discussion or create disharmony, constant gazing and/or seeking eye contact with other members. Sometimes constant vocalisations of the same aim, objective or desire, mustered support for a cause, point of view or the need for help.

The following extract from my field notes draws attention to constant gazing behaviour in order to muster support:

The Researcher believes that the person who did not agree seems to be assuming some kind of family role and ensuring the protection of those employees he deems to be in need of such safeguard. It was interesting to see the formation of the group, three versus one with three sitting closely together and one more isolated and also, the interaction between each group member who did agree when the person who did not agree was vocal. Each of the persons who did agree looked at each other on many occasions which from The Researchers point of view was to either seek support from or give support to.

In this constant gazing behaviour, looking at others, there appeared to be a means in which Newland's members would seek to make a gain that benefitted self only. Part of this self-seeking process could be to ensure that those who disagreed would, at some point in time, develop a willingness to acquiesce and capitulate to the communal demands. Whoever wanted to belong to the community would eventually relent (Trice & Beyer 1984).

Irritation and impatience were demonstrated when there was a concern about an action taken, the condition of the ongoing work processes or the attitude of another member. Annoyance manifested in red-faces, sitting in isolation from others, agitation, and on more than one occasion, abandoning the group meetings.

Additionally, in meetings, irritation and impatience were demonstrated when too much elaboration or embellishment was made on one single project matter and when too much attention was being paid to one member.

Some members indicated impatience and anxiety was greater when a 'highly focused zone' was needed in order to be able to cope with the volume and pressure of work. One congruent employee talked about a strong desire to leave the immediacy of the meeting room and return to the straightforward task of undertaking the work.

Temporarily dissolving existing integrated social roles, by means of physical withdrawal, helped Newland's members to draw the community's attention to a plight (Trice & Beyer 1984). Looking and gazing also helped Newland's members to muster the support each needed to ensure that their point of view and/or request was reciprocally accepted. Akin with rites of degradation, Newland's type physical distancing therefore, developed new group boundaries and re-affirmed the old by silently defending who belonged and who did not (Trice & Beyer 1984).

Pragmatically, distractions raised apprehension. Concerns surfaced when a Newland's member behaved in a distracting way and consequently as a result, the harmony of the group meeting suffered.

By creating distractions, sometimes a Newland's member gave the impression of wanting to dominate the group meeting. At these times, a desire to control the group through humorous distractions became evident. Making other members laugh kept the group attention upon the distracting individual and away from the serious focused content of the meeting.

For a long period of time, Newland's engineers had been managed by a leader who consistently failed to address domineering behaviours and at times, encouraged it. So early on, some Newland's members failed to recognise that creating distractions in group meetings in order to dominate, or alleviate fear, was no longer acceptable (Strachey et al 2001).

Rites of creation are the rites for establishing new roles and embedding them in ongoing social arrangements. These rites typically, therefore, help managers like myself, to create new and necessary boundaries and/or revise any tired old ones (Trice & Beyer 1984).

From experience and, more importantly, respect for the individual, I learned that when dealing with Newland's type mature engineers, who regularly and successfully survived the enduring conditions of fully operational hazardous plants worldwide and offshore, macho behaviours were best managed in ways that avoided directly confronting them.

By constructively and honestly highlighting the circumstances that manifested from the distraction, I was able to communicate to the member concerned, the impact that had been made upon the progress of the group, myself as the group leader and equally, other members. A congruent approach undoubtedly, aided me in this approach (Rogers 1951, 1980).

Rites of intercession helped me not to regard such personal conduct as a limitation of self but, as a behaviour that could eventually be worked through in terms of goals, aspirations and the recognition of particular strengths (Lopez et al 2006).

Admittedly though, sometimes my approach was successful and at other times, unsuccessful. Consistently and repeatedly highlighting and raising the salient points and the need for conformity, I was able to eventually pre-empt the types of behaviours that culminated in distractions that disturbed the focus of the group gatherings and/or meetings.

Rites of creation established new boundaries, refreshed tired old ones but also helped managers to constructively retreat from those boundaries and become a listening observer (Trice & Beyer 1984). Rites of intercession helped me to be that observing, listening and non-interfering manager, as and when necessary (Trice & Beyer 1984).

Naturally, some of Newland's employees made comparisons to other individuals who were employed in similar organisations. Staying put with Newland's however, was always a personal choice (Kivetz & Tyler 2007).

Sometimes envy was demonstrated during the process of making these comparisons, but it never extended beyond the immediate confines of the conversation into any form of confrontation with management.

If these types of conversations were in earshot, I always made a point of listening and observing in a non-intrusive way even though these were the conversations that I more often than not observed other members having without my involvement. More importantly, some of this information would later be appropriately filtered, then delivered and discussed directly with me (Neri 2006).

Significantly, the benefits of other employees in similar organisations were always brought to my attention perhaps for reasons of comparison, i.e., what benefits other employees got in SMEs elsewhere, compared to what benefits Newland's employees received.

Actual comparisons made between Newland's members, or envy of others, was never brought to my attention. I did, however, know that envy existed in Newland's workforce because I heard discussions that demonstrated its existence. Thankfully, no disturbing manifestation of envy that threatened Newland's organisational survival occurred (Trice & Beyer 1984).

Even though rites of integration help to perpetuate organisational survival through encouragement and reviving common feelings, at times, non-obtrusive styled rites of intercession helped Newland's management to remain aloof to certain topics that had potential to create disturbance.

Naturally, organisational equilibrium is disturbed when a change in argument, point of view, position or stance becomes proposed or apparent. Rites of intercession permit proposed change to manifest without the need for any conflict arising between decision makers and decision changers (Trice & Beyer 1984).

As in any organisation, there was a need for Newland's members to convincingly justify their argument for proposed change. As Newland's manager, I encouraged self-justification when changes to existing plans were set out to be modified. Reciprocally, Newland's workforce volunteered self-justification through communication and conversation thus, removing any managerial need to confront and create conflict (Trice & Beyer 1984).

Maintaining a 'relationship with the client' was always a testing ground. Realistically, the relationship with the client would always test trust and fortitude, as well as commercial vulnerability.

Meeting client deadlines and the keeping of timetables engendered difficulties when clients wanted 'rationalisations' carried out. Rationalisations were changes of options that the client directly instigated, during the course of the project work. Some changes were never initially contracted for or priced up therefore, rationalisations placed financial vulnerability upon Newland's.

Rationalisations were a way in which clients could abuse Newland's goodwill by requesting for work to be done free of charge or when extra work was carried out, that just slipped through the process unnoticed, such as:

Can you just do this?
Can you just put in this extra vessel.
We know it's out of scope but it would be useful for us.

Confidence was reduced when rationalisations emerged from the client or management interventions changed technical specifications especially, when production work was already underway and tasking processes had previously been determined. Undoubtedly, there was always a confrontational push against any changes, especially those that were deemed as unacceptable.

Even though remonstrations took place at the thought of the extra workload, demonstrating rejection, reluctance and dissatisfaction, Newland's members acted reciprocally, in the interests of the organisation, in order to preserve economic survival (Trice & Beyer 1984). A satisfied client would obviously pay their bill.

Individual or personal anxiety would arise in relation to the magnitude of the project work, especially when it was a pilot study that utilised new techniques, tools and the designing and implementation of new work methods and processes. Predictably, dealing with the unfamiliar and unresolved processes created anxiety in Newland's members.

Group and team anxiety was also invoked when the 3-D model deliverable was handed over to a client. As the model was placed outside the safety of the team boundaries, there was a sense of fear associated with 'having to let go' and place explicit trust in the completed organisational processes of production.

In the case of Newland's, proactive rites of intercession helped to reduce conflict arising by permitting the scrutinising of changes to alleviate workforce tension associated with those changes (Trice & Beyer 1984).

Following on, rites of renewal reassured organisational members that something was being done about the change problem. Aptly, rites of integration permitted the venting of fear, frustration and anxiety. Rites of enhancement spread good news about the success of the tasking arrangement and provided recognition for accomplishments and achievements (Trice & Beyer 1984).

Combined, these three rites helped to increase Newland's workforce confidence, achieve project aims and objectives and reassure members of their tasking success. Additionally, these rites demonstrate execution know-how and a manager's ability to confront inhibiting organisational and political obstacles (Hrebiniak 2006, Trice & Beyer 1984).

As Newland's manager, I generally, universally and unequivocally placed trust in the team processes and regarded emotional responses as a valued payback and faith in my leadership ability. Realistically though, I was a woman manager in an engineering world therefore, it was important for me to express reassurance in a positive way by speaking clearly, confidently and remaining assertive and supportive (Hambley, O'Neill & Kline 2007, Joshi, Sarker & Sarker 2007).

In order to regain a level of confidence at the organisational level, as Newland's manager, I reiterated and re-established existing boundaries and where necessary, established new ones.

Expectations dictate that any organisational manager is required to hold a comprehensive grasp on related work processes to facilitate the successful completion of tasks yet, team cohesion can be placed under threat by micro-managing team events (Brotheridge & Lee 2006, Collin 2006, Einarsen, Aasland & Skogstad 2007). No manager, however, is perfectly pitched. Sometimes I also had to rely upon reassuring feedback from Newland's teams that vital revenue generating project work was being correctly executed (Trice & Beyer 1984).

Pro-actively though, I could avoid Newland's members developing a sense of feeling abandoned by the influences of out of control external demands or a sense of powerlessness that could ultimately, have threatened the established processes of work and the generation of revenue (Trice & Beyer 1984).

Earlier on in this chapter, I stated that if rites of intercession were the means by which traditional authority could be placed upon a workforce by a manager, then there had to be a context in which those instructions were conveyed and received.

Newland's context was the concept of family, an organisational time and place when Newland's society interacted in ways that enabled both the formal undertaking of work and the reciprocal sharing of pleasurable events.

According to Brotheridge & Lee (2006), the concept of family is collective and encourages loyalty from the employee and also, from the employer. Undoubtedly, it was Newland's specific social inertia that enhanced a sense of community where Newland's good news could be divulged and in which familial relationships were valued and maintained (Gibb Dyer Jr 2010, Trice & Beyer 1984).

Earlier, a critical review of Trice & Beyer's (1984) rites and ceremonies permitted the invention of my own rite, rite of concession, a rite that helped to pre-empt any conflict arising in the first instance. Aided by the autonomous freedom offered in rites of concession, Newland's employees could establish and maintain their options.

Additionally, Trice & Beyer's (1984) rites of renewal improved the functioning of those choices. Both rites, however, reassured Newland's workforce that something was being done about any surfacing problems that had the potential to create conflict.

Squared up confrontation with Newland's workforce was never my management style and was to be avoided at all costs. Although, options based rites of concession helped to alleviate any conflict arising between management and workforce, it was however, rites of intercession that helped Newland's management to provide sufficient influence to implement organisational demands that simply had to be met (Trice & Beyer 1984). Consequently, when I could not use the law and/or the need for Newland's economic perpetuity as leverage, I used food to coerce the workforce.

Other interactions that encouraged commitment to the organisation and social processes stemmed from rites of integration and also, Newland's rites of intercession where the dimension of organisational feasting played a significant role (Meigs 1997, Thompson & Hassenkamp 2008, Trice & Beyer 1984).

In organisational feasting, Newland's members were both benefactor and beneficiary in the social enhancement offered during this occasion, that was not exclusively related to the ceremonial ritual of eating a cake icon (Thomson & Hassenkamp 2008, Trice & Beyer 1984).

Food was brought in that comprised of sandwiches, rolls, wraps, crisps, biscuits, fruit, and juice. There was an organisational unwritten rule, on both sides of Newland's managerial hedge: 'eat our food, take our pressure'. Twice as beneficial, this message worked both ways. In the consumption of food, Newland's members also used the opportunity to raise matters that were sensitive or 'organisationally taboo', as the food seemed to provide Dutch courage.

Over their free lunch, Newland's employees were much braver about asking for more holiday entitlement, a pay rise and/or a renegotiation of their overseas living allowance, when each held a sandwich or cream bun up to their mouths. As the question was being asked, the piece of food would quickly and discretely be thrust into an open mouth. Outwardly, the member that had raised the dilemma or asked the question, on the face of it, remained non-confrontational and non-belligerent.

At times, I felt like playing the game. Replying with a piece of food in my mouth provided me with the opportunity to 'managerially dodge' or elude any matters that I didn't wish to immediately deal with. More importantly though, as Newland's organisational manager, I never ignored the social frankness given to management staff during organisational feasting, even though the message was subdued by food.

'Successful muffling' was a ritualised behaviour during organisational feasting that worked well for Newland's employees and one that did produce intended, technical consequences of practical importance (Trice & Beyer 1984).

A gain was always to be had for Newland's management in the giving of food. Providing either a free lunch or one eleventh of a chocolate covered swiss roll, masquerading as an insect, produced more leadership influence and workforce cooperation than any amount of encouragement, war mongering or threats (Berson & Sosik 2007, Thompson & Hassenkamp 2008).

In rites of intercession, as Newland's manager, I occasionally but intentionally used food to coerce the workforce into a cooperative state. Additional to this act of wilful determination by myself as Newland's manager, the joint community reciprocally used food in one other way, which was 'to disassociate ourselves from a sense of loss'.

When an employee had decided to leave and had handed in their notice, 'the free lunch' was provided during the week in which the member was leaving.

Ceremoniously, the ritualised sharing of this food was undertaken as a farewell gesture.

Again, the sharing of food was a successful set of behaviours that did produce intended, technical consequences of practical importance. Akin with rites of renewal, the food ritual reassured Newland's other members that the loss was significantly recognised but that also, a replacement member would be found (Trice & Beyer 1984).

Within Newland's joint community, there was an innate capacity and ability to predetermine, anticipate, understand and accommodate the impact of the adverse changes, directly associated with the sense of loss of a member. Consequently, in the farewell gesture food ritual, there was always a small glimmer of hope that the member who had planned to depart Newland's employment might just be sufficiently influenced enough to change their mind, especially if that member was popular.

As Newland's members gathered around to ritualise the leaving and consume the buffet and/or cake, the more direct, cringe worthy vocalisations of what each member felt about the circumstances of the employee leaving, would begin to surface and wrangle. In the ambience of a ritual, this was 'the group voice speaking' on behalf of all others, pre-determined by the intention to share food and rattle the leaving member.

Each member said exactly what they wanted to say, whether it seemed caustic, harsh and insensitive (Mishna, Muskat & Scharness 2002, Thompson & Hassenkamp 2008, Trice & Beyer 1984). Akin with a rites of passage in reverse, the humiliating and deliberately alarming remarks facilitated the beginning of the separation of the member from Newland's employment and hence, the transition from member to ex-member (Trice & Beyer 1984).

Both new rites of concession and rites of intercession permitted and facilitated this separation and transition (Trice & Beyer 1984). Newland's remaining members retained the freedom of choice, concession, to deliberately create tension and alarm in the employee who was leaving. Purposely, Newland's management intentionally remained aloof to the ritualised 'scaring' and did not interfere or intercede, in any way whatsoever, with the process.

In this ritualised 'scaring', the sharing and consumption of food and/or cake seemed to salt rather than sweeten the tongue. Diplomacy and 'successful muffling' was set aside as interactions became a more pressurised event. A combined group effort vocalised both agreement and disagreement with the member's decision to leave and often warnings were made in relation to consequences:

An experience…of a culture shock.
It won't be like this you know.

A deliberate attempt was made to instil fear and create a perception that a new organisational world would be less caring and safe and perhaps:

Well, you should change your mind.

Using food as a creative social instrument, Newland's joint community could successfully put combined adverse pressure on any member, in any situation (Meigs 1997, Thompson & Hassenkamp 2008).

Newland's joint communal attempt aimed to make the leaving individual aware of what was being capitulated. In turn, this helped the residual members to reinforce the value of their own organisational positions, reaffirm their social importance and redefine who remained and belonged, akin with rites of degradation (Trice & Beyer 1984).

In addition to my regular attempts to use food to aid my managerial role, Newland's managing director also used food as a social instrument (Meigs 1997).

For thirty years, every Easter, Newland's owner/managing director gave each member of the workforce a chocolate bunny rabbit and every Christmas, a bottle of champagne. When asked why this was specifically done, the response was:

I thought it would be nice for people.

According to Trice & Beyer (1984), rites of enhancement help individuals to augment their social identities and more importantly, their power. The rites also help to provide public recognition of individuals for their accomplishments and to motivate others to make exemplary efforts.

In the case of Newland's managing director, whether it was the chocolate bunny rabbit or the champagne, this engineer was most certainly a popular, admired and well respected high status organisational member (Pfeffer 2010, Trice & Beyer 1984).

The next proactive dimension to the pre-cursor rites of intercession I have is called Sofa Talk.

To speak to Newland's engineers, I sometimes used Sofa Talk as a communicating technique. Using Sofa Talk, I could quickly and conveniently address Newland's engineers without having to arrange a formal meeting, disturb them too much or create unnecessary conflict by seemingly delaying the undertaking of work (Trice & Beyer 1984).

In their office section, Newland's engineers had a soft sofa area where coffee, lunch breaks and interludes from work pressures were taken. Each and every engineer made this sofa space their own. If I wanted to draw their attention towards me, without having to even speak, I would sit on the sofas and wait to be noticed.

From that vantage point, I could see into two offices and witness the employees who worked in them. If I remained there too long, I knew that these Newland's engineers would become uncomfortable with my presence. Eventually, it was not long before intrigue took over and nearly all of Newland's engineers gathered around me to ask me what I wanted.

Even though I was never given the indication of being actually unwelcomed or disrespected, I was most definitely given the signs that an intrusion had taken place. A withering look was enough. So rarely did I venture onto Newland's engineer's soft sofas, unless I wanted to provide to them, in their domain, information on a less than formal basis. In this area, and in this way, I could address them all at once, spread news about the organisation and save myself time, energy and vocal chords in the process (Trice & Beyer 1984).

Sofa Talk was very much a combination of gentle but effective rites of degradation and rites of renewal that equalised power between both manager and member. Intrusion was the social interaction that opened up the opportunity for discussion and also, the means by which both the power of the manager and the engineers was reconstituted.

According to Trice & Beyer (1984) rites of degradation can dissolve power and reaffirm the social importance and the value of roles. Rites of renewal legitimate and reinforce existing systems of power and authority.

So at the beginning of Sofa Talk, the manager would dissolve power held over the sofas by the engineers by intruding into their space and sitting on the sofa, uninvited. At the end of Sofa Talk, the engineers would renew and reinforce their power over the sofas, as the manager was given the indication that although temporarily accepted, it was time to leave (Trice & Beyer 1984).

Certainly, I never lingered there. Despite the unease sometimes associated with Sofa Talk, I did not modify nor discontinue my use of this ritualised disturbance that I deliberately created. I continued with Sofa Talk because I found it practically helpful, as the preciousness that Newland's engineers retained about their soft sofa area, I could certainly use to my advantage as well (Trice & Beyer 1984).

One intended consequence of rites of creation is to provide managers with the opportunity to use personal judgement to assess if their ritual behaviours should be continued, modified or discontinued (Trice & Beyer 1984). I regularly assessed and determined that Sofa Talk did work for me.

Pragmatically, when there was a need for me to formerly address all of Newland's engineers, I was accepted and listened to. Perplexity, however, became apparent when I simply just turned up and placed myself in this area, without giving any notice on my impending arrival.

Although, rites of renewal legitimate and reinforce existing systems of power and authority that helped Newland's engineers to reclaim their space, this was my way of making my presence felt, without the need for confrontation (Trice & Beyer 1984).

In terms of achieving desired and other related organisational consequences most associated with rites of creation, using a rites of intercession intervention of my own, as a means of communication, preserved my own time and energy (Trice & Beyer 1984). I could undoubtedly count on the fact that if I sat on Newland's engineers purple sofas, I would not be ignored.

Though I deliberately created a short disturbance, Sofa Talk helped me to more subtly communicate Newland's managerial needs without having to set up formal boundaries. Authority could be softly asserted by a manager who was willing to become vulnerable in order to gain that authority and provide important information to the workforce.

Conversely, just as I tentatively and deliberately intruded upon the precious confines of Newland's engineers soft purple sofa domain, Newland's members reciprocally encroached upon mine, the doorway of the office, that I shared with Newland's managing director.

In my field notes, I referred to this phenomenon using a simple phrase:

Vertical conversations in the doorway.

Explicitly, 'vertical conversations in the doorway' were when a member would come to the office door and remain standing in the portal of the doorway, not entering the office, but remaining on the boundaries of it. This member would then would strike up a conversation with the individuals residing in the office, who were already seated and would remain seated, throughout the course of the conversation.

Comparably, Vertical Talk mirrored the nuisance factor of Sofa Talk. Admittedly, I found these doorway conversations as an unwelcomed distraction. I could display irritation and discontent at the apparent lack of regard for the disturbances that took place, whilst the vocalisations were sustained, even though I knew these were seen as important to the group processes. I did however, give the conversations their appropriate credence and regard because of their relevance and significance to Newland's ongoing commercial activities (Rogers 1951, 1980, Trice & Beyer 1984).

Nearly every day, throughout the course of the day, Newland's members would conduct conversations in this manner with myself, the managing director and between other organisational members.

Like I created disturbance during Sofa Talk, Newland's members were able to enhance their power by using Vertical Talk, dominating the director's office doorway to spread either good or bad news (Trice & Beyer 1984).

As Vertical Talk worked for Newland's workforce, it could be regarded as a reaffirming of their social importance towards seniors and the value of their involved roles, typical of an expressive consequence of rites of degradation (Trice & Beyer 1984).

Moreover, Vertical Talk could have been a way of remaining dominant in the conversation and retaining autonomous charge over the conversation and the topic, especially if the discussion took place between a manager and a subordinate.

Additionally, these types of conversation could just have been a question of wanting to be assertive. My field note observations reflected that curiosity:

To gain one's own way
and/or:
Win the argument.

Possibly, the content of the conversation could be determined by unequal positions.

Sometimes seen in highly technical situations, one member has a greater depth of knowledge compared to another. Often, Newland's members lacked the opportunity to have a conversation that held the mutuality of a balanced or an equal view.

Rites of enhancement spread good news about an organisation and recognition of individual accomplishments and achievements (Trice & Beyer

1984). Certainly, the spot in the doorway was a place to which important topics were brought by Newland's members.

Specific requests were made that related to the negotiation of certain terms, the pricing of work, asking of permissions for the use of money, recognition of certain achievements and the desire to tentatively address sensitive issues, all dictated by personal need and organisational demands.

These important topics were freely brought to the doorway, to the attention of Newland's directors, who did not impose rules of entrance or determined too strongly defined areas of territory in need of protection. One director, however, mirrored the nuisance factor similarly linked with Sofa Talk. In spite of that director's response, bargaining in the doorway entrance certainly took place.

Even so, bargaining aside, the territorial boundaries were not freely crossed without permissions. Rites of enhancement augment the social identities of individuals and their power (Trice & Beyer 1984). Vertical Talk could be also be considered as a form of obedience and compliance, respect for the status of the individuals and the office where these individuals worked that was only to be entered into by invitation (Hodges & Geyer 2006, Trice & Beyer 1984).

At the beginning of this chapter, I laid out three salient points that Trice & Beyer (1984) say all managers should consider. First, practicing managers need to learn how to evaluate their rites and second, how to use personal judgement to continue, modify or discontinue their ceremonial activities. Last of all, manages are invited to invent new rites to provide information on how their organisational structural arrangements are working.

In this chapter, utilising Newland's organisational activities and the workforce patterns of behaviour, I have been able to address these three salient points.

I have invented a new rite called rites of intercession, as a subsystem of rites of creation. To embed their roles in ongoing social arrangements, if organisational managers use moderate intervention styles and techniques and take full note of employee interactions that follow, then this rite manifests potential to help the individual member, groups and also the involved organisation.

I have provided an explanation of how rites of intercession worked within Newland's. I have given an account of the context of family and employee patterns of behaviour, including organisational feasting, Sofa Talk and Vertical

Talk. Additionally, and where appropriate, I have compared these patterns of behaviour to other rites.

The chapter that follows is the Discussion.

Chapter 9
Discussion

In this chapter, I evaluate the study. I provide an argument for the originality of the research because it confirms that Trice & Beyer (1984) typology of rites exist in organisations like Newland Limited. I show that the typology can be extended by cultural activities that exist in the unique settings of small medium enterprises, like Newland Limited. I will then address the research validity, justification and contribution. I also provide an overview of the process. I include the Table of Results, Illustration Number TYP-01, Trice & Beyer (1984) Typology of Rites: Extended by Newland's Cultural Events.

Evaluation of the Study

Ethical consideration was an important factor for the study. Even though I was the researcher inside Newland's, I was also a director, manager and a key worker.

In the study, there were considerations that needed to be taken into account because the presence of a researcher also impacted upon the workforce. This research was focused upon Newland's organisational community that included me as an organisational worker and member. My vantage point, therefore, was different from the ethnographers who have to place themselves in locations where they can observe, without interference, their subject matter (Malinowski 1922).

Letters of consent were gained from Newland's owner and each of its employees. Newland's directors and organisational members raised no objections about the data collection which was conducted quietly and privately. Consequently, research accessibility was made possible because I had the benefit of being (a) an employee of Newland's (b) a key worker (c) a part of the whole work group and (d) research resilient enough to know that I could generate data from Newland's organisational events.

Belonging to the organisation being ethnographically studied, I had freedom to collect research data as it manifested in Newland's day-to-day cultural activities. As ethnography both describes and interprets the characteristics of a particular social setting, with the intention of capturing its cultural diversity and the multiplicity of its voices (Thomson & Hassenkamp 2008) the data collection was not intentionally hindered by access however, other factors had to be considered.

I was an established group member who made an organisational contribution in a directive and leading role. Often the incongruence of group secrets kept management in the dark as only information that had been streamlined by a sifting process was provided.

The true naturalist researcher approach was compromised by my role as a researcher, who set out to play a low-key minimalistic presence, secondly compromised and compounded by the directorial and management role that must act as leader, information giver and assessor of other employees, as each acted out their duties in direct relation to economic, strategic and organisational demands. For the sake of good ethnographic work, I had to balance the roles of participating organisational member and researcher.

As I observed the everyday happenings within Newland's organisational village, I was never alone. As I watched my work colleagues and made my field notes however, I did feel a sense of foreboding and apprehension to which Malinowski (1922) alludes when he was dumped on the beach of an island somewhere in the Western Pacific. As I made my field notes I felt alone. Yet, I was not alone because I knew that, from a directorial and managerial point of view, I was also being carefully watched.

Remaining focused and sticking with the research ethos was desired consistency however, I did always have to consider that there was not an alternative option surfacing with something new and fresh being brought to light. According to Silverman (2005), the professional researcher must have an ability to make all of the necessary changes as and when the research breaks arise from what is visible and also from what is hidden. In the case of Newland's, some interactions were hidden.

There were times when Newland's directors and members held conversations or conducted activities that I did not witness. These blind activities could have relevance to the project but are excluded, as I was unable to observe them, even though they were natural occurrences within Newland's social system. From a research point of view, these concealed processes remained elusive to the research (Silverman 2005, 2011).

I did have to take into full consideration that the closed rank approach that I sometimes experienced could have been linked to a fear of a degree of personal exposure to a managing member, which could later be associated with a compromising of employment conditions. It was, however, more realistic and highly likely that there was just a total lack of interest in what I was research doing as participation in the project was voluntary and did not form part of the research participants employment contract.

As I developed my data, I offered to show it to Newland's employees to gain their feedback. This, in turn, would ideally help to determine how accurately my findings represented the inside organisational cultural phenomena of Newland's thus testing its validity. Predictably, there was no response. I, therefore, have to admit that in my role as a researcher, I knew I was working around disinterested research participants.

It is a difficulty and a justifiable concern for any researcher to find that they have to deal with disinterested research participants, especially if the research participants have previously given informed consent to the research project. I also felt the Malinowski (1922) type gloom, hopelessness and despair, however I made absolutely certain that my attempts at collecting relevant material was fruitful. The touchstone of my own experience would be a valuable indicator for a potentially successful research endeavour as opposed to pursuing the elusive abstract (Strauss & Corbin 1998).

It was in my best interests to continue with my established research plan and negotiate the difficulties of capturing the uniqueness of Newland's internal society and its organisational action (Alvesson 2002).

Existing Typology of Rites Extended by Newland's Cultural Events

I reiterate Trice & Beyer's (1984) admission that their typology of rites is logically incomplete. Conducting this study has identified that Trice & Beyer's (1984) types of rites existed inside a small medium enterprise called Newland Limited. Consequently, examples of Newland's organisational activities, specific to the work setting, could be compared with Trice & Beyer's (1984) existing typology of rites.

Using the typology of rites as a framework, yielded insights and meaning into Newland's organisational activities. Similarly, as given in the Newland's example, rites of passage covered the recruitment training and introduction of new staff. Rites of degradation removed one of Newland's directors from office. Consequently, rites of conflict reduction managed the subsequent organisational dysfunction after which rites of renewal repaired the organisational damage.

The organisation of rites of creation aided the manifestation of a new organisational format that divested difficult circumstances to the past and opened up the opportunity for a new era to begin. A better relationship between management and workforce was enabled through balancing power and authority with popularity. Simultaneous rites of integration and rites of enhancement promoted Newland's later organisational format that manifested in the successful undertaking of work activities and the celebration of meaningful occasions.

Additionally, in their argument for the extension of their typology of rites, Trice & Beyer (1984) raise the point that rites, conducive to change, already may have been invented and could be being practiced by managers in some modern day organisations. Hence, this type of information is valuable to other organisations. In my research, I have been able to use Trice & Beyer's (1984) existing typology of rites to highlight Newland's organisational activities and in doing so, develop two new rites.

By developing two new rites, I have been able to make an original contribution to the existing body of organisational research. At the time of writing up my own study, no other full or part-time participant observer had conducted similar research and provided an insight into a small medium enterprise, like Newland Limited, as an inside key worker and a researcher of its activities at work. This point substantiates my own claim for originality of this work.

Consequently, this study adds ingredient to Trice & Beyer's (1984) typology of rites and confirms their original finding that additional types of rites are being practiced by managers, are undiscovered and worthy of research.

Newland's rituals, based in technical, practical behaviours produced intended consequences when associated with scoping, pricing and procuring paid work. Obvious negotiation, subtle renegotiation and pricing adjustments to meet client budgets produced financial results and profit for the company.

Specific to Newland's work setting, rites of passage associated with new recruits introduced the work environment and the practical use of Newland's site equipment and bespoke engineering computer software. A smooth integration process was achieved and organisational disruption lessened.

Rites of integration associated with work activities perpetuated Newland's organisational survival through vital task accomplishment. Additionally, meaningful occasions were celebrated and bonding occurred in the consumption of cake.

Because Newland's rituals and ceremonials produced the intended technical consequences, organisational survival was derived from these rituals taking place. Obviously, the output of such rituals produced financial results as Newland's traded successfully between 1983 and 2009. Organisational perpetuity was maintained.

Other new rites helped both management and the workforce. The first new rite contained in Newland's Limited, rites of concession, monitored and reviewed the status of work activities and organisational members. The manifest consequences of rites of concession permitted freedom in relation to selective choices defined by Newland's members. By allowing some freedom for organisational members, rites of concession helped to prevent conflict arising by offering agreed levels of autonomy. Rites of concession, therefore, pre-empts Trice & Beyer's (1984) rites of conflict reduction.

The second new rite is rites of intercession. Management styles and interventions, as rites of intercession, are rites that are conducive to change. A small medium enterprise is a legal entity that cannot thrive without corporate governance, directorship, successful management, and a willing workforce. Therefore, in any organisation, managers are required to offer creative influence, effective guidance and adequate supervision.

My rites of intercession highlighted the manifest consequences of my own managerial role where it was my direct responsibility to build, maintain and perpetuate inter-reliant affiliations upon which the organisation could become co-dependent.

When I set out to conduct this research my overall aim was to reveal Newland's naturally occurring organisational cultural events undertaken by personnel in their work setting. To do this, I devised three objectives, however the prime question stayed relevant "what are the threads that bind us together". I admit that I knew that certain functions and processes existed within Newland's organisational formats. Throughout the course of my involved working day, those people and processes were continually visible to me and manipulated and influenced by me.

When I started the research, Newland's was already a well-established SME, a legal entity ongoing concern that was located in an office building, inside which its employees all collectively gathered and worked in groups.

I reviewed in Kessler (2006) that organisational success does not go necessarily to the firms that set up and retain the best information systems, but to the firms that make the best use of what they know and learn. Newland's own commercial organisational success was dependent upon its workers having the ability to work and function together and retain a legal, stable existence throughout the ups and downs of the processes that were associated with that success.

Joint effort was the linked organisational strength that contributed towards the collective output however, Newland's directors and workers had to continually balance the commercially lucid and the sometimes nonsensical organisational change (Lapp & Carr 2006). In order for this to function and return success, no one person could operate as an independent individual just doing a job in singular but loyal isolation. All Newland's organisational members were expected to be able to work together in combined involvement as an instrumental and effective workforce.

I was one of two of the founding members that set up a small medium enterprise, Newland's Limited, in 1983. Back then, Turner (1983) already had drawn attention to how the use of grounded theory in organisational research keeps the researcher close to the creative and intellectual centre of their investigations, thus making research into organisations an exciting and intellectually satisfying process.

Also, Das T. Hari (1983) was seeking out improvements in the holistic, inductive and naturalistic characters of organisational research to widen the more restricted qualitative research that had prior, just focused on specific research areas and settings.

Through the conduct of all of the human relationships and interactions in the everyday activities and the application of duty, Newland's employees produced an output that was commercially viable and revenue generating for the company and its shareholders. I knew that we were successful at what we did because as a limited company trading entity, Newland's had stood the test of time, 1983 to present day, so of it and within it, I organised what I regarded as an exciting research opportunity.

Validity

It can be seen from the narrative that Newland's cultural characteristics, set in terms of rites and ceremonials (Trice & Beyer 1984) generated through the grounded theory process are representative of the inner workings of a small medium enterprise.

With the exception of the ceremonial activities that are pertinent to Newland's, such as the ritual consumption of the chocolate cake and the Crystal Celebrations, the other organisational characteristics might be expected to be seen in other organisational setups (Trice & Beyer 1984, 1993).

It is apparent in the research that rites and ceremonials are actively at work inside Newland's organisational setting. The recruitment of new staff, the undertaking of work, organisational dysfunction followed by resolution, management relationships, skills, leadership and guidance are all reported upon. Consequently, the results demonstrate that the three research objectives have been met.

In this organisation study, I have subsequently revealed, described and explained how the individuals and groups worked together; negatively and positively. I have generated an understanding of what processes are at work in the group(s) and I have revealed and made known the functions, methods and processes of the groups and the underlying "threads that binds us together".

Today, and spanning Newland's lifetime, we still see research interest emerging on the understanding of organisational culture. It is still defined as one of the major issues in academic research and education, in organisation theory as well as in management practice, because the cultural dimension is central in all aspects of organisational life (Alvesson 2002, 2012).

Justification

Justification for organisational cultural research like my own is based upon the common sense fact that SMEs, like Newland's Limited, are rich sources of organisational, strategic, functional, cultural, and social information just waiting to be plucked from their orchards of economic existence and researched (Fineman, Gabriel & Sims 2010). Organisational ethnography involves research into these organisations of modern day society (Eberle & Maeder 2011, Silverman 2011).

According to Eberle & Maeder (2011), work in the field of organisational ethnography has markedly expanded in recent years alongside an increased focus on the use of qualitative methods and ethnography more generally. In addition, the use of grounded theory also makes a contribution to organisational ethnography as many of the Glaser & Strauss (1967) approaches are still used today.

Earlier on, in the literature review chapter, I made reference to Kessler (2006) and Kessler & Bailey (2007) who conclude that the research spotlight in terms of organisational wisdom, human management and strategic implications has been narrowly placed upon ethical behaviour, corporate social responsibility and strategic complexities leaving out the other factors associated with the organisational cultures. These authors raise the call for new research perspectives and approaches to be taken on the behaviours within organisations, as well as the stewardship of such organisations.

In addition, I refer to Muncey's (2010) view on the increased creation of autoethnographies. Yet, in spite of this increase, we still see very few studies of organisational culture within small to medium-sized enterprises existing and even fewer use ethnographic methods to explore the complex phenomenon of these working environments (Brooks 2008, Fineman, Gabriel & Sims 2010, Gingrich-Philbrook 2005). More autoethnographies, therefore, should be conducted because obviously too few studies on culture use ethnographic methods to explore the potential of these common organisational environments.

My literature review shows that Storey (1994) says there still remains the need for organisational researchers to focus on studies of universal definitions of organisational cultures within SMEs. Due to the complexities of organisational cultures and their unique standings within the organisation that they apply to, the establishment of a universal definition for such cultures could be too complex to organisation.

Peel (2006) is ambitiously seeking out the organisational researcher who can help to provide the universal definition for an SME. Although, my work may not necessarily provide a universal definition of an SME, as an organisational researcher, I was able to conduct a study on an organisational culture within an SME, Newland's. My research justification also stems from the earlier review of Schein (2010).

It can be seen that the Schein (2010) focus is on the organisational interior where it defines organisational culture as a pattern of shared basic assumptions that have been learned by a group, as it problem solved its needs for external adaptation and internal integration, that include the influences of leadership.

In line with these authors, I have given illustration to the unique complexities that can exist within the functional and social cultural interiors of an SME, Newland's. I, therefore, add ingredient to the definitions for organisational culture and their shared and reciprocal patterns of working and thus, the domain of organisational wisdom.

I justify my research finally by re-visiting the work of Trice & Beyer (1984) who have appealed to organisational researchers to conduct studies that place the micro-detail of their organisational phenomena into a framework concept of culture. Later, Trice & Beyer (1993) extend these concepts by offering the opportunity for organisational researchers to review the cultural processes that underlie much of the daily activities of modern day organisations.

Their work makes reference to substance, a network of meanings, from which practices emerge that express and communicate those meanings. These authors state clearly that they do not expect that their typology of six major characteristics of organisational culture is exhaustive, but it is a very good starting point from which organisational researchers could add refinements and enhancements.

In particular, there has been an increase in the focus of the use of qualitative methods to gain understandings of the work practices used in software engineering based SMEs, the genre in which Newland's traded (Bodan, Muller & Nett 2011).

Contributing

The literature showed that organisational wisdom is an emerging research domain because it reflects the complex, diverse, fluid and interdependent aspects and realities of business climates. Included in this, is the individual wisdom linked with organisational structure, culture and leadership (Kessler 2006).

From the point of view of my research, using organisational ethnography and constructivist grounded theory method, I justify an opportunity to further reveal, illustrate and describe Newland's internal functions and processes and its organisational ways of working and communing and make a contribution in line with the calls for the more within research that still exists.

My work does not focus solely on certain narrowed aspects of Newland's organisational functionality as it provides a wider inside picture of the functional and social internal workings of Newland's Limited derived from the use of constructivist grounded theory (Charmaz 2006, Das T. Hari 1983, Kessler 2006, Kessler & Bailey 2007, Turner 1983). In doing so, it adds to the Eberle & Maeder (2011) reference to the ongoing expansion of organisational ethnography and the Muncey (2010) recognition that few ethnographic studies exist of organisational cultures within SMEs.

As per Storey (1994), I can offer up the functional and social complexities of Newland's to support a need to focus on studies that will make a contribution to defining organisational cultures within SMEs, yet because of their unique complexities, not necessarily universally define them (Peel 2006).

In placing the micro-detail of Newland's organisational culture into a socially organisational framework of work using rites and ceremonials, I am able to satisfy the call for research from Trice & Beyer (1984, 1993) who request that researchers arrange their organisational phenomena into a framework concept of culture and identify the cultural processes that underlie much of the daily activities and complexities of modern day organisations.

As my work focuses on the organisational interior of Newland's, the within, I am able to demonstrate the shared basic assumptions of its members, patterns of working, including the influences of my own leadership (Schein 2010).

Finally, in disclosing the social organisation of Newland's, I am also able to illustrate the more detailed work practices used in a software engineering based SME (Bodan, Muller & Nett 2011).

Because of the diverse activities that are included in this research, this study will add to the emerging research domain of organisational wisdom.

Overview

From the data that I gathered and analysed in the grounded theory approach, what emerged was a depiction of the "organise us" in terms of Newlands organisational characteristics or an answer to my original researcher question "what are the threads that bind us together" or more appropriately "Newland Limited together".

What I identified related with Newland's social organisation, a framework system that perpetuated its economic survival. I questioned if, because in my role as an employed person, director of the company and manager, that this survival concept was already prevalent in my being because that was what I was employed to do, to ensure that everything that mattered business wise was well taken care of. So there was already an emotive structure in place in which I was functioning, therefore the presence of an economical perception that survival was imperative, could have coloured my research view of what was happening.

I justify this in my role as the researcher to say that at some point in this research the sense of organisational survival undoubtedly would have raised its head and could not be ignored in terms of the research study of a small medium enterprise and the organisation of the activities and processes of doing things in organisations (Fineman, Gabriel & Sims 2010).

Likened to a river, viewed from a helicopter above, looking calm, smooth and tranquil, yet the closer view shows the turbulence and choppy waters, Fineman, Gabriel & Sims (2010) encourage organisational researchers, as people who know the river waters well, to present their stories and learn from their adventure. I likened Newland's to a swan swimming on a lake, serenely sat on crystal water, yet paddling like mad underneath!

I take this justification one step further by also stating that all organisations are set up to survive and are regulated as a legally organisational concern that aspires for an economic future and I do not know of any company that strives for failure rather than success.

I followed the grounded theory principle of dealing with the data as it emerged and Newland's organisational characteristics were revealed. It was the ways in which I unravelled those complexities, represented them and reported these unique organisational characteristics that would be important to my ethnographic success.

From Newland's unique organisational cultural characteristics (Fineman, Gabriel & Sims 2010, Schein 2010, Trice & Beyer 1984) all of what emerged from the grounded theory has been encompassed from the interactions of the caring human being, to the involvement of being a group member, through to the commitment and obligations of being employed.

In summary, Newland's organisational framework could organise the whole of its workforce in order to do its bidding. Springing the legal entity into organisational cultural life, we could manifest what needed to be done, we could man up the work, we could commune in doing so, we knew what we were doing and we could gain knowledge from doing it, we could interact with each other.

I could manage and lead when and where I needed to govern and we could do everything that was necessary for our corporate governance, commercial undertaking, production output and ultimately, the economic survival of an organisational swan. Sometimes we could just celebrate and eat cake and have access to and the fun of using the latest computer technology that we didn't have to buy for ourselves.

I believed that I could design and develop a research project based upon my personal experiences at work as a director, a manager, a leader, a group member and a close working colleague of the individuals with whom I worked. Contained within Newland's organisational environment were the everyday activities that were worthy of research recognition and the effort that would be required to fulfil that objective.

I set out to discover those everydayness activities connected with what we all compliantly did to ensure that the medium-sized enterprise in which we all worked would be continuously organisationally successful. I affectionately thought of these ways of doing as—the threads that bound us together.

Our organisational cultural characteristics were very unique to our SME setup. It did not surprise me that what I identified also related with our organisational survival. I wondered that because in my role as an employed person, director of the company and manager that this was always prevalent in my being anyway because that was what I was employed to do, to ensure that everything that mattered business wise was well taken care of.

So there was already an emotive structure in place in which I was functioning anyway and the presence of my perception that survival was imperative could have coloured my view of what was happening. I justify this in my role as the researcher to say that at some point in this research the sense of organisational survival undoubtedly would have raised its head and could not be ignored.

Out of this research something sadly also emerged for me. I felt that some of my work as a manager did fall below organisational expectations. I arrived at the feeling that The Group of Uncertainty had failed. I introduced this group because after we lost someone whose management style was different to mine, there was a need to open up a place where our employees could discuss matters that they felt were in need of discussion, comparison or support.

Unfortunately, the group space never seemed to be used for that, there were blank faces that said very little that left me with a sense of loss of purpose for even having the group at all. I would like to add here as well that although I used the group as one of the groups in which I collected my research data, I did not introduce the group for that purpose.

The GUD group was introduced for the purpose to assist the company only, its employees and the actions and progresses that were required to make the company operate successfully. I did this in the role of a director and a manager. I have mentioned earlier that the group had the ability and versatility to use itself for different purposes as long as the main purpose of survival was maintained.

I had a different sense associated with it as well which was a gloomy feeling that the first half of the meeting was successful and the second half of the meeting had failed. This question I raised with the managing director in an email and the response of the managing director is given here:

Email, 20 April 2009 9:54, Response to "A Research Question: Has The Monday Morning Group Failed":

I am sorry that you feel that the second half of the Monday Morning group had failed. I disagree with this assumption of yours. Engineers do not normally like to discuss very much else than technical/progress subjects in front of the group and their peers. What has happened is they have taken their feelings away with them from the meeting and have to trusted colleagues discussed and taken action on the subjects brought up at the meetings. This has produced actions that then benefitted the company by the colleagues taking successful action without going back to the group meeting to discuss these actions.

It is also the loss of the group that these were not taken up at the meeting. It also could mean that the group was happy with the results and actions of the first part of the meeting and therefore, did not believe that they had to say anything from the first part of the meeting. They are very content with the way you have run the meetings and did not need to respond to anything when requested to do so in the second part of the meeting. I hope this helps you in carrying on with the meeting knowing it is a constructive part of the company method of working.

My view on this is that although, it can be seen from the managing director's response email that there was also a perception that the second half of the meeting was a success as staff members used "Outside Groups" to "take their feelings" and discuss related matters, there was also the sense that there was a lack of trust in the leadership of the meeting. There could also have been an apprehension that the meeting was deemed as being unsafe and staff members preferred to hold other discussions elsewhere.

The group became outmoded by the other groups that naturally came into existence and therefore the Group of Uncertain Diversity had no purpose attached to it at all.

I cared very much about my work, protecting the company as an ongoing concern in my role as an officer of it. I cared about my work colleagues, wishing to be a part of the whole group structures and being accepted in both roles as director, manager and an individual at work.

I cared about doing this internal research and ensuring that the level of commitment that was required I could fulfil. At the start, I was fifty-three years of age and took on the commitment to do the study with full consideration of the rigorous work that would be involved and to be honest, I wondered if I would have the stamina for it.

I also placed the same level of commitment in my work effort, yet I often felt unaccepted by the rest of the natives which sometimes left me bereft of any sense of belonging. There was my own personal motivation to succeed and I would not deliberately try to undo any of those processes that enabled me to aspire for success and not failure. I could yield to the requirements of the obligation that was needed to do all of my work and have a voice in doing so.

To sum up the whole of this, it is necessary to address work where and how these findings would and could fit into existing research. The diversity of this study on an SME called Newland Limited will add to the existing body of literature on organisational wisdom. Additionally, some of the content might interest researchers who study discrete aspects of organisations like gender, groups, knowledge management, leadership, teams, team working and how virtual teams function.

This study has also considered the work of Malinowski, Heidegger, Bion and the founding grounded theorists Glaser & Strauss. Primarily though, the organisational cultural characteristics I have associated with the work of Trice & Beyer (1984, 1993).

When I made commitment to Newland's in 1983, I knew we could succeed at this new enterprise through combining both business and personal ambition, giving it the required level of commitment and working hard using all of our previous experiences and paying attention to any new opportunities and developments that signposted themselves along our road to achieving success. I left my position with Newlands Limited in 2009.

Dissemination

There will be no opportunity to disseminate this work in Newland's because in 2009, I retired as one of the primary directors. Its content, however, would still remain useful to Newland's if the current owner declared an interest.

Newland's was a small medium enterprise of longevity and financial integrity. Between 1983 and 2009, it held innovative creative people in employment and developed market leading 3-D engineering data services. Because this study is based upon the commercial activities of Newland's and its cultural events, it would remain relevant to other organisations who could, in the future, allocate interest, time, finances and resources to conduct internal research.

If private or public enterprise, large, medium or small demonstrated interest in gaining further insight into their organisational cultures, this type of study could also address problematic discrete aspects. For instance, leadership issues that contribute to dysfunction within the workplace can create serious grievances. Consequently, employees under grievance, who set out to sue are an organisational financial risk.

Highlighting early damage done by non-constructive leadership approaches could lessen disruption to employee **well-being** thus, reducing the need for the allocation of time and monetary resources to the grievance and legal process. The early identification of such disruptive leaders and managers could help to pre-empt any arising conflict.

Table of Results

The following table TYP-01, is an illustration of Newland's cultural events, social organisation, that have been compared with and have further developed Trice & Beyer's (1984) types of rites:

TRICE & BEYER (1984) TYPOLOGY OF RITES: EXTENDED BY NEWLAND'S CULTURAL EVENTS

Type of Rites	**Newland's Example**	**Manifest, Expressive Social Consequence**	**Examples of Possible Latent, Expressive Consequence**
Rites of Passage	Recruitment, training, introduction of new staff	Ensure smooth integration process	Disruption lessened as 'Best Fit' and 'Technical Ability' assimilates
Rites of Degradation	Removal of director from office	Arbitrate with existing workforce to redeem management image	Alter perceptions of management; recover workforce relations
Rites of Concession *	Monitor and review status of work activities and members	Permit freedom in relation to selective choices defined by members	Prevents conflict arising by offering levels of autonomy
Rites of Conflict Reduction	Organisational dysfunction	Divest loss to past; communicate proposed changes	Recognition of loss; promote change to alleviate member anxiety
Rites of Renewal	Repair organisational damage	Promote new organisational era; endorse confidence in workforce	Make reparation; acknowledge difficulties; address anxiety; refresh company image
Rites of Creation and, Rites of Integration and, Rites of Enhancement	New organisational format	Balance power and authority with popularity	Proactive involvement to invoke organisational needs; interpret events and members attitudes; integrate all factors
	Undertaking work activities	Perpetuate organisational survival through vital task accomplishment	Work activities enabled; provision for formal and social gatherings

	Celebrate meaningful occasions	Tell stories, eat cake; crystallise time	Recognise traditional events; pass on important social knowledge; temporarily equalise status; bond using food
Rites of Intercession *	Management styles and interventions	Build, maintain and perpetuate inter-reliant affiliation upon which organisation can become co-dependent	Creative influence, effective guidance and adequate supervision aid organisational functionality; use food to persuade; food used for recognition

Illustration Number TYP-01

*** New Rite**

Chapter 10
Conclusion

In this organisational ethnography about Newland's, I have achieved what I set out to achieve. Using Trice & Beyer's (1984) typology of rites, I have revealed how Newland's organisational members functioned reciprocally, including their social interactions.

The typology of rites was utilised as a framework and I have highlighted the rituals and ceremonial processes that existed in Newland's groups and teams.

The overall aim of the study was to reveal Newland's naturally occurring organisational cultural events undertaken by personnel in their work setting. By extending Trice & Beyer's (1984) existing typology, it has revealed and made known Newland's organisational functions, methods and processes and hence, the threads that bound a small medium enterprise, like Newland's together, in line with the aims and objectives.

In the case of Newland's, rites and ceremonials were able to be applied to staff recruitment, training and introduction. Undertaking work activities and celebrating meaningful occasions were able to be framed in existing types of rites, including management styles, monitoring and interventions. Additionally, rites revealed the process associated with a significant organisational dysfunctional event and the promotion of a new era. As all research asks for originality in the work, two new rites were developed. Newland's cultural events were therefore, revealed, described, understood and made known in terms of rites and ceremonials.

One point that needs addressing in this study is the interpretation of Newland's data. Even though other researchers undoubtedly would place different interpretations and illustrations on the Newland's data, it is realistic to accept that for a modern day small medium enterprise, trading in the competitive field of engineering data management services, the concept of organisational survival would not have escaped the ethnographic field notes of these other researchers.

Rites and ceremonials are not limited by the size and scale of the organisation in which they function. Generally speaking, if organisational researchers conducted similar studies that extended types of rites, a universal definition of an SME, based upon such typologies, could be developed over time. Regardless of headcount, turnover or balance sheet total, many organisations could make comparisons, develop key strategy, monitor the performance of management and examine workforce production based on insights provided from existing rites.

Research perspectives need to be extended in terms of organisational wisdom that link people and their behaviours inside organisations. A broader view would give the socially organised patterns of people and their behaviours in organisations rather than the discrete aspects that seem to be popular with current organisational researchers.

Reference List

ACAS, www.acas.org.uk

Agazarian, Y., Peters, R. (1981) *The Visible and Invisible Group*, London: Routledge.

Al-Anon (1992) *Courage to Change One Day at a Time in Al-Anon II*, Virginia Beach, VA., USA: Al-Anon Family Groups Headquarters Inc.

Alavi, M., Kayworth, T. R., Leidner, D. E. (Winter 2005-6) 'An Empirical Examination of the Influence of Organisational Culture on Knowledge Management Practices', *Journal Of Management Information Systems*, vol. 22, no. 3, p.p. 191-224.

Alvesson, M. (2002) *Understanding Organisational Culture*, London: Sage Publications Limited.

Alvesson, M. (2010) 'Self-Doubters, Strugglers, Storytellers, Surfers and Others; Images of Self Identities in Organisation Studies', *Human Relations*, vol. 63, part 2, p.p. 193-217.

Alvesson, M. (2012) *Understanding Organisational Culture 3rd Edition*, London: Sage Publications Limited.

Ambrosini, V., Bowman, C., Burton-Taylor, S. (2007) 'Inter-Team Coordination Activities as a Source of Customer Satisfaction', *Human Relations*, vol. 60, no. 1, p.p. 59-98.

Andersen, J. A. (2009) 'When a Servant-Leader Comes Knocking', *Leadership & Organisation Development Journal*, vol. 30, no. 1, p.p. 4-15.

Anderson, J. (2007) 'Forgiveness: A Relational Process: Research and Reflections', *European Journal of Psychotherapy and Counselling*, vol. 9, part 1, p.p. 63-76.

Anderson, L. (2006) 'Analytic Autoethnography', *Journal of Contemporary Ethnography*, vol. 35, no. 4, p.p. 373-395.

Anderson, N. (1923) *The Hobo: The Sociology of the Homeless Man*, Chicago, USA: University of Chicago Press.

Anderson, N., Ones, D. S., Sinangil, H. K., Viswesvaran, C. (Eds.) (2001) *Handbook of Industrial, Work and Organisational Psychology Volume 2 Organisational Psychology*, London: Sage Publications Limited.

Andersson, L. M., Giacalone, R. A., Jurkiewicz, C. L. (2007) 'On the Relationship of Hope and Gratitude to Corporate Social Responsibility', *Journal of Business Ethics*, vol. 70, p.p. 401-409.

Arthur, M. B., Defillippi, R. J., Lindsay, V. J. (2008) 'On Being a Knowledge Worker', *Organisational Dynamics*, vol. 37, no. 4, p.p. 365-377.

Armstrong, D. (2005) 'The Work Group Revisited: Reflections on the Practice of Group Relations', In: French, R. (ed.) *Organisation in the Mind: Psychoanalysis, Group Relations and Organisational Consultancy: Occasional Papers 1989-2003,* London: Karnac, p.p. 139-150, Cited in French, R. B., Simpson, P. (2010) 'The 'Work Group': Redressing the Balance in Bion's Experiences in Groups', *Human Relations*, vol. 63, no. 12, p.p. 1859-1878.

Ashleigh, M. J., Nandhakumar, J. (2007) 'Trust and Technologies: Implications for Organisational Work Practices', *Decision Support Systems*, vol. 43, p.p. 607-617.

Ashman, I., Lawler, J. (2008) 'Existential Communications and Leadership', *Leadership*, vol. 4, no. 3, p.p. 253-269.

Atchison, T. J. (1991) 'The Employment Relationship: Un-Tied or Re-Tied', *Academy of Management Executive*, vol. 5, p.p. 52-62 Cited in Brotheridge, C. M., Lee, R. T. (2006) 'We are Family: Congruity Between Organisational and Family Functioning Constructs', *Human Relations*, vol. 59, no. 1, p.p. 141-161.

Atkinson, P. (2006) 'Rescuing Autoethnography', *Journal of Contemporary Ethnography*, vol. 35, no. 4, p.p. 400-404.

Atkinson, P., Delamont, S. (2006) 'Rescuing Narrative from Qualitative Research', *Narrative Inquiry*, vol. 16, no. 1, p.p. 164-172.

'Women in Racing', *Autosport Magazine,* vol. 189, no. 8, 23 August 2007, p.p. 44-47.

'Matrix System Left Coughlan Disenchanted with McLaren', *Autosport Magazine,* vol. 189, no. 13, 27 September 2007, p.p. 6.

'Patrick Head John Bolster Award', *Autosport Magazine,* vol. 190, no. 10, 6 December 2007, p.p. 53.

Ayre, M., Mill, J., Gill, J. (2011) 'Two Steps Forward, One Step Back: Women in Professional Engineering in Australia', *International Journal of Gender, Science and Technology*, vol. 3, no. 2, p.p. 293-312.

Baker, W. E., Sinkula, J. M. (1999) 'The Synergistic Effect of Market Orientation and Learning Orientation on Organisational Performance', *Academy of Marketing Science Journal*, vol. 27, p.p. 411-427, Cited in Siu Loon Hoe (2007) 'Is Interpersonal Trust a Necessary Condition for Organisational Learning?', *Journal of Organisational Transformation and Social Change*, vol. 4, no. 2, p.p. 149-156.

Barnes, B., Ernst, S., Hyde, K. (1999) *An Introduction to Groupwork a Group Analytic Perspective Basic Texts in Counselling and Psychotherapy Series Editor: Stephen Frosh*, New York, NY 10010, USA: Palgrave Macmillan.

Bass, B. M., Avolio, B. J. (1994) *Improving Leadership Effectiveness Through Transformational Leadership*, Thousand Oaks, CA, USA: Sage Publications.

BBC (2005) *Homes Colour, Psychology of Colour*, [online]. Available from: <http://www.bbc.co.uk> [Accessed on 15 August 2005].

Beaver, G., Hutchings, K. (2005) 'Training and Developing an Age Diverse Workforce in Small Medium Enterprises: The Need for a Strategic Approach', *Education and Training*, vol. 47, no. 8/9, p.p. 592-604.

Beech, N. (2011) 'Liminality and the Practices of Identity Reconstruction', *Human Relations*, vol. 64, no. 2, p.p. 285-302.

Behr, H., Hearst, L. (2005) *Group Analytic Psychotherapy a Meeting of Minds*, London: Whurr Publishers Limited.

Belbin, R. M. (2003) *Team Roles at Work*, London: Elsevier Butterworth Heinemann, Cited in Thomson, D., Hassenkamp, A. (2008) 'The Social Meaning and Function of Food Rituals in Healthcare Practice: An Ethnography', *Human Relations*, vol. 61, no. 12, p.p. 1775-1802.

Berson, Y., Sosik, J. J. (2007) 'The Relationship Between Self-Other Rating Agreement and Influence Tactics and Organisational Processes', *Group & Organisation Management*, vol. 32, no. 6, p.p. 675-698.

Bierly III, P. E., Kessler, E. H., Christensen, E. W. (2000) 'Organisational Learning, Knowledge & Wisdom', *Journal of Organisational Change Management*, vol. 13, no. 6, p.p. 595-618.

Billington, J. (2002) *Colour Your Garden*, London: Quadrille Publishing Limited.

Bion, W. R. (1961) *Experiences in Groups and Other Papers*, First published in 1961 by Tavistock Publications Limited; Re-printed 2001 Hove, East Sussex: Brunner-Routledge.

Bion, W. R. (1962) *Learning from Experience*, Northvale, NJ, USA: Jason Aronson, Cited in Fraley, K. (2007) 'Bion's Model of the Mind', *Psychoanalytic Social Work*, vol. 14, no. 1, p.p. 59-76.

Bion, W. R. (1965) *Transformations*, First published in 1965 by William Heinemann Medical Books Limited; Re-printed 1984, With Permission of Francesca Bion, London: H. Karnac (Books) Limited.

Birks, M., Mills, J. (2011) *Grounded Theory: A Practical Guide*, London: Sage.

Birksted-Breen, D., General Editor, Abel-Hirsch, N., Edited By (2007) *Yesterday, Today And Tomorrow Hanna Segal*, London: Routledge.

Blake, W., English Poet, Painter, Printmaker, Born in London, Lived 1757-1827, *The Marriage of Heaven And Hell*, Composed in London Between 1790 and 1793: Dover Publications Inc.

Blaxter, L., Hughes, C., Tight, M. (2001) *How to Research*, Maidenhead: Open University Press.

Bochner, A. P., Ellis, C. (2001) *Ethnographically Speaking: Autoethnography, Literature, and Aesthetics*, Walnut Creek, CA, USA: AltaMira Press.

Boden, A., Muller, C., Nett, B. (2011) 'Conducting a Business Ethnography in Global Software Development Projects of Small German Enterprises', *Information and Software Technology*, vol. 53, p.p. 1012-1021.

Bolle, E. (2006) 'Existential Management', *Critical Perspectives on International Business*, vol. 2, no. 3, p.p. 259-268.

Bosch-Sijtsema, P. (2007) 'The Impact of Individual Expectations and Expectation Conflicts on Virtual Teams', *Group and Organisation Management*, vol. 32, no. 3, p.p. 358-388.

Bourne, P. G. (1967) 'Some Observations of the Psycho-Social Phenomena Seen in Basic Training', *Psychiatry*, vol. 30, p.p. 187-196, Cited in Trice, H. M., Beyer, J. M. (1984) 'Studying Organisational Cultures Through Rites and Ceremonials', *Academy of Management Review*, vol. 9, no. 4, p.p. 653-669.

Bowlby, J. (1969) *Attachment and Loss: Attachment*, New York, USA: Basic Books.

Bowlby, J. (1973) *Attachment and Loss: Separation*, New York, USA: Basic Books.

Bowlby, J. (1980) *Attachment and Loss: Sadness and Depression*, New York, USA: Basic Books.

Brackman, B. (2006) *Facts and Fabrications, Unravelling the History of Quilts and Slavery*, Lafayette, CA, USA: C&T Publishing Inc.

Brooks, B. (2008) 'The Natural Selection of Organisational and Safety Culture Within a Small to Medium-Sized Enterprise (SME)', *Journal of Safety Research*, vol. 39, p.p. 73-85.

Brotheridge, C. M., Lee, R. T. (2006) 'We are Family: Congruity Between Organisational and Family Functioning Constructs', *Human Relations*, vol. 59, no. 1, p.p. 141-161.

Brouthers, K. D., Brouthers, L. E. (2003) 'Why Service and Manufacturing Entry Mode Choices Differ: The Influence of Transaction Cost Factors, Risk and Trust', *Journal of Management Studies*, vol. 40, no. 5, p.p. 1179-1204, Cited in Zimmerman, M. A., Barksy, D., Brouthers, K. D. (2009) 'Networks, SMEs and International Diversification', *Multinational Business Review*, vol. 17, Issue 4, p.p. 143-162.

Burns, E., Bouchard, S. (2003) *Underground Railroad Sampler*, San Marcos, CA, USA: Eleanor A. Burns Family Trust.

Carman, T. (2001) 'On Making Sense (And Nonsense) of Heidegger', *Philosophy and Phenomenological Research*, vol. 63, no. 3, p.p. 561-572.

Cegarra-Navarro, J. G., Dewhurst, F. W. (2006) 'Linking Shared Organisational Context and Relational Capital Through Unlearning: An Initial Empirical Investigation in SMEs', *The Learning Organisation*, vol. 13, no. 1, p.p. 49-62.

Cerulo, K. A. (1997) 'Technologically Generated Communities, Reframing Sociological Concepts for a Brave New (Virtual?) World', *Sociological Inquiry,* vol. 67, part 1, p.p. 48-58, Cited in Ashleigh, M. J., Nandhakumar, J. (2007) 'Trust and Technologies: Implications for Organisational Work Practices', *Decision Support Systems*, vol. 43, p.p. 607-617.

Charmaz, K. C. (2006) *Constructing Grounded Theory a Practical Guide Through Qualitative Analysis*, London: Sage Publications Limited.

Chambers, J. C. (2001) 'Culture and Psychotherapy: Towards a Hermeneutic Approach', *Psychotherapy-Theory-Research-Practice-Training*, vol. 38, no. 2, p.p. 115-128.

Cialdini, R. B. (1984) *The Psychology Influence of Persuasion*, New York, NY 100222, USA: Harper Collins.

Cialdini, R. B. (2009) *Influence Science and Practice, Fifth Edition*, Boston, MA 02116, USA: Pearson/Allyn and Bacon.

Clair, J. A., Dufresne, R. L. (2007) 'Changing Poison into Medicine: How Companies Can Experience Positive Transformation from a Crises', *Organisational Dynamics*, vol. 36, no. 1, p.p. 63-77.

Clargo, P., Tunstall, R. (2011) 'Leading an Entrepreneurial Workforce: Development or Decline', *Education + Training*, vol. 53, no. 8/9, p.p. 762-783.

Coffey, A. (1999) *The Ethnographic Self: Fieldwork and the Representation of Identity*, London: Sage.

Collin, K. (2006) 'Connecting Work and Learning: Design Engineers' Learning at Work', *Journal of Workplace Learning*, vol. 18, no. 7/8, p.p. 403-413.

Colman, A. M. (2006) *Oxford Dictionary of Psychology Second Edition*, Oxford: Oxford University Press.

Colour Affects (2005) *Colour Psychology*, [online]. Available from: <http://www.colour-affects.co.uk> [Accessed on 15 August 2005].

Conger, J. A., Lawler III, E. E. (2009) 'Sharing Leadership on Corporate Boards: A Critical Requirement for Teamwork at the Top', *Organisational Dynamics*, vol. 38, no. 3, p.p. 183-191.

Croft, A., Castle, T. (2008) *Brown Fires Ally Over Contest Call*, [Online] Reuters, Available from: http://uk.news.yahoo.com/rtrs/20080913/tpl-uk-britain-politics- 20b2d2f.html [Accessed on 13 Sept 2008].

Crowell, S. (2007) 'Sorge or Selbstbewusstsein? Heidegger and Korsgaard on the Sources of Normativity', *European Journal of Philosophy*, vol. 15, no. 3, p.p. 315-333.

Crown Paints (Akzo Nobel nv) (2005) *Experience Colour, Colour Experience*, [online]. Available from: <http://www.crownpaints.co.uk> [Accessed on 20 July 2005].

Das, T. Hari (1983) 'Qualitative Research in Organisational Behaviour', *Journal of Management Studies*, vol. 20, Issue 3, p.p. 301-314.

Dasborough, M. T., Ashkanasy, N. M. (2002) 'Emotion and Attribution of Intentionality in Leader-Member Relationships', *The Leadership Quarterly*, vol. 13, p.p. 615-634, Cited in Game, A. M. (2008) 'Negative Emotions in Supervisory Relationships: The Role of Relational Models', *Human Relations*, vol. 61, no. 3, p.p. 355-393.

Davies, C. A. (1999) *Reflexive Ethnography: A Guide to Researching Selves and Others*, London: Routledge.

Delahaye, B. (2005) 'Knowledge Management in an SME', *International Journal of Organisational Behaviour'*, vol. 9, no. 3, p.p. 604-614.

Den Hartog, D. N., Koopman, P. L. (2001) 'Leadership in Organisations', Cited in Anderson, N., Ones, D. S., Sinangil, H. K., Viswesvaran, C. (Eds.) *Handbook of Industrial, Work and Organisational Psychology Volume 2 Organisational Psychology*, vol. 2, p.p. 166-167, London: Sage Publications Limited.

Den Hartog, D. N., De Hoogh, A. H. B., Keegan, A. E. (2007) 'The Interactive Effects of Belongingness and Charisma on Helping and Compliance', *Journal of Applied Psychology*, vol. 92, no. 4, p.p. 1131-1139.

Denzin, N. K., Lincoln, Y. S. (2005) *The Sage Handbook of Qualitative Research Third Edition*, London: Sage Publications Limited.

Dey, J. (1999) *Grounding Grounded Theory Guidelines for Qualitative Inquiry*, London: Academic Press Inc.

Dias, W. P. S. (2007) 'Philosophical Grounding and Computational Formalisation for Practice Based Engineering Knowledge', *Knowledge-Based Systems*, vol. 20, p.p. 382-387.

DiBella, A. J., Nevis, E. C. (1998) *How Organisations Learn: An Integrated Strategy for Building Learning Capability*, San Francisco, CA, USA: Jossey-Bass, Cited in Siu Loon Hoe (2007) 'Is Interpersonal Trust a Necessary Condition for Organisational Learning?', *Journal of Organisational Transformation and Social Change*, vol. 4, no. 2, p.p. 149-156.

Dixon, K. R., Panteli, N. (2010) 'From Virtual Teams to Virtuality in Teams', *Human Relations*, vol. 63, no. 8, p.p. 1177-1197.

Dubreuil, B. (2008) 'Strong Reciprocity and the Emergence of Large-Scale Societies', *Philosophy of the Social Sciences*, vol. 38, no. 2, p.p. 192-210.

Dulux (ICI PLC) (2005) *Colour Chemistry*, [online]. Available from: <http://www.duluxchemistry.co.uk> [Accessed on 19 July 2005]

Dunn, M. (2000) *The Good Grief Guide*, Oxford OX4 1RE: Pathways, How To Books Limited.

Durst, S., Edvardsson, I. R. (2012) 'Knowledge Management in SMEs: A Literature Review', *Journal of Knowledge Management*, vol. 16, no. 6, p.p. 879-903.

Dyer Jr., W. G. (2006) 'Examining the 'Family Effect' on Firm Performance', *Family Business Review*, vol. 19, no. 4, p.p. 253-273.

Dyer Jr., W. G. (2010) 'Are You the Right Type of Family Business?', *Organisational Dynamics*, vol. 39, no. 3, p.p. 269-278.

Easterby-Smith, M., Lyles, M. A. (Eds.) (2003, 2005) *The Blackwell Handbook of Organisational Learning and Knowledge Management,* Oxford, UK: Blackwell Publishing Limited.

Eberle, T. S., Maeder, C. (2011) 'Organisational Ethnography' Chapter 4, p.p. 52-73, Cited in Silverman, D. (Eds.) (2011) *Qualitative Research Third Edition*, London: Sage.

Edwards, P., Belanger, J. (2008) 'Generalising from Workplace Ethnographies from Induction to Theory', *Journal of Contemporary Ethnography*, vol. 37, no. 3, p.p. 291-313.

Einarsen, S., Aasland, M. S., Skogstad, A. (2007) 'Destructive Leadership Behaviour: A Definition and Conceptual Model', *The Leadership Quarterly*, vol. 18, p.p. 207-216.

Ellis, C. (2004) *The Ethnographic I: A Methodological Novel About Autoethnography*, Walnut Creek, CA, USA: AltaMira Press.

Elsbach, K. D., Cable, D. M., Sherman, J. W. (2010) 'How Passive "Face-Time" Affects Perceptions of Employees: Evidence of Spontaneous Trait Influence', *Human Relations*, vol. 63, no. 6, p.p.735-760.

Espedal, B. (2007) 'Why Rules Rather Than Discretion', *Journal of Organisational Change Management*, vol. 20, no. 1, p.p. 95-108.

Families Anonymous (1999) *Today a Better Way*, Culver City, CA, USA: Families Anonymous Inc.

Farrow & Ball Limited (2005) *The Very Best Brand in Paint & Paper, unrivalled colours, finest products, great service,* [online]. Available from: http://farrow-ball.co.uk> [Accessed on 15 August 2005].

Ferrin, D. L., Bligh, M. C., Kohles, J. C. (2007) 'Can I Trust You to Trust Me? A Theory of Trust, Monitoring and Cooperation in Interpersonal and Intergroup Relationships', *Group & Organisation Management*, vol. 32, no. 4, p.p. 465-499.

Fetterman, D. M. (1998) *Ethnography Second Edition Step By Step*, London: Sage Publications Limited.

Fiennes, R. (2007) *Ranulph Fiennes, Mad, Bad and Dangerous to Know*, London: Hodder and Stoughton.

Filson, A., Lewis, A. (2000) 'Cultural Issues in Implementing Changes to New Product Development Process in a Small to Medium-Sized Enterprise (SME)', *Journal of Engineering Design*, vol. 11, no. 2, p.p. 149-157.

Fineman, S., Gabriel, Y., Sims, D. (2010) *Organising Organisations Fourth Edition,* London: Sage Publications Limited.

Fischer, A. R. (2007) 'Parental Relationship Quality and Masculine Gender-Role Strain in Young Men: Mediating Effects of Personality', *The Counselling Psychologist*, vol. 35, no. 2, p.p. 328-358.

Floyd, D., McManus, J. (2005) 'The Role of SMEs in Improving the Competitive Position of the European Union', *European Business Review*, vol. 17, no. 2, p.p. 144-150.

Fraley, K. (2007) 'Bion's Model of the Mind', *Psychoanalytic Social Work*, vol. 14, no. 1, p.p. 59-76.

Franklin, P. (2007) 'Explication: Working to Discover and Share New Knowledge from Prior Experience', *Journal of Workplace Learning*, vol. 19, no. 1, p.p. 45-54.

French, W. L., Bell, C. H. (1978) *Organisational Development Second Edition*, Englewood Cliffs, NJ, USA: Prentice-Hall, Cited in Trice, H. M., Beyer, J. M. (1984) 'Studying Organisational Cultures Through Rites and Ceremonials', *Academy of Management Review*, vol. 9, no. 4, p.p. 653-669.

French, R. B., Simpson, P. (2010) 'The "Work Group": Redressing the Balance in Bion's Experiences in Groups', *Human Relations*, vol. 63, no. 12, p.p. 1859-1878.

Freud, S. (1938) *An Outline of Psychoanalysis, The Standard Edition*, London: W. W. Norton & Company Limited (1 April 1970), p.p. 141-207.

Freud, S. (1941) *The Psychopathology of Everyday Life*, London: Penguin Books Limited.

Fried, G., Polt, R., New Translation By (2000) *Martin Heidegger: Introduction to Metaphysics*, USA: Yale University Press.

Friedman, R. (2006) 'Who Contains the Group and Who is the Leader? A Relational Disorders Perspective', *European Journal of Psychotherapy and Counselling*, vol. 8, part 1, p.p. 21-32.

Frost, J., Osterloh, M., Weibel, A. (2010) 'Governing Knowledge Work: Transactional and Transformational Solutions', *Organisational Dynamics*, vol. 39, no. 2, p.p. 126-136.

Gadamer, H. G. (1975) *Truth and Method*, New York, USA: Seabury Press.

Gallos, J. V. (2006) *Organisation Development*, San Francisco, CA, USA: Jossey-Bass.

Game, A. M. (2008) 'Negative Emotions in Supervisory Relationships: The Role of Relational Models', *Human Relations*, vol. 61, no. 3, p.p. 355-393.

Gardner, H. E., Laskin, E. (1995) *Leading Minds: An Anatomy Leadership*, New York, USA: Basic Books.

Garfinkel, H. (1956) 'Conditions of Successful Degradation Ceremonies', *American Journal of Sociology*, vol. 61, no. 5, p.p. 420-424.

Gatongi, F. (2007) 'Person-Centred Approach in Schools: Is it the Answer to Disruptive Behaviour in Our Classrooms?', *Counselling Psychology Quarterly*, vol. 20, no. 2, p.p. 205-211.

Geddes, D., Konrad, A. M. (2003) 'Demographic Differences and Reactions to Performance Feedback', *Human Relations*, vol. 56, p.p. 1485-1513.

Gephart, R. P. (1978) 'Status Degradation and Organisational Succession: An Ethnomethodological Approach', *Administrative Science Quarterly*, vol. 23, no. 4, p.p. 553-581.

Gerstel, N., Gross, H. E. (Eds.) (1987) *Families and Work*, Philadelphia, USA: Temple University Press.

Gibbons, J. (2001) 'Knowledge in Action', *Philosophy and Phenomenological Research*, vol. 62, no. 3, p.p. 579-600.

Gingrich-Philbrook, C. (2005) 'Autoethnography Family Values: Easy Access to Compulsory Experiences', *Text and Performance Quarterly*, vol. 25, no. 4, p.p. 197-314, Cited in Muncey, T. (2010) *Creating Autoethnographies*, London: Sage.

Glaser, B. G. (1978) *Theoretical Sensitivity Advances in the Methodology of Grounded Theory*, Mill Valley, CA 94942, USA: Sociology Press.

Glaser, B. G. (1998) *Doing Grounded Theory: Issues and Discussions*, Mill Valley, CA 94942, USA: Sociology Press.

Glaser, B. G. (2001) *The Grounded Theory Perspective: Conceptualisation Contrasted with Description*, Mill Valley, CA 94942, USA: Sociology Press.

Glaser, B. G., Strauss, A. L. (1967) *The Discovery of Grounded Theory: Strategies for Qualitative Research*, Chicago, New York, USA: Aldine de Gruyter.

Goffman, E. (1967) *Interaction Ritual: Essays on Face-To-Face Behaviour*, Garden City, New York, USA: Anchor Books, Cited in Summers-Effler, E. (2007) 'Vortexes of Involvement Social Systems as Turbulent Flow', *Philosophy of the Social Sciences*, vol. 37, no. 4, p.p. 433-448.

Goldmintz, Y., Schaefer, C. E. (2007) 'Why Play Matters to Adults', *Psychology and Education: An Interdisciplinary Journal,* vol. 44, no. 1, p.p. 12-25.

Goldstein, N. J., Martin, S. J., Cialdini, R. B. (2007) *Yes! 50 Secrets from the Science of Persuasion*, London: Profile Books Limited.

Goleman, D. (1998) *Working with Emotional Intelligence*, London: Bloomsbury Publishing PLC.

Goncalo, J. A., Staw, B. M. (2006) 'Individualism-Collectivism and Group Creativity', *Organisational Behaviour and Human Decision Processes*, vol. 100, p.p. 96-109.

Gordon, P. R. (2001) *A Study of Group Psychotherapy: An Empirical Study of The Whole Group*, University of Melbourne, Department of Psychology, Melbourne, Australia.

Gorman, E. (2008) 'Dennis Drives Away His Darkest Moments', *The Times*, Monday, 17 March 2008, Sport, p.p. 83.

Goulding, C. (2002) *Grounded Theory: A Practical Guide for Management, Business and Market Researchers*, London: Sage Publications Limited.

Gray, D. E. (2004) *Doing Research in the Real World*, London: Sage Publications Limited.

Greenhaus, J. H., Powell, G. N. (2003) 'When Work and Family Collide: Deciding Between Competing Role Demands', *Organisational Behaviour and Human Decision Processes*, vol. 90, p.p. 291-303.

Greenleaf, R. (1970) *The Servant as Leader*, New York, NY, USA: Paulist Press.

Greenhaus, J. H., Powell, G. N. (2006) 'When Work and Family are Allies: A Theory of Work-Family Enrichment', *Academy of Management Review*, vol. 31, p.p. 72-92.

Greenleaf, R. K. (1998) *The Power of Servant Leadership'*, Edited by Larry C. Spears, Foreword By Peter B. Vaill, San Francisco, CA, USA: Berrett-Koehler Publishers Inc.

Griffiths, M., Light, B. (2009) 'Innovation in ICT Adoption By SMEs: An Investigation into Resistance Practices at an SME Consultancy', *Journal of Enterprise Information*, vol. 22, no. 1/2, p.p. 119-136.

Griffiths, P. (2008) *Brown Sacks Second Party Dissident*, [online], Available from: Reuters http://uk.news.yahoo.com/rtrs/2OO8O913/tpl-uk-britain-brown-87aacO6.html [Accessed on 13 Sept 2008].

Guadagno, R. E., Cialdini, R. B. (2007) 'Persuade Him by Email, But See Her in Person: Online Persuasion Revisited', *Computers in Human Behaviour*, vol. 23, p.p. 999-1015.

Gubrium, J., Holstein, J. (1987) 'The Private Image: Experiential Location and Method in Family Studies', *Journal of Marriage and the Family*, vol. 49, p.p. 773-786, Cited in Silverman, D. (2005) *Doing Qualitative Research Second Edition*, London: Sage.

Hacking, I. (2002a) *Historical Ontology*, Cambridge, MA, USA: Harvard University Press, Cited in Sugarman, J. (2009) 'Historical Ontology and Psychological Description', *Journal of Theoretical and Philosophical Psychology*, vol. 29, no. 1, p.p. 5-15.

Hackman, J. R. (1990) *Groups That Work (and Those That Don't)* San Francisco, CA, USA: Jossey-Bass, Cited in Thomson, D., Hassenkamp, A. (2008) 'The Social Meaning and Function of Food Rituals in Healthcare Practice: An Ethnography', *Human Relations*, vol. 61, no. 12, p.p. 1775-1802.

Hambley, L. A., O'Neil, T. A., Kline, T. J. B. (2007) 'Virtual Team Leadership: the Effects of Leadership Style and Communication Medium on Team Interaction Styles and Outcomes', *Organisational Behaviour and Human Decision Processes*, vol. 103, part 1, p.p. 1-20.

Hamilton, R., Vohs, K. D., Sellier, A., Meyvis, T. (2011) 'Being of Two Minds: Switching Mindsets Exhausts Self-Regulatory Resources', *Organisational Behaviour and Human Decision Processes*, vol. 115, p.p. 13-24.

Hannabuss, S. (1997) 'Counselling Approaches and the Workplace', *Library Management*, vol. 18, no. 8, p.p. 373-379.

Hansen, R. S. (2006) 'Benefits and Problems with Student Teams: Suggestions for Improving Team Projects', *Journal of Education for Business*, p.p. 11-19.

Hardin, A., Fuller, M. A. Davison, R. M. (2007) 'I Know I Can, But Can We?', *Small Group Research*, vol. 38, no. 1, p.p. 130-155.

Hatch, M. J., Kostera, M. Kozminski, A. K. (2006) 'The Three Faces of Leadership: Manager, Artist, Priest', *Organisational Dynamics*, vol. 35, no. 1, p.p. 49-68.

Haxton, B., Translated by (2001) *Heraclitus Fragments*, London: Penguin Books Limited.

Hayano, D. (1979) 'Autoethnography: Paradigms, Problems and Prospects', *Human Organisation*, vol. 38, no. 1, p.p. 99-104.

Heidegger, M. (1962) *Being and Time,* Translated by J. Macquarrie & E. Robinson, Oxford: Blackwell.

Heidegger, M. (1966) *Discourse on Thinking*, New York, NY, USA: Harper and Row.

Heidegger, M. (This English Translation 2010) *Phenomenology of Intuition and Expression*, Athlone Contemporary European Thinkers, London: Continuum International Publishing Group; First Published In German as *Phanomenologie Der Anschauung Und Des Ausdrucks*, Vittorio Klostermann GmbH, Frankfurt am Main, 1993.

Heidegger, M. (This English Translation 2010) *Logic the Question of Truth*, Translated by Thomas Sheehan, Bloomington, Indiana, USA: Indiana University Press; First Published in German as Heidegger, M., Biemel, W., Klostermann, V. (Eds.) (1976) *Gesamtausgabe 21: Logik: Die Frage Nach Der Wahrheit (WS 1925-26)* Frankfurt am Main.

Hermans, H. J. M. (2006) 'Moving Through Three Paradigms, Yet Remaining the Same Thinker', *Counselling Psychology Quarterly*, vol. **19**, part 1, p.p. 5-25.

Higdon, J. (2005) 'Freud at the Glasgow Empire', *Counselling and Psychotherapy Journal*, vol. 16, part 6, p.p. 16-18.

Hinshelwood, R. D. (1991) *A Dictionary of Kleinian Thought*, London: Free Association Books.

Hodges, B. H., Geyer, A. L. (2006) 'A Nonconformist Account of the Asch Experiments: Values, Pragmatics and Moral Dilemmas', *Personality and Social Psychology Review*, vol. 10, no. 1, p.p. 2-19.

Holland, J. L. (1997) *Making Vocational Choices: A Theory of Vocational Personalities and Work Environments (3rd Edition)* Odessa, Florida, USA: Psychological Assessment Resources.

Holstein, J. A. Gubrium, J. F. (1995) *The Active Interview, Qualitative Research Methods Series 37*, London: Sage Publications Limited.

Holstein, J. A. Gubrium, J. F. (1997) *The New Language of Qualitative Method*, New York, New York 10016, USA: Oxford University Press Inc.

Holt, N. L. (2003) 'Representation, Legitimation and Autoethnography: An Autoethnographic Writing Story', *International Journal of Qualitative Methods*, vol. 2, no. 1, p.p. 1, Cited in Muncey, T. (2010) *Creating Autoethnographies*, London: Sage.

Holtom, R. (2011) BT Life, *Are You Suffering from Technostalgia?* [online]. Available from: http://www.btlife.bt.com/technology-and-communications/are-you-suffering- from-tech [Accessed on 27 March 2011].

Horrocks, S. (2004) 'Saving Heidegger from Benner and Wrubel', *Nursing Philosophy*, vol. 5, p.p. 175-181.

Hrebiniak, L. G. (2006) 'Obstacles to Effective Strategy Implementation', *Organisational Dynamics*, vol. 35, no. 1, p.p. 12-31.

Husserl, E. (1991) *On the Phenomenology of the Consciousness of Internal Time (1893-1917)* Repr. New York, USA: Springer, Cited in Summers-Effler, E. (2007) 'Vortexes of Involvement Social Systems as Turbulent Flow', *Philosophy of the Social Sciences*, vol. 37, no. 4, p.p. 433-448.

Islam, G., Zypher, M. J. (2009) 'Rituals in Organisations: A Review and Expansion of Current Theory', *Group & Organisation Management*, vol. 34, no. 1, p.p. 114-139.

Jaworski, J. (1998) *Synchronicity the Inner Path of Leadership,* Introduction by Peter Senge, San Francisco, USA: Berrett-Koehler Publishers, Inc.

Jenkins, P. (1994) 'It's a Kind of Magic…', *The Therapist*, p.p. 40-41.

Jeske, D. (2001) 'Friendship and Reasons of Intimacy', *Philosophy and Phenomenological Research*, vol. 63, no. 2, p.p. 329-346.

Johnson, S. Cited in Al-Anon (1992) *Courage to Change One Day at a Time in Al-Anon II*, Virginia Beach, USA: Al-Anon Family Group Headquarters Inc.

Jorgensen, F., Ulhoi, J. P. (2010) 'Enhancing Innovation Capacity in SMEs Through Early Network Relationships', *Creativity and Innovation Management*, vol. 19, Issue 4, p.p. 397-404.

Joshi, K. D., Sarker, S., Sarker, S. (2007) 'Knowledge Transfer Within Information Systems Development Teams: Examining the Role of Knowledge Source Attributes', *Decision Support Systems*, vol. 43, p.p. 322-335.

Kaplan, M. (2000) 'To What Must an Epistemology Be True?', *Philosophy and Phenomenological Research*, vol. 61, no. 2, p.p. 279-304.

Keeley, M. (1995) 'The Trouble with Transformational Leadership: Towards a Federalist Ethic for Organisations', *Business Ethics Quarterly*, vol. 5, no. 1, p.p. 67-96, Cited in Andersen, J. A. (2009) 'When a Servant-Leader Comes Knocking', *Leadership & Organisation Development Journal*, vol. 30, no. 1, p.p. 4-15.

Kelly, M. (2005) 'The Ethics Revolution', *Business Ethics,* vol. 19, part 2, p.p. 6, Cited in Velthouse, B., Kandogan, Y. (2007) 'Ethics in Practice: What are Managers Really Doing?', *Journal of Business Ethics*, vol. 70, p.p. 151-163.

Kelly, J. R., Barsade, S. G. (2001) 'Mood and Emotions in Small Groups and Work Teams', *Organisational Behaviour and Human Decision Processes*, vol. 86, no. 1, p.p. 99-130.

Kenwright, B., Everton Football Club Chairman (2008) *Labour Donors Turn Against Brown*, [online], Available from: MSN News & Weather http://news.uk.msn.com/article.aspx?cp-documentid=8741779 [Accessed on 25 July 2008].

Kessler, E. H. (2006) 'Organisational Wisdom Human, Managerial and Strategic Implications', *Group & Organisation Management*, vol. 31, no. 3, p.p. 296-299.

Kessler, E. H., Bailey, J. R. (2007) *Handbook of Organisational and Managerial Wisdom*, London: Sage Publications Limited.

Kets De Vries, M. F. R. (2007) 'Decoding the Team Conundrum: The Eight Roles Executives Play', *Organisational Dynamics*, vol. 36, no. 1, p.p. 28-44.

King, G. A. (2004) 'The Meaning of Life Experiences: Application of a Meta-Model to Rehabilitation Sciences and Services', *American Journal of Orthopsychiatry*, vol. 74, p.p. 72-78, Cited in Lightsey Jr., O. R. (2006) 'Resilience, Meaning, and Well-Being', *The Counselling Psychologist*, vol. 34, no. 1, p.p. 96-107.

Kirchler, E., Hoelzl, E., Wahl, I. (2008) 'Enforced Versus Voluntary Tax Compliance: the "Slippery Slope" Framework', *Journal of Economic Psychology*, vol. 29, p.p. 210-225.

Kivetz, Y., Tyler, T. R. (2007) 'Tomorrow I'll Be Me: The Effect of Time Perspective on the Activation of Idealistic Versus Pragmatic Selves', *Organisational Behaviour and Human Decision Processes*, vol. 102, p.p. 193-211.

Klein, M. (1997) *Melanie Klein Envy and Gratitude and Other Works 1946-1963*, London: Vintage (First Published in Great Britain by the Hogarth Press Limited 1975).

Knox, R. (2007) 'Experiencing Risk in Person-Centred Counselling: A Qualitative Exploration of Therapist Risk Taking', *British Journal of Guidance and Counselling*, vol. 35, no. 3, p.p. 317-330.

Koch, S. C. (2005) 'Evaluative Affect Display Towards Male and Female Leaders of Task-Oriented Groups', *Small Group Research,* vol. 36, no. 6, p.p. 678-703.

Krueger, R. A., Casey, M. A. (2000) *Focus Groups Third Edition: A Practical Guide for Applied Research*, London: Sage Publications Limited.

Kutz, C. (2000) 'Acting Together', *Philosophy and Phenomenological Research*, vol. 61, no. 1, p.p. 1-31.

Kyriakidou, O. (2012) 'Negotiating Gendered Identities Through the Process of Identity Construction, Women Managers in Engineering', *Equality, Diversity and Inclusion: An International Journal*, vol. 31, no. 1, p.p. 27-42.

Laing, R. D. (1969) *The Divided Self*, London: Penguin Books Limited.

Lagos, C. M. (2007) 'The Theory of Thinking and the Capacity to Mentalise: A Comparison of Fonagy's and Bion's Models', *The Spanish Journal of Psychology*, vol. 10, no. 1, p.p. 189-198.

Lapp, C. A., Carr, A. N. (2006) 'To Have to Halve: "Being" in the Middle in Changing Time's Space', *Journal of Organisational Change Management*, vol. 19, no. 5, p.p. 655-687.

Ledgerwood, L., *The Apprentice*, BBC, Week 5, Broadcast on 24 April 2009.

Leonard, N., Beauvais, L., Scholl, R. (1999) 'Work Motivation: The Incorporation of Self-Concept-Based Processes', *Human Relations*, vol. 52, p.p. 1339-1357, Cited in Alvesson, M. (2010) 'Self-Doubters, Strugglers, Storytellers, Surfers and Others; Images of Self Identities in Organisation Studies', *Human Relations*, vol. 63, part 2, p.p. 193-217.

Levine, D. P. (2010) *Object Relations, Work and the Self*, London: Routledge.

Lewin, K. (1935) *A Dynamic Theory of Personality*, New York, USA: McGraw Hill.

Lipgar, R. M. (2006) 'Learning from Bion's Legacy to Groups', *European Journal of Psychotherapy and Counselling*, vol. 8, no. 1, p.p. 79-91.

Lightsey Jr., O. R. (2006) 'Resilience, Meaning, and Well-Being', *The Counselling Psychologist*, vol. 34, no. 1, p.p. 96-107.

Lister, R. (2008) *What Can Chaucer Teach the Captains of Industry?*, [online] Available from: <http://www.salford.ac.uk/news/details/674> [Accessed on 26 March 2008].

Locke, K. D. (2000) *Grounded Theory in Management Research (Sage Series in Management Research)*, London: Sage Publications Limited.

Loewenthal, D. (2006a) 'Editorial: The Leader and the Group: Freud, Bion, Europe and the Journal', *European Journal of Psychotherapy and Counselling*, vol. 8, no. 1, p.p. 1-2.

Loewenthal, D. (2006b) 'Editorial: Therapeutic Training After Freud', *European Journal of Psychotherapy and Counselling*, vol. 8, no. 4, p.p. 363-367.

Lopez-Corvo, R. E. (2003) *The Dictionary of the Work of W. R. Bion*, English Edition First Published in 2003, London: H. Karnac (Books) Limited.

Lopez, S. J., Magyar-Moe, J. L., Petersen, S. E., Ryder, J. A., Krieshok, T. S., O'Byrne, K. K., Lichtenberg, J. W., Fry, N.A. (2006) 'Counselling Psychology's Focus on Positive Aspects of Human Functioning', vol. 34, no. 2, p.p. 205-227.

Lopez-Corvo, R. E. (2006) *Wild Thoughts Searching for a Thinker: A Clinical Application of W. R. Bion's Theories*, London: Karnac Books Limited.

Lyonette, C., Crompton, R. (2008) 'The Only Way is Up? An Examination of Women's "Under-Achievement" in the Accountancy Profession in the UK', *Gender in Management: An International Journal*, vol. 23, no. 7, p.p. 506-521.

Malinowski, B. (First Published 1922, Transferred to Digital Printing 2005) *Argonauts of the Western Pacific,* With a Preface by Sir James Fraser, Oxon: Routledge.

Malpas, J. (2006) *Heidegger's Topology: Being, Place, World*, Cambridge, MA, USA: Massachusetts Institute of Technology.

Manzoni, J., Barsoux, J. (2009) 'The Interpersonal Side of Taking Charge', *Organisational Dynamics*, vol. 38, no. 2, p.p. 106-116.

Marcus, E. (2001) 'Mental Causation: Unnaturalised But Not Unnatural', *Philosophy and Phenomenological Research*, vol. 63, no. 1, p.p. 57-83.

Manz, C. C., Pearce, C. L., Sims Jr., H. P. (2009) 'The Ins and Outs of Leading Teams: An Overview', *Organisational Dynamics*, vol. 38, no. 3, p.p. 179-182.

May, R. (1983) *The Discovery of Being*, New York, NY 10110, USA: W. W. Norton & Company Inc.

McAllister, D. J. (1995) 'Affect- and Cognition-Based Trust as Foundations for Interpersonal Cooperation in Organisations', *Academy of Management Journal*, vol. 38, p.p. 24-59.

McColl-Kennedy, J. R., Anderson, R. D. (2005) 'Subordinate-Manager Gender Combination and Perceived Leadership Style Influence on Emotions, Self-Esteem and Organisational Commitment', *Journal of Business Research*, vol. 58, p.p. 115-125, Cited in Game, A. M. (2008) 'Negative Emotions in Supervisory Relationships: the Role of Relational Models', *Human Relations*, vol. 61, no. 3, p.p. 355-393.

McNeill, W., Walker, N., Translated by (1995) *Martin Heidegger: The Fundamental Concepts of Metaphysics World, Finitude, Solitude*, Bloomington, Indiana, USA: Indiana University Press.

Meigs, A. (1997) 'Food as a Cultural Construction', In C. Counihan & P. Van Esterick (Eds.), *Food and Culture: A Reader*, London: Routledge, p.p. 95-106, Cited in Thomson, D., Hassenkamp, A. (2008) 'The Social Meaning and Function of Food Rituals in Healthcare Practice: An Ethnography', *Human Relations*, vol. 61, no. 12, p.p. 1775-1802.

Melita Prati, L., McMillan-Capehart, A., Karriker, J. H. (2009) 'Affecting Organisational Identity a Manager's Influence', *Journal of Leadership & Organisational Studies*, vol. 15, no. 4, p.p. 404-415.

Menzies-Lyth, I. (1988) *Containing Anxiety in Institutions, Selected Essays, Volume 1,* London: Free Association Books.

Meyer, J. W., Rowan, B. (1977) 'Institutionalised Organisations: Formal Structure as Myth and Ceremony', *American Journal of Sociology*, vol. 83, no. 2, p.p. 340-363.

Mishna, F. M., Muskat, M. S., Scharness, M. S. S. (2002) 'Food for Thought: the Use of Food in Group Therapy with Children and Adolescents', *International Journal of Psychotherapy*, vol. 52, no. 1, p.p. 27-47, Cited in Thomson, D., Hassenkamp, A. (2008) 'The Social Meaning and Function of Food Rituals in Healthcare Practice: An Ethnography', *Human Relations*, vol. 61, no. 12, p.p. 1775-1802.

Mitroff, I. I., Kilman, R. H., On Organisation Stories: An Approach to the Design and Analysis of Organisations Through Myths and Stories. In Kilman, R. H., Pondy, L. R., Sleven, D. P. (Eds.) (1976) *The Management of Organisation Design,* vol. 2, New York, USA: North Holland, p.p. 189-207, Cited in Trice, H. M., Beyer, J. M. (1984) 'Studying Organisational Cultures Through Rites and Ceremonials', *Academy of Management Review*, vol. 9, no. 4, p.p. 653-669.

Morgan, D. (1997) *Focus Groups As Qualitative Research Second Edition, Qualitative Research Methods Series 16*, London: Sage Publications Limited.

Morris, M., Nadler, J., Kurtzberg, T., Thompson, L. (2002) 'Schmooze or Lose: Social Friction and Lubrication in Email Negotiations', *Group Dynamics*, vol. 6, no. 1, p.p. 89-100, Cited in Taylor, H., Fieldman, G., Altman, Y. (2008) 'Email at Work: A Cause for Concern? The Implications of the New Communication Technologies for Health, Well-being and Productivity at Work', *Journal of Organisational Transformation and Social Change*, vol. 5, no. 2, p.p. 159-173.

Muncey, T. (2010) *Creating Autoethnographies*, London: Sage.

Naranjo-Valencia, J. C., Jimenez-Jimenez, D., Sanz-Valle, R. (2011) 'Innovation or Imitation? The Role of Organisational Culture', *Management Decision*, vol. 49, no. 1, p.p. 55-72.

Neri, C. (2006) 'Leadership in Small Groups: Syncretic Sociality and the Genius Loci', *European Journal of Psychotherapy and Counselling*, vol. 8, no. 1, p.p. 33-46.

Neufeld, J. E., Rasmussen H. N., Lopez, S. J., Ryder, J. A., Magyar-Moe, J. L., Ford, A. I., Edwards, L. M., Bouwkamp, J. C. (2006) 'The Engagement Model of Person-Environment Interaction', *The Counselling Psychologist*, vol. 34, no. 2, p.p. 245-259.

Neyland, D. (2008) *Organisational Ethnography*, London: Sage.

Nunes, M. B., Annansingh, F., Eaglestone, B., Wakefield, R. (2006) 'Knowledge Management Issues in Knowledge-Intensive SMEs', *Journal of Documentation*, vol. 62, no. 1, p.p. 101-119.

Oborn, E., Dawson, S. (2010) 'Knowledge and Practice in Multidisciplinary Teams: Struggle, Accommodation and Privilege', *Human Relations*, vol. 63, no. 12, p.p. 1835-1857.

O'Regan, N., Ghobadian, A. (2006) 'Perceptions of Generic Strategies of Small and Medium-Sized Engineering and Electronics Manufacturers in the UK: The Applicability of the Miles and Snow Typology', *Journal of Manufacturing Technology Management*, vol. 17, no. 5, p.p. 603-620.

Parsons, F. (1909) *Choosing a Vocation*, Boston, USA: Houghton-Mifflin.

Peacock, M. S. (2007) 'The Conceptual Construction of Altruism Ernst Fehr's Experimental Approach to Human Conduct', *Philosophy of the Social Sciences*, vol. 37, no. 1, p.p. 3-23.

Peel, D. (2006) 'An Analysis of the Impact of SME Organisational Culture on Coaching and Mentoring', *International Journal of Evidence Based Coaching and Mentoring,* vol. 4, no. 1, p.p. 9-19.

Pfeffer, J. (1981) *Power in Organisations*, Boston, Massachusetts, USA: Pitman.

Pfeffer, J. (2010) *Power Why Some People Have It, and Others Don't,* New York, NY 10022, USA: HarperCollins Publishers.

Phillips, B. (2007) 'Nursing Care and Understanding the Experiences of Others: A Gadamerian Perspective', *Nursing Inquiry*, vol. 14, no. 1, p.p. 89-94.

Philipse, H. (2001) 'How are We to Interpret Heidegger's Oeuvre? A Methodological Manifesto', *Philosophy and Phenomenological Researcher*, vol. 63, no. 3, p.p. 573-586.

Piaget, J. (1932) *The Moral Judgement of the Child*, London: Paul Kegan.

Pinter, H. (2005) *Art, Truth and Politics*, Nobel Lecture, [online], Available at: http://nobelprize.org/nobel prizes/litrature/laureats/2005/pinter-lecture-e.html [Accessed July 2006].

Podsakoff, P. M., MacKenzie, S. B., Paine, J. B., Bachrach, D. G. (2000) 'Organisational Citizenship Behaviours: A Critical Review of the Theoretical and Empirical Literature and Suggestions for Future Research', *Journal of Management*, vol. 26, p.p. 513-563, Cited in Den Hartog, D. N., De Hoogh, A. H. B., Keegan, A. E. (2007) 'The Interactive Effects of Belongingness and Charisma on Helping and Compliance', *Journal of Applied Psychology*, vol. 92, no. 4, p.p. 1131-1139.

Potter, R. E., Balthazard, P. A. (2002) 'Virtual Team Interaction Styles: Assessment and Effects', *International Journal of Human-Computer Studies*, vol. 56, p.p. 423-433.

Potter, R. E., Balthazard, P.A., Cooke, R. A. (2000) 'Virtual Team Interaction: Assessment, Consequences and Management', *Team Performance Management: An International Journal*, vol. 6, parts 7/8, p.p. 131-137.

Powell, W. W., DiMaggio, P. J. (Eds.) (1991) *The New Institutionalism in Organisational Analysis*, London: The University of Chicago Press Limited.

Powell, G. N., Eddleston, K. A. (2013) 'Linking Family-to-Business Enrichment and Support to Entrepreneurial Success: Do Female and Male Entrepreneurs Experience Different Outcomes?', *Journal of Business Venturing*, vol. 28, no. 2, p.p. 261-280.

Ramdani, B., Kawalek, P., Lorenzo, O. (2009) 'Knowledge Management and Enterprise Systems Adoption by SMEs: Predicting SMEs' Adoption of Enterprise Systems', *Journal of Enterprise Information Management*, vol. 22, no. 1/2, p.p. 10-24.

Rapport, N. (2008) 'Gratuitousness: Notes Towards an Anthropology of Interiority', *The Australian Journal of Anthropology*, vol. 19, no. 3, p.p. 331-349.

Rey, G. (2001) 'Review: Digging Deeper for the a Priori, Reviewed Work(s): In Defence of Pure Reason by Laurence Bonjour', *Philosophy and Phenomenological Research*, vol. 63, no. 3, p.p. 649-656.

Richardson, M. S. (1993) 'Work in People's Lives: A Location for Counselling Psychologists', *Journal of Counselling Psychology*, vol. 40, p.p. 425-433.

Ringer, T. M. (2007) 'Viewpoint Leadership for Collective Thinking in the Workplace', *Team Performance Management*, vol. 13, no. 3/4, p.p. 130-144.

Robinson, G., Sir (2008) *Labour Donors Turn Against Brown*, [online], Available from: MSN News & Weather http://news.uk.msn.com/article.aspx?cp- documentid=8741779 [Accessed on 25 July 2008].

Robbins, B. D., Parlavecchio, H. (2006) 'The Unwanted Exposure of the Self: A Phenomenological Study of Embarrassment', *The Humanistic Psychologist*, vol. 34, no. 4, p.p. 321-345.

Robitschek, C., Woodson, S. J. (2006) 'Vocational Psychology: Using One of Counselling Psychology's Strengths to Foster Human Strength', vol. 34, no. 2, p.p. 260-275.

Rogers, C. R. (1951) *Client-Centred Therapy*, London: Constable and Company Limited.

Rogers, C. R. (1980) *A Way of Being: The Founder of the Human Potential Movement Looks Back on a Distinguished Career*, New York, New York 10003, USA: Houghton-Mifflin Company.

Rogers, C. R., Freiberg, J. (1994) *Freedom to Learn*, Englewood Cliffs, New Jersey, USA: Prentice Hill.

Roldan, A. A. (2002) 'Writing Ethnography. Malinowski's Fieldnotes on Baloma', *Social Anthropology*, vol. 10, no. 3, p.p. 377-393.

Roper, J. M., Shapira, J. (2000) *Ethnography in Nursing Research*, London: Sage Publications Limited.

Roth, J. A. (1963) *Timetables: Structuring the Passage of Time in Hospital Treatment and Other Careers*, Indianapolis, USA: Bobbs-Merrill.

Rowley, J. (2006) 'What Do We Need to Know About Wisdom', *Management Decision*, vol. 44, no. 9, p.p. 1246-1257.

Rowley, J., Gibbs, P. (2008) 'From Learning Organisation to Practically Wise Organisation', *The Learning Organisation*, vol. 15, no. 5, p.p. 356-372.

Roy, D. E. (1959/1960) '"Banana-Time": Job Satisfaction and Informal Interaction', *Human Organisation*, vol. 18, p.p. 158-168.

Royal Horticultural Society (2005) *RHS Online*, [online]. Available from: <http://www.rhs.org.uk> [Accessed on 22 August 2005].

Russell, J. S. (2008) 'Engineering Professional Growth and Quality and Cultivating the Next Generation', *Leadership and Management in Engineering*, vol. 8, Issue 2, p.p. 57-60.

Rycroft, C. (1995) *A Critical Dictionary of Psychoanalysis Second Edition*, London: Penguin Books Limited.

Safranski, R. (1998) *Martin Heidegger: Between Good and Evil*, Cambridge, MA, USA: Harvard University Press, Cited in Bolle, E. (2006) 'Existential Management', *Critical Perspectives on International Business*, vol. 2, no. 3, p.p. 259-268.

Sagan, O. (2008) 'The Loneliness of the Long-Anxious Learner: Mental Illness, Narrative Biography and Learning to Write', *Psychodynamic Practice*, vol. 14, no. 1, p.p. 43-58.

Schreiber, R. S. Stern, P. N. (2001) *Using Grounded Theory in Nursing*, New York, USA: Springer Publishing Company Inc.

Schaubroeck, J., Walumbwa, F. O., Ganster, D. C., Kepes, S. (2007) 'Destructive Leader Traits and the Neutralising Influence of an "Enriched" Job', *The Leadership Quarterly*, vol. 18, p.p. 236-251.

Schein, E. H. (2010) *Organisational Culture and Leadership Fourth Edition*, San Francisco, CA, USA: Jossey-Bass.

Schein, E. (1998) 'The Family as Metaphor', *Journal of Management Inquiry*, vol. 7, p.p. 131-132, Cited in Brotheridge, C. M., Lee, R. T. (2006) 'We are Family: Congruity Between Organisational and Family Functioning Constructs', *Human Relations*, vol. 59, no. 1, p.p. 141-161.

Schmid, H. B. (2008) 'Plural Action', *Philosophy of the Social Sciences*, vol. 38, no. 1, p.p. 25-54.

Schon, D. A. (1987) *Educating the Reflective Practitioner Towards a New Design for Teaching and Learning in the Professions*, San Francisco, CA, USA: Jossey-Bass.

Schrire, S. (2006) 'Knowledge Building in Asynchronous Discussion Groups: Going Beyond Quantitative Analysis', *Computers and Education*, vol. 46, p.p. 49-70.

Schwartzman, H. B. (1993) *Ethnography in Organisations*, Newbury Park, CA, USA: Sage.

Schulz, K. P. (2005) 'Learning in Complex Organisations as Practicing and Reflecting: A Model Development and Application from a Theory of Practice Perspective', *Journal of Workplace Learning*, vol. 17, no. 8, p.p. 493-507.

Sciarra, D. (1999) 'The Role of the Qualitative Researcher', Cited in Kopala, M., Suzuki, L. A. (Eds.) *Using Qualitative Methods in Psychology*, Thousand Oaks, CA, USA: Sage Publications.

Scott, M. (1968) *The Racing Game*, Chicago, USA: Aldine.

Scott, K. A., Brown, D. J. (2006) 'Female First, Leader Second? Gender Bias in the Encoding of Leadership Behaviour', *Organisational Behaviour and Human Decision Processes*, vol. 101, p.p. 230-242.

Scott, W. R. (2008) *Institutions and Organisations Third Edition*, London: Sage Publications Limited.

Senge, P., Scharmer, C. O., Jaworski, J., Flowers, B. S. (2005) *Presence Exploring Profound Change in People, Organisations and Society*, First Published in Great Britain by Nicholas Brealey Publishing in 2005, London: Nicholas Brealey Publishing.

Seibert, C. H. Translated by (1970) *Martin Heidegger and Eugen Fink Heraclitus Seminar*, Evanston, Illinois 60208-4170, USA: Northwestern University Press.

Servon, L. J., Visser, M. A. (2011) 'Progress Hindered: The Retention and Advancement of Women in Science, Engineering and Technology Careers', *Human Resource Management Journal*, vol. 21, no. 3, p.p. 272-284.

Sekiguchi, T., Huber, V. L. (2011) 'The Use of Person-Organisation Fit and Person Job Fit Information in Making Selection Decisions', *Organisational Behaviour and Human Decision Processes*, vol. 116, p.p. 203-216.

Sheard, G., Kakabadse, A. P., Kakabadse, N. K. (2011) 'Organisational Politics: Reconciling Leadership's Rational-Emotional Paradox', *Leadership and Organisation Development Journal*, vol. 32, no. 1, p.p. 78-97.

Sijtsema, P. B. (2007) 'The Impact of Individual Expectations and Expectation Conflicts on Virtual Teams', *Group and Organisation Management,* vol. 32, no. 3, p.p. 358-388.

Silverman, D. (2005) *Doing Qualitative Research Second Edition*, London: Sage.

Silverman, D. (Eds.) (2011) *Qualitative Research Third Edition*, London: Sage.

Simpson, A., Barker, P. (2007) 'The Persistence of Memory: Using Narrative Picturing to Cooperatively Explore Life Stories in Qualitative Inquiry', *Nursing Inquiry*, vol. 14, part 1, p.p. 35-41.

Singh, R. K., Garg, S. K., Deshmukh, S. G. (2008) 'Strategy Development by SMEs for Competitiveness: a Review', *Benchmarking: An International Journal*, vol. 15, no. 5, p.p. 525-547.

Siu Loon Hoe (2007) 'Is Interpersonal Trust a Necessary Condition for Organisational Learning?', *Journal of Organisational Transformation and Social Change*, vol. 4, no. 2, p.p. 149-156.

Sky News (2008) *Third Brown Plotter Sacked*, [online], Available from: http://news.sky.com/skynews/Home/Politics/Prime-Minister-Gordon-Brown-In- Turmoil, [Accessed on 15 September 2008].

Sky News (2008) *Sir Ian Blair: Boris Made Me Quit*, [online], Available from: http://news.sky.com/skynews/Home/UK-News/Sir-Ian-Blair-Steps-Down-As-Metropolitan [Accessed on 03 October 2008].

Sky News (2008) *Smith's Anger Over Blair Ousting*, [online], Available from: http://news.sky.com/skynews/Home/Politics/Sir-Ian-Blair-Resignation-Home-Secretary [Accessed on 03 October 2008].

Sleeth, D. B. (2006) 'The Self and the Integral Interface: Towards a New Understanding of the Whole Person', *The Humanistic Psychologist*, vol. 34, no. 3, p.p. 243-261.

Smith, A. D. (2001) 'Perception and Belief', *Philosophy and Phenomenological Research*, vol. 62, no. 2, p.p. 283-309.

Smith, D. L. (2007) 'A Phenomenological Reflection on the Experience of Hope', *The Humanistic Psychologist*, vol. 35, no. 1, p.p. 81-104.

Smith, J., Gardner, D. (2007) 'Factors Affecting Employee Use of Work-Life Balance Initiatives', *New Zealand Journal of Psychology*, vol. 36, no. 1, p.p. 3-12.

Smythe, E., Norton, A. (2007) 'Thinking as Leadership/Leadership as Thinking', *Leadership*, vol. 3, no. 1, p.p. 65-90.

Soanes, C., Stevenson, A. (Eds.) (2003) *Oxford Dictionary of English Second Edition*, Oxford: Oxford University Press.

Sosik, J. J. (2001) 'Self-Other Agreement on Charismatic Leadership: Relationships with Work Attitudes and Managerial Performance', *Group & Organisation Management*, vol. 26, p.p. 484-511.

Sosik, J. J., Jung, D. I. (2003) 'Impression Management Strategies and Performance in Information Technology: The Role of Self-Other Rating Agreement on Charismatic Leadership', *Management Communication Quarterly*, vol. 17, no. 2, p.p. 233-268.

Sosik, J. J., Megerian, L. E. (1999) 'Understanding Leader Emotional Intelligence and Performance: The Role of Self-Other Agreement on Transformational Leadership Perceptions', *Group & Organisation Management*, vol. 25, p.p. 291-317.

Stake, R. E. (1995) *The Art of Case Study Research*, Thousand Oaks, CA, USA: Sage Publications.

Stensaker, I., & Falkenburg, J. (2007) 'Making Sense of Different Responses To Corporate Change', *Human Relations*, vol. **60**, no. 1, 2007, p.p. 137-177.

Storey, D. J. (1994) *Understanding the Small Business Sector*, London: Routledge.

Strachey, J. (Translated from German Under the General Editorship of J. Strachey) In Collaboration with A. Freud, Assisted by Alix Strachey and Alan Tyson (2001) *The Standard Edition of the Complete Psychological Works of Sigmund Freud, the Ego and the Id and Other Works, Volume XIX (1923-1925)* London: Vintage (First Published in Great Britain in 1961 by the Hogarth Press Limited).

Strauss, J., Corbin, J. (1998) *Basics of Qualitative Research, Techniques and Procedures for Developing Grounded Theory*, London: Sage Publications Limited.

Summers-Effler, E. (2007) 'Vortexes of Involvement Social Systems As Turbulent Flow', *Philosophy of the Social Sciences*, vol. 37, no. 4, p.p. 433-448.

Sugarman, J. (2009) 'Historical Ontology and Psychological Description', *Journal of Theoretical and Philosophical Psychology*, vol. 29, no. 1, p.p. 5-15.

Suzuki, L. A., Ahluwalia, M. K., Arora, A. K., Mattis J. S. (2007) 'The Pond You Fish in Determines the Fish You Catch', *The Counselling Psychologist*, vol. 35, no. 2, p.p. 295-327.

Sveningsson, S., Alvesson, M. (2003) 'Managing Managerial Identities', *Human Relations*, vol. 56, p.p. 1163-1193, Cited in Alvesson, M. (2010) 'Self-Doubters, Strugglers, Storytellers, Surfers and Others; Images of Self Identities in Organisation Studies', *Human Relations*, vol. 63, part 2, p.p. 193-217.

Taylor, H., Fieldman, G., Altman, Y. (2008) 'Email at Work: A Cause for Concern? The Implications of the New Communication Technologies for Health, Well-being and Productivity at Work', *Journal of Organisational Transformation and Social Change*, vol. 5, no. 2, p.p. 159-173.

Taggar, S., Neubert, M. (2004) 'The Impact of Poor Performers on Team Outcomes: An Empirical Examination of Attribution Theory', *Personnel Psychology*, vol. 57, p.p. 935-968.

Tekosis, P. (2008) 'I Choose, You Choose, We Choose, Towards an Understanding of Effected Possibility', *Existential Analysis*, vol. 19, no. 1, p.p. 33-45.

Tepper, B. J. (2000) 'Consequences of Abusive Supervision', *Academy of Management Journal*, vol. 43, no. 2, p.p. 178-190.

Tews, M. J., Michel, J. W., Bartlett, A. (2012) 'The *Fun*damental Role of Workplace Fun in Applicant Attraction', *Journal of Leadership & Organisational Studies*, vol. 19, no. 1, p.p. 105-114.

The Colour Therapy Information Resource (2005) *What is Colour Therapy*, [online]. Available from: <http://www.colourtherapyhealing.com> [Accessed on 19 July 2005].

Thomson, D., Hassenkamp, A. (2008) 'The Social Meaning and Function of Food Rituals in Healthcare Practice: An Ethnography', *Human Relations*, vol. 61, no. 12, p.p. 1775-1802.

Tierney, P., Tepper, B. J. (2007) 'Editorial, Introduction to the Leadership Quarterly Special Issue: Destructive Leadership', *The Leadership Quarterly*, vol. 18, p.p. 171-173.

Tobin, J. l., Dobard, R. G. (1999) *Hidden in Plain View a Secret Story of Quilts and the Underground Railroad*, New York, USA: Anchor Books, A Division of Random House Inc.

Trice, H. M. (1984) 'Rites and Ceremonials in Organisational Cultures', Cited in Bacharach, S. B., Mitchell, S. M. (Eds.) *Perspectives on Organisational Sociology: Theory and Research,* vol. 4, Greenwich, Conn, USA: JAI Press.

Trice, H. M., Beyer, J. M. (1984) 'Studying Organisational Cultures Through Rites and Ceremonials', *Academy of Management Review*, vol. 9, no. 4, p.p. 653-669.

Trice, H. M., Beyer, J. M. (1993) *The Cultures of Work Organisations*, Upper Saddle River, NJ 07458, USA: Prentice-Hall Inc.

Troth, A. (2009) 'A Model of Team Emotional Intelligence, Conflict, Task Complexity and Decision Making', *International Journal of Organisational Behaviour*, vol. 14, no. 1, July to December, p.p. 26-40.

Turner, B. A. (1983) 'The Use of Grounded Theory for the Qualitative Analysis of Organisational Behaviour', *Journal of Management Studies*, vol. 20, Issue 3, p.p. 333-348.

Turner, R. (1947) 'The Navy Disbursing Officer as a Bureaucrat', *American Sociological Review*, vol. 12, p.p. 342-348.

Turner, V. (1969) *The Ritual Process*, London: Routledge and Kegan Paul.

Turner, R., Ledwith, A., Kelly, J. (2010) 'Project Management in Small to Medium-**Sized** Enterprises: Matching Processes to the Nature of the Firm', *International Journal of Project Management*, vol. 28, p.p. 744-755.

Tyler, T. (2006) 'Psychological Perspectives on Legitimacy and Legitimation', *Annual Review of Psychology*, vol. 57, p.p. 375-400.

UN (2005) *United Nations. It's Your World*, [online]. Available from: <http://www.un.org> [Accessed on 12 August 2005]

University of Salford (Date of Issue: September 2009 [Updated August 2009]) *Code of Practice for the Conduct of Post-graduate Research Degree Programmes 2009-2010*, Post-graduate Student Administration, The University of Salford, Humphrey Booth House, Salford, Greater Manchester M5 4WT, United Kingdom www.salford.ac.uk

Van Dierendonck, C., Haynes, C., Borrill, C., Stride, C. (2007) 'Effects of Upward Feedback on Leadership Behaviour Towards Subordinates', *Journal of Management Development*, vol. 36, no. 3, p.p. 228-238.

Van Gennep, A. (1960) *The Rites of Passage*, London: Kegan Paul.

Van Kaam, A. (1961) 'Clinical Implications of Heidegger's Concept of Will, Decision and Responsibility', *Review of Existential Psychology and Psychiatry*, vol. 1, pp. 205-216.

Velthouse, B., Kandogan, Y. (2007) 'Ethics in Practice: What are Managers Really Doing?', *Journal of Business Ethics*, vol. 70, p.p. 151-163.

Vogelgesang, G. R., Lester, P. B. (2009) 'Transparency: How Leaders Can Get Results by Laying It on the Line', *Organisational Dynamics*, vol. 38, no. 4, p.p. 252-260.

Von Eckartsberg, R. (2005) 'How Will I Proceed? What is My Method?', *The Humanistic Psychologist*, vol. 33, no. 4, p.p. 259-270.

Von Eckartsberg, R. (2008) 'Dasein-Synthesis', *The Humanistic Psychologist*, vol. 36, p.p. 9-18.

Vryan, K. D. (2006) 'Expanding Analytic Autoethnography and Enhancing Its Potential', *Journal of Contemporary Ethnography*, vol. 35, no. 4, p.p. 405-409.

Wageman, R., Fisher, C. M., Hackman, J. R. (2009) 'Leading Teams When the Time is Right: Finding Best Moments to Act', *Organisational Dynamics*, vol. 38, no. 3, p.p. 192-203.

Watzlawick, P., Beavin Bavelas, J., Jackson, D. D. (1967) *Pragmatics of Human Communication a Study of Interactional Patterns, Pathologies and Paradoxes*, New York, USA: W. W. Norton & Company Inc.

Whitaker, D. S., Lieberman, M. A. (1964) *Psychology Through the Group Process*, Chicago, Illinois, USA: Aldine Publishing, Cited in Ringer, T. M. (2007) 'Viewpoint Leadership for Collective Thinking in the Workplace', *Team Performance Management*, vol. 13, no. 3/4, p.p. 130-144.

Whitty, M. T., Carr, A. N. (2006) 'New Rules in the Workplace: Applying Object Relations Theory to Explain Problem Internet and Email Behaviour in the Workplace', *Computers in Human Behaviour*, vol. 22, p.p. 235-250.

Wilhelmson, L. (2006) 'Transformative Learning in Joint Leadership', *Journal of Workplace Learning*, vol. 18, no. 7/8, p.p. 495-507.

Wilkinson, C. E., Rees, C. E., Knight, L. V. (2007) '"From the Heart of My Bottom": Negotiating Humour in Focus Group Discussions', *Qualitative Health Research*, vol. 18, no. 3, p.p. 411-422.

Williams, H., Parker, S. K., Turner, N. (2007) 'Perceived Dissimilarity and Perspective Taking Within Work Teams', *Group & Organisation Management*, vol. 32, no. 5, p.p. 569-597.

Wilks, F. (1998) *Intelligent Emotion: How to Succeed Through Transforming Your Feelings*, London: William Heinemann.

Wolcott, H. F. (2001) *Writing Up Qualitative Research, Second Edition,* London: Sage Publications Limited.

Woodhouse, D., Pengelly, P. (1991) *Anxiety and the Dynamics of Collaboration,* Aberdeen: Aberdeen University Press, Cited in Barnes, B., Ernst, S., Hyde, K. (1999) *An Introduction to Groupwork a Group Analytic Perspective Basic Texts in Counselling and Psychotherapy Series, Editor: Stephen Frosh*, New York, NY 10010, USA: Palgrave Macmillan.

Wolfensberger, W. (2007) 'The Fruitlessness of Trying to Convey Competencies To People While Ignoring Their Image', *Intellectual and Developmental Disabilities*, vol. 45, no. 2, p.p. 138.

Worden, J. W. (1991) *Grief Counselling and Grief Therapy, A Handbook for the Mental Health Practitioner, Second Edition*, London: Routledge.

Wulf, V., Rhode, M. (1995) 'Towards an Integrated Organisation and Technology Development', *Designing Interactive Systems*, vol. 55, Cited in Boden, A., Muller, C., Nett, B. (2011) 'Conducting a Business Ethnography in Global Software Development Projects of Small German Enterprises', *Information and Software Technology*, vol. 53, p.p. 1012-1021.

Yahoo Extra News (2009) *Security for Key Stepped Up at Waitangi*, [online], Available from: http://nz.news.yahoo.eom/a/-/top-stories/53O3921 [Accessed on 06 Feb 2009].

Yahoo Extra News (2009) *Festival Atmosphere at Waitangi*, [online], Available from: http://nz.news.yahoo.eom/a/-/top-stories/5303642 [Accessed on 06 Feb 2009].

Yalowitz, S. (2000) 'A Dispositional Account of Self Knowledge', *Philosophy and Phenomenological Research*, vol. 61, no. 2, p.p. 249-278.

Yang, Shih-ying (2011) 'Wisdom Displayed Through Leadership: Exploring Leadership Related Wisdom', *The Leadership Quarterly*, vol. 22, no. 4, p.p. 616-632.

Ybema, S., Yanor, D., Wels, H., Kamsteeg, F. (2009) *Organisational Ethnography: Studying the Complexities of Everyday Life*, London: Sage.

Yellowlees, P. M., Marks, S. (2007) 'Problematic Internet Use or Internet Addiction', *Computers in Human Behaviour*, vol. 23, p.p. 1447-1453.

Yuanmeng, X. (2011) 'Trade Finance in the Post-Crisis Era', *Banker 2011: How to Run a Bank*, p.p. 122-123.

Yukl, G. A. (2002) *Leadership in Organisations Fifth Edition,* Upper Saddle River, New Jersey, USA: Prentice-Hall.

Ziegler, R. (2008) 'What Makes the Kula Go Round? A Simulation Model of the Spontaneous Emergence of a Ceremonial Exchange System', *Social Networks*, vol. 30, p.p. 107-126.

Zimmerman, D. (2001) 'Thinking with Your Hypothalamus: Reflections on a Cognitive Role for the Reactive Emotions', *Philosophy and Phenomenological Research*, vol. 63, no. 3, p.p. 521-541.

Zimmerman, M. A., Barksy, D., Brouthers, K. D. (2009) 'Networks, SMEs and International Diversification', *Multinational Business Review*, vol. 17, Issue 4, p.p. 143-162.

Zook, D. C. (2008) 'The Irony of It All: Soren Kierkegaard and the Anxious Pleasures of Civil Society', *British Journal for the History of Philosophy*, vol. 16, no. 2, p.p. 393-419.